STALKED

Breaking the Silence on the Crime of Stalking in America

The National Coalition Against Domestic Violence reports that, every five years, the death toll of persons killed by relatives or acquaintances equals that of the entire Vietnam War.

Advocates estimate that victims who leave a battering relationship have a 75 percent higher chance of being killed by their partners—and, in the vast majority of cases, stalking precedes the fatal attack.

What are the chances stalking might happen to you? *STALKED: Breaking the Silence on the Crime of Stalking in America* explores every pertinent aspect of the stalking phenomenon. You'll discover:

- that most stalking arises from interpersonal relationships.
- why you *must* document all stalking activity *and* keep a copy of all evidence in a safe place (with the police, with your attorney, or in a safe deposit box)
- the efficiency of bodyguard services and electronic monitoring of stalkers (now being tested nationwide)
- the pros and cons of owning a handgun for self-defense
- the results of forensic psychology studies of the stalking of celebrities and politicians
- the impressive success rate of the Model Mugging Women's Self-Defense course, created by martial arts expert Matthew Thomas and available nationwide

STALKED

Breaking the Silence on the Crime of Stalking in America

Melita Schaum and Karen Parrish

POCKET BOOKS
New York London Toronto Sydney Tokyo Singapore

We would like to acknowledge the following sources for permission to quote material:

Wendy Collier. Material from "The Cycle of Stalking" flier, "Stalking: An Overview" pamphlet, and "My Story," by Wendy Collier. Written by Wendy L. Collier, © 1993, Victim Protection Services.

Gavin de Becker. © 1994 Gavin de Becker. Reprinted by permission of the author.

William R. Kordenbrock, Legislative Specialist for Michigan State Senator R. Robert Geake, sponsor of the Michigan Anti-stalking Law.

JurisMonitor, 5757 Central Ave., #200, Boulder, CO 80301.

Jane McAllister. © 1994 Jane McAllister. Used by permission of the author.

Northwestern National Life Insurance Company, "Fear and Violence in the Workplace," 1993.

Paxton Quigley. From *Armed and Female* by Paxton Quigley. Copyright © 1989 by Paxton Quigley Productions. Used by permission of Dutton Signet, a division of Penguin Books USA Inc.

Silvija A. Strikis. © 1994 Silvija A. Strikis. Used by permission of the author.

An *Original* Publication of POCKET BOOKS

POCKET BOOKS, a division of Simon & Schuster Inc.
1230 Avenue of the Americas, New York, NY 10020

ISBN: 0-671-88710-6

First Pocket Books printing January 1995

10 9 8 7 6 5 4 3 2 1

POCKET and colophon are registered trademarks of Simon & Schuster Inc.

Printed in the U.S.A.

We would like to acknowledge the generosity, insight and courage of victims and their families who came forward to share with us their stories, their pain and their amazing strength of spirit. This book is for them.

ACKNOWLEDGMENTS

We are grateful to the University of Michigan–Dearborn, Office of Sponsored Research and the University of Michigan–Ann Arbor, Office of the Vice President for Research for grant assistance, and we appreciate the energy and effort of Leslie Tarnacki and Linda Briglio, our research assistants on the project.

Special thanks go to the many people whose encouragement and expertise helped this project along, in particular:

Wendy Collier
Beverly Crawford
Gavin de Becker
Robert Fein
Donna Hunzeker
William Kordenbrock
John Lane
Jane McAllister and the members of
  Citizens Against Stalking
Beth Miller
Silvija A. Strikis
RoseAlyce Thayer
Michele Ward
Ron Ward

CONTENTS

Introduction

On July 18, 1989, America was horrified by the murder of Rebecca Schaeffer, the talented twenty-one-year-old star of television's *My Sister Sam.* For two years prior to that fatal day, a self-professed admirer, Robert Bardo, had been following the actress, twice even trying to enter the Warner Bros. studio lot where she worked. Turned away by security both times, once Bardo brought along a five-foot-tall teddy bear for Schaeffer. But on the morning he finally located her, Bardo was ready to deliver a very different kind of gift. As she opened her apartment door, Bardo grabbed her arm and, holding her fast, aimed his .357 Magnum at point-blank range. Rebecca Schaeffer died within minutes, of a massive bullet wound to the heart.

Now serving a life sentence with no chance of parole, Robert Bardo gave us more than just another senseless murder on that grim day. As no one had done before, this deranged young man galvanized the public into having to face a range of criminal activities previously considered invisible. With the squeeze of a trigger, Robert Bardo gave us a glimpse into the distorted and potentially deadly mind of the stalker.

In part as a result of Rebecca Schaeffer's death, in 1990 California became the first state to pass antistalking legislation, which made it a crime for any person to repeatedly follow or harass, credibly threatening another person's physical safety. Within three years, forty-seven states and the District of Columbia had followed suit. Senators Barbara Boxer and Bob Krueger introduced legislation into Congress that would make stalking a federal crime. Concerned about the pervasive and dangerous nature of stalking —Krueger from personal experience—the senators called for strong legislative measures to address this seemingly new "crime of the nineties."

Yet for those who study stalking, this crime is anything but new. According to Lieutenant John Lane of the Los Angeles Police Department, "These behaviors have existed in our society for a long time, but we're just now starting to put a label on them." Since 1990, Lane has directed the LAPD's Threat Management Unit, the only police unit in the country designed exclusively to assess, monitor, and provide assistance in cases of unwanted pursuit or harassment. Since its inception, the TMU has worked extensively with forensic psychiatrists and independent security experts to monitor and document such crimes.

The work of Lane and others has yielded provocative and fascinating clues about stalking. Gavin de Becker, a prominent expert on stalking and a consultant to the LAPD, has collected over 300,000 unusual pieces of communication sent to Hollywood stars, including items like stones and postage stamps, shampoo coupons, a half-eaten candy bar, vials of blood and semen, animal feces, and, in one instance, the head of a coyote. Yet despite the sensational nature of these bizarre objects, de Becker is quick to point out that the number of celebrities currently being stalked is vastly smaller than the high number of cases in which stalking victims are ordinary citizens. Indeed, it is estimated that the number of people who are being stalked right now exceeds twice the number of people who will die in a given year from all accidents combined, including motor vehicle accidents.

UCLA professor of forensic psychiatry Park Dietz, who has conducted extensive studies of stalking and obsessive behavior, predicts that one in twenty American women will become victims of stalking at some time in their lives. Although occasionally the victim of stalking is a man or a public figure, most targets of stalkers are ordinary women who are followed, threatened, or repeatedly harassed by men they have known—often by men they have lived with and loved. Some experts estimate that 75 to 80 percent of stalking cases emerge from domestic situations. Frequently their outcome is tragic. According to the FBI's Uniform Crime Reports, 30 percent of female homicide victims in 1990 were killed by intimate partners. As to how many of these women were stalked prior to their deaths, some authorities put the number as high as 90 percent.

What are the chances that stalking might happen to you? What constitutes this crime, and what can you do about it? What are the psychological and social factors that impel stalkers to stalk? Who are their victims, and how do the new laws work to protect us all? The following chapters attempt to answer these questions, bringing together the voices of victims and advocates, legal experts and psychologists, security consultants and social analysts.

Stalking is not a new phenomenon. Strictly speaking, it is no more a crime of the nineties than it is of the eighties, seventies, or sixties. What *is* new about stalking is the extent to which the public is hearing from victims of the crime. On talk shows and radio programs, in magazine and newspaper articles, these victims tell us about a variety of experiences endured and trauma suffered. Some of the first victims to be heard were those who spoke at legislative hearings around the country. We begin by presenting some of their stories, both to show the range of criminal activities constituting the crime and the widespread extent of stalking in this country.

As these victims' stories demonstrate, stalkers can engage in everything from phone harassment to vandalism, from the sending of letters and gifts to theft, from pursuit behavior to assault, rape, even murder. As victims and their families know, stalking can happen in rural Indiana as well as in Washington, D.C. It occurs with teenage victims and child victims as well as adults. A victim can be stalked over a period of days or weeks, or she can be pursued for years. Indeed, perhaps the only encompassing feature of the crime is that *it is different in each case.*

Though they were presented with these many faces of stalking, state legislators nonetheless needed to define the crime as simply and clearly as possible. How did they do so, and what general features do most laws in the country now share? We take a look at those features, so that victims of stalkers and their families know clearly the actions and attributes that constitute the crime.

Who are the victims of stalkers? A statistically

small—but prominently visible—number are celebrities: Hollywood actors and actresses and highly visible athletes. Performing on television, in concerts, or in sports arenas, these figures are familiar to countless people worldwide. According to Gavin de Becker, many highly publicized stars—like Madonna, for example—achieve such international prominence, they may be known to more than *one billion* people. In an audience of such astronomical proportions, there are undoubtedly those who will be powerfully drawn to the star, impelled to find—and perhaps even harm—that star.

Who are some of the stars and public figures who have suffered under this crime, and what are the current findings of forensic psychiatrists who examine the motives that might turn a fan into a fanatic? Although we may think that invasion of personal life goes with the territory of celebrity prominence, the criminal behavior of these stalkers to the stars clearly crosses the line between devotion and dangerous obsession.

While the stalking of celebrities often draws the most media attention, however, the vast majority of stalking takes place between ordinary people—often ordinary people who have known each other intimately. By looking at case studies, we examine the connection between domestic violence and stalking, a link that makes up by far the highest percentage of stalking cases in this country. What are some of the danger signals to look for, signs that might point to a partner's potential stalking? What patterns and cycles do stalking and domestic abuse have in common?

A broad arena of remaining cases exists in which victims are either casual acquaintances or random targets. These cases include the stalking of co-workers and, often most tragically, the stalking of children. The stories of numerous victims illustrate the wide range and seemingly inexplicable nature of this form of stalking, which seems to come out of the blue, invading and even destroying lives at random.

Clearly, stalking is not just a statistical event. It is a daily reality for thousands of women and a smaller but equally victimized number of men. Victims of stalking may feel vulnerably alone with their reactions, but the peculiar invasiveness of the crime elicits common emotional responses in many victims. By combining the experience of victims' rights advocates, therapists, and survivors of stalking, we move into a practical discussion of strategies and resources for dealing with—or helping someone else deal with—stalking behavior. We also explore sensitive and practical ways to organize support from family, friends, and victim organizations.

A wider circle of support involves the judicial system, an arena that often seems remote and difficult for the average person to negotiate. In an easy-to-follow fashion, we move through the steps involved in dealing with the complexities of attorneys, police, and the court system, and clarify the legal protection against stalking available to all citizens.

To date, antistalking laws are not identical from state to state, and federal legislation, though proposed, has not been enacted. How each stalking victim chooses to use available legal protection depends in part on where she lives. We help clarify the situation by highlighting some key differences among antistalking laws from state to state. We also trace potential civil liberties issues raised by such laws, including controversial applications of the law to public protest, as well as ways in which antistalking laws may be effectively used in cases of child molestation, gang warfare, and cults.

Numerous programs and articles of self-defense are available today, presenting a confusing, often contradictory array of options for victims. We provide an overview of basic home security measures, including the use of the telephone and the pros and cons of guard dogs. In more extreme cases, some victims may opt to use weapons. We examine the pros and cons of various nonlethal and lethal weapons and outline the numerous personal, legal, and practical issues surrounding the use and ownership of handguns. We also explore the rise in personal protection or bodyguard services for ordinary citizens, along with some of the new technologies for monitoring stalkers currently being tested across the country. For anyone interested in an added measure of personal security today, we provide an overview of combat and self-defense skills programs, showing how such courses offer victims a chance to regain personal control and strength. For those victims whose situations have become the most extreme and dangerous, we end with recommendations from top private investigators on how to disappear, providing a chilling look at the easily-followed paper trail most citizens unknowingly leave behind them.

Why is stalking currently so prevalent in our society? Our final chapter seeks to answer this question by looking at other cultural phenomena: media portrayals of romance and sexuality, the cult of celebrity, teen violence, stress in the modern workplace, and the new anonymity of electronic communications, the latest arena for interpersonal invasion.

For some, the word *stalking* conjures images of ski-masked maniacs slipping in through unlocked bedroom windows, of serial killers idling along behind their victims on dark country roads, of voyeurs lurking in alleyways or behind bushes. But what of the man next door, the ex-husband, the landlord, the client, the person on the exercycle next to you at the health club, the supermarket clerk, the random acquaintance? Focusing on the more sensational portrayals of this crime may be blinding us to the dangerously everyday face of stalking—and to its very real prevalence in society today. In this book we hope to dispel myths and provide new insights, in part by exploring stalking's many faces and the social and psychological complexities the crime reveals.

CHAPTER 1

"What Does He Have to Do, Shoot Me?"

A Brief Overview of the Crime

This is terrorism, pure and simple. . . . Somebody's life is destroyed by it, somebody's life becomes enveloped by it. Everything that they do—when they are asleep, when they are awake—is somehow connected to it. . . . There is somebody constantly focused on them with an obsession.

Ira Reiner, former District Attorney,
Los Angeles County

This society makes these people, and America makes more of them than any country in the world.

Gavin de Becker, expert on stalking

In six brief weeks, between January 5 and February 18, 1990, Orange County, California, newspapers ran the now-famous stories of four local women murdered by their former boyfriends or husbands. Three had been to the police to protest their abuse and, desperately seeking protection, had taken out restraining orders. One victim was Patricia Kastle, a U.S. Olympic skier—fatally shot in the head and back by her former husband, Lee Strumer. Another was Manijeh Bolour, a nurse hounded for ten years by a former boyfriend, Hossein Ghaffari, who had followed her to California from Austria. Ghaffari caught up with Bolour one morning and rammed his car into hers, causing a fatal explosion. Brenda Thurman had left her boyfriend, Rodney Terry Cornegay, at the end of 1989, moving with her two children to a women's shelter and then to a new apartment. Cornegay hired a private detective to find her, then three weeks later gunned her down. Nineteen-year-old Tammy Marie Davis had been beaten and terrorized by her ex-boyfriend, Brian Framstead, who had also assaulted their twenty-one-month-old child, sending both of them to the hospital. In the weeks before Framstead shot her to death, Davis had desperately questioned the police's inability to act before a crime was committed. "What does he have to do," she cried, "*shoot* me?"

A few miles north in Los Angeles County, a different group of people was asking similar questions. "The entertainment community was very much up in arms and very concerned about Rebecca Schaeffer's murder in 1989," recalls Lieutenant John Lane of the Los Angeles Police Department. The details of Schaeffer's death, shocking enough in themselves, were particularly troubling because they seemed to be representative of a growing national trend. By 1989, according to a National Institute of Justice report, as many attacks on public figures by people with mental disorders had occurred in the previous twenty years *as had occurred in the preceding 175 years.*

Increasingly concerned about the rise in attacks,

one group of celebrities' agents, the Conference of Personal Managers, decided to act. In late 1989, the group hosted a meeting to present its concerns to members of the Los Angeles Police Department and security experts, and to learn about all available protective options for its clients. That meeting, recalls Lane, helped form a special group within the LAPD, one that would be responsible for assessing and managing cases of repeated harassment throughout the city of Los Angeles. In July of 1990 the Threat Management Unit, the first of its kind in the nation, was born.

Meanwhile, California State Senator Ed Royce, in tandem with Judge John Watson of Orange County, was sponsoring Senate Bill 2184, which was then being shaped, debated, and revised in committee. On January 1, 1991, SB 2184 became California Penal Code 646.9, better known as the nation's first antistalking law. Using language that would set a precedent for every antistalking law that followed it, California's legislation defined stalking as the "willful, malicious, and repeated harassing or following of another" combined with the making of a credible threat toward that person of great bodily harm or death.

On May 24, 1991, the first felony stalking arrest in California occurred when police charged Mark David Bleakley of Sherman Oaks with stalking his ex-girlfriend, Leslie Wein. According to documents filed in court, Bleakley and Wein had dated for two years; however, when Wein broke off the relationship, Bleakley simply wouldn't let go. Wein alleged that Bleakley made numerous hangup calls to her home, slashed her car's tires, poured acid on her car and other cars she used, and stole her dog. In all, Wein filed thirteen separate charges with the police, and she sought and obtained a restraining order to prevent Bleakley from calling or approaching her. But it wasn't until Bleakley explicitly threatened Wein that police felt they could intervene, testing the new legislation. On May 17, 1991, Bleakley phoned Wein at work with the message: "I am ready to play hardball now—are you? Consider this an advance warning. I'm not just coming after your possessions, you'll be the next thing damaged." The threat was not only explicit, it was also eminently credible: after Bleakley was taken into custody, police found a .357 Magnum revolver in his apartment, under his bed. Bleakley was sentenced to one year in jail and six months in a rehabilitation facility.

"I Don't Know If You Can Understand the Fear"

The quick passage of California's antistalking law was due in no small part to the emotional, often dramatic testimony given by victims of stalkers at that state's legislative hearings. Kathleen Baty was one of the courageous witnesses who helped impel the passage of the law. Wife of professional football player Greg Baty, Kathleen had been stalked for years by a man she barely remembered from high school. Her story appears in full in Chapter 8, detailing how the harassment and threats culminated in an attempted gunpoint kidnapping and a terrifying standoff with police SWAT teams. Ed Royce, in a televised interview, spoke to the importance of Kathleen's testimony in helping to pass the law: "It was her documentation of her experiences over eight years with this individual who was obsessed with her. . . . That expression of what she'd been through, you could see it on the faces of the members of the committee."

Lawmakers were soon to learn that Baty's ordeal was mirrored in the lives of countless others. At state legislative hearings held around the country over the next twenty-four months, hundreds of people who had been similarly terrorized came forward to tell legislators what it was like to live imprisoned in the vise of a stalker's obsession. Some victims described how vengeful ex-boyfriends would follow them by car, phone them tirelessly, make death threats. Others spoke of the eerie terror of being targeted by someone they barely knew, or by total strangers. Such victims described rambling letters, disturbing phone messages, and incomprehensible, erratic behavior. All spoke of additional crimes their stalkers had committed against them, their families and friends: trespassing, breaking and entering, property damage, theft, rape, assault, kidnapping, attempted murder.

One woman from Montana spoke at length of the repercussions of leaving an abusive spouse, who then began to hunt her down:

> I received my first protection order in 1982, granting me temporary protection from my physically abusive, alcoholic husband. When he refused treatment for his alcohol problem, we divorced. . . . [Then] the stalking began. I was followed everywhere I went from morning till night, to and from work, to and from night classes, to and from church, anywhere, everywhere. I was threatened, beaten and told repeatedly that he would ruin my life forever. I received my second protection order. My ex-husband was ordered

> to stay five hundred yards away from me or my property for an indefinite period of time. [He] refused to comply. . . . Vandalism began happening to my car, to my mobile home, the office where I worked, to my friends' cars, to my son's car. Every window in my car was broken at least once, the radiator punctured at least three times, tires slashed numerous times, the brakes cut, acid poured on the exterior of the car three times, something poured into my gas tank, ruining my motor. . . . Windows were broken in my mobile home, trees uprooted in the yard, the wood burner was chucked full of wood and turned on high, burning a hole in the ceiling of my mobile home. The list goes on and on.

A woman in Hawaii described the impact of living under siege, tormented both by her stalker and by a group of the stalker's friends:

> I suffered many personal problems. I had migraine headaches. I could not sleep. I lost my job. My current relationship was almost destroyed. I felt driven to the point of insanity. I had thoughts of actually killing my abuser to escape further harassment. . . . My abuser got help from friends. Strangers would call and make obscene sexual comments. I was terrorized after midnight once by a man who came to my house and stood outside yelling and threatening to harm me, if not right at that moment, then tomorrow. I was afraid to leave my house, especially at night, not knowing if my abuser or any [of the abuser's] friends might be outside.

Another woman from the same state found that even her young son was not immune to her ex-husband's surveillance and intimidation:

I'm going through this alone with a child I have to protect. . . . [Once] I caught [my ex-husband] videotaping us as we were having dinner. . . . He made a cut-throat action which came across to my son and me that we were dead. My son asked me, "Why is he doing this to us, Mom?" My son is twelve years old. What do you say to your child when they ask you a question like that?

A Connecticut teenager testified about what it was like to be the target of a stranger's unwanted attentions:

For a year and a half I've been stalked by an older man in a maroon car, to and from school, every day. It started in my freshman year [of high school]. . . . I was walking to school with a girlfriend one day, and we . . . noticed him. I was in such shock that I always kept forgetting to get his license plate, but [this time] I got it. He noticed that I had gotten it and he became very frustrated . . . [so then he] followed me very closely. . . . I didn't know what to do. I ran to the nearest Burger King, and I called my mother and I said, "Here's his license plate number, call the police . . . I'm going to walk to [school] when I think it's safe. I waited . . . five minutes and [when] I hadn't seen him, I started to cross the street and he pulled out from behind a bank and almost hit me. I began to run and he rolled down his window in front of everybody, just stopped his car in the middle of the road, and said, "I'll see you after school, little girl." . . . I had heard about people following children, or offering them candy, but I never thought it would be happening to me in any way. And then it did and now I have to watch who I talk to or where I go. . . . My whole life has changed.

Even the mother of a murdered child described what it was like to have to witness, helplessly, the stalking that preceded her daughter's death:

> Six months before she was killed, that man stalked her. I saw the man when I waited for the bus in the morning. When I met that bus after school, very often he was up there at the corner, never saying anything, just staring at us.

Individual bill sponsors also testified that conversations with victims and their families had had a profound effect on them. In Illinois, Representative Tom Homer referred to the astonishing number of victims' relatives in his state who had spoken on behalf of the antistalking bill he was sponsoring:

> First . . . there was Elizabeth Cohan of Springfield, who, even after seven years, still trembles when she testifies and recounts the activities leading up to the shooting death of her boyfriend, Mark Vasconcelles, here in Springfield. . . . Then there was the testimony . . . from Lynette Barth, whose sister, in Peoria, was a nurse at the Good Samaritan Nursing Home in East Peoria. . . . [Less] than a week after she had moved out on her boyfriend . . . and after he had threatened her repeatedly, disabled her automobile, threatened to kill her, [he] did, in fact, show up at the nursing home and repeatedly stabbed Sandra Mason to death. . . . Then, perhaps the most compelling testimony was made just a few weeks ago at the Judiciary Committee, when Grace Beach of Elmhurst and Barbara Erjavich of Orland Park sat together as the parents of two children who had been buried just in February. . . . Beach's son, Glen, and . . . Erjavich's daughter,

> Karen, were boyfriend and girlfriend. . . . [A] man by the name of Ken Kopecky . . . gunned down both of these young, beautiful people in the prime of their life. Then, in March, there was a case up in Mt. Prospect of Connie Chaney, whose husband had followed and harassed her for months. . . . He shot her to death. . . . The list goes on and on.

Springing from a vast well of public anguish, fear, and outrage, such testimony impelled legislators to respond quickly. By the end of 1992, twenty-nine states had new antistalking legislation in place. By the end of 1993, eighteen additional states and the District of Columbia had followed suit, and other states had amended existing laws—such as those prohibiting terroristic threats—to take into account the repetitive, often escalating nature of crimes like stalking. By New Years' Day of 1994, forty-eight states had antistalking laws, and California had amended its law for the second time.

As further evidence of an increasing public awareness of the crime, the United States Senate Judiciary Committee conducted its own hearings on stalking in September of 1992. As with state legislative hearings, testimony from victims and their families offered glimpses into the way stalkers destroy lives. One witness, Sandra Poland of Maine, described to committee members how her daughter Kimberly had been harassed and terrorized for eight years by a mentally ill man. Seeing her daughter's picture in the newspaper one day in 1984, the harasser, whom Poland would only identify as John Doe, began to visit Kimberly at home and at her job, sending her letters and phoning her incessantly. Though the man was advised repeatedly that Kimberly had no interest in him and that he was unwelcome to contact her, he continued his intrusions in the girl's life. In 1986, while Kimberly recuperated from surgery in a local hospital, "Doe" entered her room and had to be forcibly evicted. In what appeared to be escalating danger for the young woman, he began sending Kimberly threatening letters, including one with drawings of dripping blood. The day after that drawing appeared, the Polands found an arrow lodged in a tree on their lawn.

Through the late 1980s, Doe continued to harass and follow Kimberly, seemingly willing to travel great distances to try to make contact with her. Tracking her to her college in Massachusetts, Doe would appear in Kimberly's dormitory, asking for her and leaving bizarre, rambling notes. Ultimately, Kimberly, fearing for her safety, withdrew from the school. Though the Polands successfully took out a restraining order and were able to have him involuntarily committed in two psychiatric institutions, they were unable to assure Kimberly's safety. When asked by a sheriff why he couldn't get on with his life and get a job, Doe replied, in words which reflect the sentiments of so many stalkers, "This *is* my job."

In her testimony to the Senate Judiciary, Sandra Poland attempted to find words for how this ordeal had changed her family's life:

> There is no way to describe to you the fear that our family has of this individual, no way to describe what it is like to live a life of constantly being on guard. Kimberly, her dad, and I all suffer from stress-related symptoms, including headaches, backaches, nervousness, restlessness, as well as fright. We have installed new locks on our doors and keep them locked at all

times. We have all obtained concealed weapons permits. We go to bed with a gun under our pillow. . . . We who are hardworking, law-abiding, tax-paying citizens are the ones who have become imprisoned.

Despite the threats Doe has made against our lives, despite his repeated violations of restraining orders, despite the professional assessment of him as dangerous, both the district attorney and our attorney have said that nothing can be done until Doe does something. What is the something that they must wait for him to do—kidnap Kimberly, rape Kimberly, or kill her? Would you be willing to sit back and wait for that to happen to your son or your daughter?

Defining Stalking

The testimony is vivid; the life-damaging effects of this crime are graphic and real. But what exactly constitutes stalking? How is it legally defined? In Chapter 7 we examine how the details in antistalking laws vary by state, as well as how the language in those laws is currently subject to revision—even constitutional challenge. Here we'll look at the main provisions, the constants in defining the crime.

Because states looked to California as a precedent for drafting their own legislation, two key elements from California's law have surfaced in laws throughout the country:

1. The *repeated* pattern of harassing or following another person.
2. The *element of threat* made or posed against that person.

The issue of *intent* poses a third facet relevant to antistalking legislation. In order to understand the crime better, then, let's look at each of these elements in turn.

Course of Conduct

The repetitive nature of incidents that make up stalking behavior is the first important component of this crime. For a person to be charged with stalking, he must engage in a *course of conduct* where specific acts of harassment or following occur on more than one distinct occasion—that is, they create a *pattern* of behavior. In many states, this pattern is further defined as one that shows "a continuity of purpose."

As an example, an angry employee who follows her co-worker home from work for a week has, by the second evening, engaged in a "course of conduct." A stranger who one day sends someone a harassing letter and a month later leaves several menacing messages on her answering machine also satisfies the element, as does a person who follows his ex-wife's new boyfriend to the grocery store one morning and returns to harass him in the afternoon. On the other hand, no antistalking law would apply to a man who, for example, approaches and angrily accosts his ex-wife *on one occasion,* or to a fan who threatens a celebrity in *one letter.* Such actions, no matter how objectionable, do not in the eyes of the law suggest a *course* of conduct in which a *continuity* of purpose is displayed.

Must a course of conduct occur within any specific period of time? Legislators grappled with this question in trying to define fully the course of conduct requirements. In Michigan, for example, legislators considered requiring that the two acts be on separate days, or that the conduct continue for at least thirty days, but rejected these approaches. Instead, writes David Cahill, former legal counsel to the House of Representatives Judiciary Committee, Michigan's law requires only that *at least two distinct acts occur,* which could even be "separated by an hour or less." Most states write the law this broadly, though there are exceptions. In Arkansas, for example, the law requires that "two or more acts [must be] separated by at least 36 hours, but [occur] within one year." In Chapter 7 we detail some of these exceptions more fully.

Threats Made or Implied

Most antistalking laws around the country discuss threats or threatening behavior. Most antistalking laws require, at minimum, that the victim *feel* threatened by the stalker's actions. In these states, the stalker may explicitly threaten the victim, but the law does not require that such a threat take place. As long as the stalker's other actions create a threatening climate for the victim, the law can be applied.

In other states, however, repeated harassment or following must be accompanied by an *explicit threat.* Most states that require a threat also require that it be "credible." In many states that require a credible threat, the defendant must have the "intent and/or apparent ability" to carry out the threat. Someone who clearly could not carry out the threat would not fit this requirement. For instance, if a mentally ill stalker threatens to blow up North America if a celebrity does not answer his letters, that would be considered an incredible threat. (Of course, such a threat consequently might suggest that the stalker's actions be carefully monitored.) As with the course of conduct requirements, many threat requirements vary by state. Chapter 7 examines some of these differences and looks at how some laws have already been modified.

Intent

Most criminal laws in this country—including antistalking laws—require some form of *intent* on the part of the crime's perpetrator. Intent requirements seek to identify that the behavior is "willful," "knowing," or "purposeful," or they refer to behavior undertaken "intentionally" or "maliciously." While the phrasing varies, the requirement remains the same. For example, California penalizes a course of conduct that is *"willful, malicious* and repeated," while Washington prohibits *"intentionally* and repeatedly" following another. In these definitions, "willful," "malicious," and "intentional" speak to the perpetrator's conscious desire to undertake a particular action, such as following or harassing.

The intent requirement creates a type of reference point in defining guilt and degrees of guilt. Consider, for example, the difference between murder in the first degree and manslaughter. Someone who actively plots —and carries out—the murder of another is viewed under the law quite differently than one who accidentally and *unintentionally* causes a death. The two types of crime—and the severity of their respective punishments—are measured by the difference between wanting to bring about death, on the one hand, and having no such intention on the other.

Because it is impossible to get into the mind of a defendant, however, the law requires that the prosecution prove to a judge or jury that the circumstances surrounding a case point to a defendant's intent. In a stalking case, for example, the prosecutor might present evidence that a man had followed his ex-wife on the highway and rammed her car with his own. If the prosecutor can convincingly show that the defendant had *deliberately* used his car as a weapon—that is, that this was not simply the result of bad brakes or wet roads—then he can claim that the actions were calculated, that they were not accidental but performed with intent.

In addition to requiring that a defendant had the intent to commit a certain *action,* many states require proof that he intended to bring about a certain *result.* Some few states require only that the stalker intend to *alarm* or *annoy,* but most states require that he intend to cause *fear or great emotional distress* in his victim. Such an intent to cause fear—and the fear that results—is a characteristic of stalking as described by victims around the country. As we'll see in Chapter 5, victims describe a range of emotions and responses to stalkers' invasions, many of which center on fear and the uncertainty that exposure to such an emotion can bring. Whether describing themselves as afraid, terrified, petrified, scared to death, or frozen with fear, victims are recounting a near-universal response to stalking and its intended effects.

Men as Victims of Stalking

Because women comprise the overwhelming majority of stalking victims, and men make up most stalking perpetrators, we refer to stalking victims throughout this book as "she" and "her" and to stalkers as "he" and "him." By speaking generally of the crime's victims and perpetrators this way, we do not mean to dismiss male stalking victims or minimize their fear, anger, and suffering. These emotional responses to stalking occur regardless of gender, and we believe the practical suggestions that follow in later chapters are equally applicable to male victims of stalking as they are to women.

Men *are* stalked, of course, as accounts from magazine and newspaper articles suggest. As we will see in Chapter 2, male celebrities are harassed and followed by disturbed female fans. Drs. Michael Zona and Kaushal Sharma of the USC School of Medicine and John Lane of the LAPD have studied such cases; in one study, the authors examined 74 cases of obsessional pursuit drawn from the LAPD files. The results of this study, though performed on a very small sample, are provocative. According to the authors, seven of the cases involved stalkers who suffer from erotomania (examined in Chapter 2), and of those seven cases, five stalking victims were men stalked by women.

Much more disturbingly common are those cases involving domestic violence-related or intimate partner stalking, where a man—as well as a woman—is stalked. In domestic violence cases, the new male partners of women who have left an abusive spouse or boyfriend may well be at risk themselves. A case from West Point, Utah, grimly illustrates this dynamic. Early in the morning of July 3, 1994, a woman desperately phoned 911. On the taped call that resulted, while a child cries in the background, the woman can be heard begging her husband not to kill her boyfriend. Tragically, both the woman, thirty-two-year old Misty Marchant, and her boyfriend, Kirt Swann, were shot to death by Misty's husband, Kenneth Marchant. Marchant, who had previously threatened his wife, later killed himself at his father's home.

Stalking cases that arise from prior domestic violence can themselves become violent in the extreme, exacting a price from male and female victims. In the August 1994 issue of *Self* magazine, writer Charles C. Mann documents the nightmare endured by the Brantley and Mary Ann Sweat family of Springfield, Massachusetts. Mann recounts how in 1987, David Wilhite, the ex-boyfriend of teenage daughter Korinna, shattered the family irrevocably. Having left Wilhite months earlier due to his violence, Korinna was making a new life for herself, taking high school equivalency classes and dating a new boyfriend, Michael. But on October 9, Wilhite ambushed Korinna and Michael as they sat together in Michael's car in front of Korinna's home. Wilhite shot and killed Korinna and seriously wounded Michael; then, when Korinna's younger sister Tammy rushed out to help, he murdered her, too. A few moments later Mary Ann was shot through the torso, arm, and abdomen; she barely survived her injuries. Wilhite later killed himself.

Mann's chilling account shows the rippling effects of such extreme violence, noting that for every actual victim, untold other family members and friends are affected. In this family's case, Mary Ann endured years of physical and psychological therapy, and Brantley had to be hospitalized several times, finally losing his job. Ultimately, the couple's marriage dissolved under the weight of their ordeal.

Even in cases where no prior domestic abuse has

been documented, men are at risk. Recall the testimony of Representative Tom Homer of Illinois, who recounted how Glen Beach and his girlfriend Karen Erjavich were stalked and murdered. In that case, Karen Erjavich had known Kenneth Kopecky since high school. But it wasn't until they both attended Kopecky's sister's wedding that Kopecky began to be obsessed with Erjavich. Deciding that in order to win Erjavich he would have to move Glen aside, Kopecky began sending the thirty-one-year-old paramedic threatening letters and insisting that Erjavich date him. When Erjavich refused, Kopecky armed himself with a Colt .380 handgun and a bayonet and ambushed the couple, killing both of them. He, like Kenneth Marchant and David Wilhite, later committed suicide.

Male stalking victims help bring home the point that no one is immune to the potential violence of a stalker's obsession. Whether stalked directly or because of their proximity to stalking victims, men suffer the effects of this crime and its often profound consequences. In writing about gunshot victims generally, Charles Mann notes that perhaps the most terrible effect of this nationwide violence is that it has become so commonplace. "It's like a steady fall of snow," he writes. "We notice when it begins, but then we forget that the flakes are drifting down. Soon the landscape is blanketed with white. In this case the drifts are of pain and waste, and we walk right through them, unaware that the season has turned to winter."

Ultimately we all share in the wastefulness of this particular crime: in its causes, its effects, and its solutions. Ultimately our success in combating stalking will be measured by our willingness to confront, condemn, and penalize the behaviors that constitute it. To do that will take more than quick legislative fixes, more than cursory glimpses at the crime provided by talk-show interviews with victims and made-for-TV accounts of their suffering. Real progress toward stopping the crime will come when we take a long, hard look at why stalking occurs and begin to understand the many forms it takes.

CHAPTER 2

Fame's High Price

The Stalking of Celebrities

> The celebrity in some ways is like, to some people, what Jesus Christ is to them. They're very religious about Jesus Christ. They've never met the guy, they've never seen the guy, but they want to have a personal relationship with him.
>
> Robert Bardo, convicted of the murder of actress Rebecca Schaeffer

> I realize that you aren't going to come looking for me. So I'm going to have to go looking for you. Please don't be frightened. I am not a nut.
>
> Anonymous "fan's" letter to a star

From the superstar rock musician to the local news anchor, celebrities seem to be natural targets for stalkers. As figures, they are visually—and repeatedly—made available to the public. They come into our homes, are part of our lives; even ordinary people tend to follow their favorite stars devotedly. Fanzines, fan clubs, and movie magazines, loved by the public (and essential to a star's success), allow all fans a sort of access to *their* stars. But when a *fan* turns *fa-*

natic, such publicity, benign for a general viewing audience, can begin to feed dangerous obsessional fantasies.

One fantasy often found at the core of celebrity stalking is that the fan actually "knows" the star. Such was the case for Robert Bardo, the nineteen-year-old who stalked and murdered actress Rebecca Schaeffer in 1989. In a prison interview, when asked why he picked and hunted down Schaeffer, a perfect stranger, Bardo spoke directly about this twisted sense of affinity: "It happens 'cause they're in the limelight. . . . She was very open with her personality. . . . When I read those magazine articles, I feel like I know them [the stars]. . . . It's like they've been with you their whole life. . . . *To me, my victim wasn't a stranger."* (Italics added)

Talk show host David Letterman was also apparently not a stranger to Margaret Ray, the woman who has hounded him since 1988, believing that she and Letterman are "married." As of July 1993, Ray has been arrested eight times for allegedly breaking into Letterman's home, once with her son in tow, and for trespassing and sleeping on his property. On one occasion when the star was out of town, she broke into his car and drove it around for several days. In an interview, Letterman expressed dismay that the mental health system has yet to successfully treat Ray, a woman he believes to be confused and in need of help.

In the case of soap opera star Andrea Evans, overt hostile gestures, death threats, and a suicide attempt by her stalker made the actress actually fear for her life. In a 1993 interview with *People* magazine, Evans detailed her ordeal, which began in 1987 when she was roughly accosted by a strange man in the lobby of her New York apartment building. Shortly thereafter this man appeared at the studio where she worked and publicly slashed his wrists. At that point, Evans began working closely with the FBI, who had a file on the man for having threatened former President Ronald Reagan. For a time, Evans tried to maintain a fairly normal life by hiring others to shop and run errands, taking private cars to and from work, and by occasionally using twenty-four-hour security guards. Yet this facade of security and normality was soon to be punctured: Evans began receiving terroristic letters, some written in blood, some covered in swastikas. On holidays her stalker would send her cards describing his fantasy of their wedding—in a cemetery.

In 1990, Evans's stalker was caught trying to enter the office of the Secretary of State in Washington. He was armed with a meat cleaver—and a picture of the star. Evans moved away from New York, returning just once in 1991 to attend a celebrity tennis tournament, where her stalker again found and accosted her. At the time of this writing, Evans has gone into hiding and will not disclose where she lives.

Andrea Evans has good reason to adopt such a low profile. Rebecca Schaeffer's tragic case, though it received considerable public attention, was not the only celebrity stalking case to end in extreme violence. In May 1982 actress Theresa Saldana was hunted down and brutally attacked by Arthur Richard Jackson, a drifter who flew from Scotland to Los Angeles to locate her. Ambushed by Jackson in her apartment's parking lot, Saldana was saved only by the intervention of a bystander. Nonetheless, she had suffered ten serious stab wounds to the chest, arms, and legs, and spent years in physical, psychological, and emotional recovery. As a result of her ordeal, she went on to found Victims for Victims, an advocacy and support group. For his part, Jackson had written in his journal that he wanted to send Saldana "to heaven," then to request execution for himself so he could join her in paradise. This evil world, wrote Jackson, was too ugly for such a "beautiful angel." Jackson seems to still believe in his mission: Even from prison he has repeatedly threatened to kill Saldana when he is released.

In the Limelight: Stars and Their Fans

The list of celebrities who have been harassed, threatened, stalked, or assaulted is long—and growing longer. In the 1980s and '90s alone, the names of those who have been targets of a fan's unwanted or dangerous attentions read like a seating chart to the Academy Awards or Grammy ceremonies: Michael J. Fox, Michael Jackson, Sheena Easton, Cher, Johnny Carson, Vanna White, Sylvester Stallone, Justine Bateman, Olivia Newton-John, Sharon Gless, Teri Garr, Janet Jackson, Donna Mills, Sonny Bono, Tanya Tucker, Stephanie Zimbalist, James Olmos, Anne Murray, Eric Soldo, Tiffany, Debbie Gibson, among others. Because many stars so strongly guard their privacy, the details of their stalking typically remain confidential. But the *numbers* of stars who hire private security groups for consultation, occasional protection, even round-the-clock security indicate that the problem is severe—and getting worse.

Gavin de Becker, an expert on stalking and private consultant on security issues in southern California, works to protect celebrities faced with such harassment. De Becker currently provides services for about 170 individual celebrities, sports and religious figures, and acts as security consultant to forty major corporations. Altogether his staff has assessed some 16,000 people who may pose a threat to clients. De Becker believes that the phenomenon of celebrity stalking is on the rise, fueled in part by the media and the public's growing access to the stars' professional and private lives. "Nowhere in history," says de Becker, "could you completely 'know' someone like you can now 'know' Johnny Carson."

Since his organization began operation, de Becker and his staff have collected over 300,000 bizarre letters and gifts sent to stars by clearly obsessed fans. These items offer a glimpse into strange territory, the regions of the obsessed mind, and help de Becker assess the potential threat posed by any particular fan. Ranging from the strange but mundane (five one-cent postage stamps in one mailing) to the flagrant and expensive (a motorcycle), these items are a catalogue of the perplexing, the disordered, or the deranged. As individual gifts, some items seem merely odd: disposable razors, a half-eaten candy bar, a sample tube of toothpaste, a stone, a Rubic's Cube key chain, a map of the subject's hometown or a photo of the star's home, a pencil, a passport, locks of human hair. Others have more disturbing implications: a thousand-page letter, animal feces, a bed pan, a facsimile bomb. Still others are downright frightening: a syringe of blood, pieces of blood-smeared paper, a coyote's head, photos of corpses with the star's face superimposed on them, containers of urine or semen, dead animals, even human body parts.

Some items are disturbing because they arrive in overwhelming volume, suggesting a fan's passionate attachment through sheer force of numbers. Michael J. Fox experienced just such an obsessive onslaught. In 1988, when Fox and actress Tracy Pollan married, the actor began receiving letters—some explicitly threatening—from a young woman named Tina Marie Ledbetter, who called herself Fox's "Number One fan." In the course of about a year, Fox received *6,200* such letters from Ledbetter. In some, Ledbetter demanded that Fox and Pollan separate; otherwise, she claimed, Fox would die.

Such threats may be disturbing, but for Dr. Park Dietz, a forensic psychiatrist at the UCLA School of Medicine and an expert on criminal pathology, they are no fail-safe method for predicting actual violence from a fan. In two companion studies—one on inappropriate letters mailed to celebrities, the other on inappropriate letters to members of Congress—Dietz and his colleagues claim some interesting discoveries. First, their data indicated that the presence of a threat provided *no clear prediction* as to whether the celebrity would eventually be approached or put in danger of physical harm. In itself, according to Dietz's research team, a written threat did not reliably predict contact. However, writers who *expressed a desire for contact* were more likely to actually approach the stars than those who did not express such a desire; similarly, those who mentioned *sharing a special destiny or fate* with the celebrity were more likely to approach the victim than those who did not. Further, the mention of a *specific date or place* where something "would happen to the celebrity" was positively correlated with approaching behavior, as was the presence of *more than ten letters* written to the celebrity. Other positive indicators of approach were (1) mentioning a weapon, (2) writing from more than one address, (3) writing to the same celebrity for more than one year, and (4) attempting to telephone as well as write. Taken together, these indicators of potential harm are now used in assessing the threat to any targeted star.

Local Celebrities: Ready Targets

Celebrity status and the privileges that accompany it may offer only a thin veneer of protection against a fanatic's attempts to make contact. Moreover, celebrities needn't be nationally known in order to become targets of obsession. Unlike Hollywood celebrities, whose publicity extends widely, even internationally, local TV and radio personalities may only be known to a regional audience. Yet some members of that audience may also stalk—a fact that can have terrifying repercussions. Kelly Minton, formerly a TV anchor for WDAF-TV in Kansas City, Missouri, experienced such terror. In the spring of 1992, Minton, who anchored the six P.M. and ten P.M. newscasts, began receiving strange letters, which became increasingly threatening. "He sent pictures of female celebrities—Paula Abdul, Ivana Trump—and they started coming with limbs cut off. Then they were headless, or they had no torsos. He kept saying he wanted to meet me. Then he wrote, 'We'll see Jesus together.' "

When Minton received a letter with bloody fingerprints on it, she alerted management, who increased security at the station. Ultimately, the repeated contact—which grew to include phone calls traced to local pay phones and messages traced in the dirt on her car—drove Minton to quit her job and leave town. "I don't know if I'll stay in the business—I'm not sure I want to go back into public life and risk going through that again."

Valerie Martin's story also illustrates the disturbing extent to which an audience member can affect a local celebrity. A disc jockey in Fargo, North Dakota, Martin became aware she was being targeted in the summer of 1992. Working her station's seven-to-midnight call-in request show, Valerie received a call one night from a man who would not identify himself. "I had no idea who this guy was," she recalls, but the caller's message suggested he knew her. "I apologize for being rude to you," he said, "I want to give you the opportunity to date me." Believing him merely goofy or weird, Valerie told the man firmly she didn't know him and that she had no interest in dating him. When she hung up the phone, she remembers, she laughed about the incident with her station manager, who had heard her side of the conversation and found it amusing.

Valerie had forgotten about the first call by the time the second came in September. This time she found herself speaking with a man who repeatedly asked, "Hey, Valerie, what's with the overtures? What's with the overtures?" Martin's station plays a mix of easy listening rock, love songs and ballads, and so the caller's question at first seemed a misplaced pun. Valerie recalls thinking it was just her luck to get "some disgruntled public radio listener" on the line.

The next day it became clear she was wrong. A fax arrived at the station which described in detail the physical attributes of a man whom we will call "Dave." Valerie knew of a Dave, a man who occasionally visited her neighbors downstairs in the house where she rented an apartment. Once or twice she had seen him in passing; occasionally she would see his bicycle parked outside the house. She had never thought much about him, but in this fax it became clear that *he* was thinking of *her*. "He told his height, his weight, his preferences, he explained his likes and dislikes," Valerie recalls. The fax noted that Valerie would receive a call later in the day. Written at the bottom of the page were the sentences, "You've been propositioned. Get ready." When he did call, she firmly insisted that he was offending her and that she had no interest in him.

Once again, Dave seemed to disappear, and it was not until October that he contacted her again. On reading his third fax sent to her at the station, Valerie began to feel nervous about the man and his state of mind. Far from dropping out of her life, Dave seemed to suggest that Valerie was actually controlling his own. "What did I do to you," the message asked, "for you [to] play with me like this?" On November 16 a messenger delivered to Valerie one dozen red roses and a lengthy letter. In it Dave casually observed that he wanted to date Valerie three or four times; by then he noted, "we should both know whether or not there's a future in it. If we don't, we both should be shot." Later in the letter he warned her that if she didn't "come back" to him, he would kill her. Valerie was terrified.

At this point Valerie embarked on a journey filled with confusion, fear—and self-education. Initially pressing her case solely with the police, Valerie later would work with detectives, a private lawyer, and staff from area groups concerned with victims' rights and women's issues. Over the next six months—a period in which she continued to receive numerous faxes and letters—she worked to protect herself by learning about her available legal options. Hoping to erase any clues for her stalker, Valerie moved to a new address and had identifying information about herself erased from public records. She experienced additional relief when Dave was arrested on harassment charges and when she was granted an order of protection, and she was happy to learn that Dave had moved out of the state. In a turn of events familiar to many victims of stalkers, however, Valerie has since learned that Dave has returned to the area and has been asking about her.

Men in the public eye may also become targets of pursuit. Indeed, according to John Lane, a significant number of minor or local celebrities who are targeted are male. Lane cites a case in which a television game show host in California began receiving anonymous, repeated phone calls. The calls were especially disturbing because the caller referred to the host's and his wife's out-of-state relatives, seeming to know an uncanny amount about their names and whereabouts. Finally, with the assistance of the LAPD, the calls were traced to their source. Astonishingly, the caller was a successful phone company supervisor in Texas who had used her position to access personal information on the celebrity. She was married and had a family; she seemed, in Lane's words, "a normally functioning member of society." When confronted, however, she admitted to making the calls and agreed to undergo counseling.

Public Officials

Like other stalkers of the stars, this woman had an obsession that spurred her to risk her job and family to pursue with single-minded determination a person she had never met. U.S. Senators, members of Congress, and U.S. Supreme Court Justices, like celebrities, also have been at the receiving end of such obsession. Park Dietz's study of inappropriate letters sent to members of Congress helps clarify the nature and extent of these threats. Dietz selected a hundred cases drawn randomly from the archives of the U.S. Capitol Police to study and assess the dangers posed to this one group of prominent public figures.

In addition to leading high-profile lives, members of Congress may be targets because of the nature of their work. Dietz notes that these individuals "must take public positions on such charged issues as abortion, gun control, capital punishment, gay rights, aid to the Contras, and military spending. . . . Not surprisingly, members of Congress receive a steady stream of hostile and inappropriate mail, telephone calls, and visitors." Like individuals who send gifts to Hollywood celebrities, those who write to members of Congress often include bizarre enclosures, some of a disturbingly personal nature, including "birth certificates, passports, photographs of the subject masturbating, and containers of blood or semen."

Moreover, the content of the letters themselves often proves highly provocative. One writer, who demanded "the unconditional arrest and impeachment of the President of the United States," also claimed that one evening, while watching the news, he had been able telepathically to make the anchor blink his eyes. "I am sure," he continued, "[that] millions of people witnessed this occurrence." One woman frequently wrote, called, and visited the offices of a member of Congress. In one letter she noted that she had lost her daughter, and that "generally I don't lose my tempor [sic] But when I do I start to slam things . . . I'll wait one year and if I don't get Lilian Back—slam—I'll destroy them. Slam. Because what happened to me was true—slam—They called me a Liar—slam—and if I have to slam—I'll destroy them all." Another writer claimed to have stabbed herself in the eye with a pen while composing her letter.

In studying outcomes, Dietz and his colleagues found some interesting similarities between these and letters sent to celebrities. As with celebrities, threats seemed to be no reliable indication of possible approach and violence. In fact, Dietz observed, letter writers who threatened a member of Congress were statistically less likely to approach that public figure.

But what of someone who does attempt to make physical contact with a public figure and engages in harassment that goes beyond annoyance to become intimately invasive? Kathleen and Bob Krueger's story puts a human face on the fear that such public figures experience. In 1993, Texas Senator Bob Krueger and his wife Kathleen made public their ongoing struggle with an ex-campaign worker, Thomas Michael Humphrey. Their story began nine years earlier, in 1984, during Krueger's campaign for a seat in the U.S. Senate. The Kruegers had hired Humphrey and his plane to take them to campaign stops around the state. When Krueger lost the Democratic primary, Humphrey seemed much more distraught than other campaign workers. Seemingly unable to accept the loss, Humphrey would repeatedly show up at the couple's home, until they finally felt compelled to tell him, "Go on with your life as we have ours." At that moment, Kathleen recalls, Tom snapped. Humphrey began phoning the Kruegers incessantly. Threatening notes and letters began appearing at their doorstep, evidently hand-delivered. One day Humphrey himself appeared and gripped the startled Kathleen in a long, eerie hug. At that point the Kruegers decided not to open their door to him again.

At one stage in the Krueger's ordeal, Humphrey had moved to California, and the couple felt they might be free of him. But the phone calls kept coming, escalating to as many as 120 per day—and so did the threats. In one call Humphrey told Krueger, "I'm going to kill you, I'm going to kill you . . . I've hired a killer to put a .22-caliber to your head while you lay sleeping next to your wife." Because the threat was explicit and made across state lines, the FBI was able to intervene and arrest Humphrey. It was stories like the Kruegers' —and their courage to go public—that helped pass antistalking legislation and impel Congress to consider guidelines for developing a model for state antistalking laws.

Athletes

Interestingly, one of the first documented cases of celebrity stalking in this country did not involve a Hollywood celebrity, but a professional athlete, baseball player Eddie Waitkus. In 1949 a deranged fan of Waitkus's, Ruth Steinhagen, approached Waitkus in his hotel room in Philadelphia and shot him with a rifle. Described in detail in Chapter 11, the Waitkus/Steinhagen case can be seen as a cautionary tale about the dangers of idolatry and the deluded fans it encourages.

Like other celebrities, athletes today are viewed by enormous television audiences whose members may include the deluded and the obsessional. Ice skater Katarina Witt was victimized for months by a man who seemed willing to go to any lengths to locate her. In 1990, after having sent Witt a catalogue of disturbing items—strange letters, proposals of marriage, nude photos—her perpetrator traveled from California to the ice skater's home in Altendorf, Germany. Jumping over her fence, he pounded on her door yelling, "I love you." Once, according to his letters, he even masturbated at her door. Witt pleaded with him to be left alone. FBI agents finally arrested the man after he mailed Witt a letter that read, "Please don't be afraid when God allows me to pull you out of your body to hold you tight! Then you'll know there is life beyond the flesh."

In an even more disturbing case which received enormous media attention, tennis champion Monica Seles was attacked at a tennis tournament in Hamburg, Germany, on April 30, 1993, by Gunther Parche, a knife-wielding assailant who claimed to be a fan of Steffi Graf's. Apparently eager to take Seles out of competition, Parche walked up behind Seles as she sat at courtside between games, stabbed her in the back with a nine-inch boning knife, and attempted to stab her a second time before being subdued by courtside authorities. Fortunately, the man's aim was not as deadly as his intent, and Seles survived the attack. The attack appears to have done more than injure her physically, however, and at the time of this writing, the former champion has not returned to competitive tennis.

Mental Illness and Stalking: The Case of Ralph Nau

What accounts for the extreme behavior exhibited by stalkers of the famous? According to forensic psychiatrists, celebrity stalkers may suffer from three categories of disorder: (1) a mental illness such as schizophrenia, (2) a mental illness such as a delusional disorder, or (3) a personality or characterological disorder. Clearly, not all people who suffer from a major mental illness or a personality disorder engage in stalking. Those who do, however, may pose especially serious challenges for celebrities, their security staffs, and law enforcement. The case of Ralph Nau—conceivably Hollywood's most notorious stalker—illustrates the risk posed to celebrities by mentally ill fans. It also points up our legal system's shortcomings in dealing with mentally ill stalkers.

As Bruce Rubenstein reported in his detailed, three-part series in the *Illinois Legal Times,* Ralph Nau's childhood in a Wisconsin farming family was anything but normal. "My parents," Nau wrote to Rubenstein, "had a very active sex life"—Nau claims that they organized "swing" parties for couples at their home, which often culminated in bedroom orgies. Ralph, his older brother, and younger sister shared a room directly above their parents' room. The children's room was heated by an open grate, through which they had full view of the parents' activities.

Nau's own initiation to sex occurred when, at the age of sixteen, his father forced the teenager to engage in incest with his mother. "It was the worst moment I ever had," Nau wrote, "It was my first and last time in bed with a girl." Shortly thereafter, Nau began exhibiting disturbing behavior. He took up writing fan letters to singer-actresses Cher and Olivia Newton-John, often amounting to several letters a day. At the same time, he joined a pen pal club for "mature men"—his correspondent, "Candy," would, for a fee, describe pornographic sex. The rules of the club led Nau to believe that another woman, "Maria," was watching over these letter-writing interchanges and would punish any unruly correspondent.

In 1980, Nau apparently became so inspired by Candy's descriptions that he traveled to the letter club's Indiana mailing address in an attempt to track down his fictional correspondent. However, he discovered that his letters—as well as those written by others—were being forwarded to an address in Arizona. Attempting to continue his search to Arizona, he later told psychiatrists, he somehow ended up in the desert, where he encountered a vision of Maria, who instructed him to find Cher and Newton-John. Nau set out for Los Angeles to do just that.

For three years Nau lived under the facade of a normal life. Employed in a veterinary hospital, he proved to be a diligent, trustworthy worker. He was, however, nightly writing long letters to Cher, Newton-John, and Sheena Easton. When they did not respond, Nau grew increasingly frustrated, believing that Maria had turned them against him. In the meantime, both Cher and Newton-John had contacted Gavin de Becker, whose security agents ultimately located and began shadowing Nau. They observed him frequenting gun shops, and they were able to surveille Nau's room, which appeared to be "a shrine to Olivia Newton-John."

In late 1981, Nau killed a puppy at the veterinary hospital, extracted its teeth, and sent them to Newton-John. In an enclosed letter he explained that he had determined that the puppy was an "agent" sent by

Maria, and added, "Whoever is in charge of this shit, they're going real low when they start in on a defenseless little puppy. They should all be six feet under." Ominously, by this time Nau was also referring to Newton-John as already dead; he believed she had been killed by her evil double, whom Nau believed it was his responsibility to kill next.

In 1983, Nau went so far as to travel to Australia, believing that Newton-John was there. When in 1984 he returned to his parents' farm in Wisconsin, Nau's troubling behavior became even more deranged. Bizarre reports of his activities surfaced from neighbors and family: Nau would wander about the farm, screaming; Nau had gutted a dead cow and slept for a night inside its body; Nau was committing acts of bestiality with his dog. Still, no one seemed willing to intervene—until events took a lethal turn.

When Nau's parents divorced that same year, Nau moved to the farm of his mother's new husband, Kenneth Gerkin. Gerkin had an eight-year-old son by a former marriage, Dennis, a reportedly autistic boy. One night Nau told his mother and Gerkin that Dennis had disappeared from his bed. A search by the local sheriff's office revealed the boy's body in a shallow grave. In a statement made to police, Nau claimed that he had taken a walk with Dennis, "but when we got outside, he wasn't human anymore. . . . When we got by the tree, the animal tried to get away and started crying, and I swung at it with the ax and hit it in the head."

Interviewed on several occasions by psychiatrists, Nau was diagnosed as suffering from paranoid schizophrenia, an illness whose symptoms can include severely disordered thinking and behavior. Nau's delusions included convictions that evil others were out to persecute and control him by inserting thoughts into his mind.

At the time of Dennis's murder in 1984, Nau reportedly believed himself to be telepathically communicating with the entire 1984 Rumanian national gymnastics team, and he was writing to Nadia Comaneci. Since then he has mailed thousands of letters to forty different celebrities. Nau has written to Marie Osmond, Madonna, Heather Locklear, and Whitney Houston. He has written to Vanna White, who he believed sent him messages through *Wheel of Fortune* puzzles. He has claimed that a variety of stars, such as Joan Lunden and Sheena Easton, have communicated with him via the television, and that others speak to him through their album covers. He has claimed to be the father of Farrah Fawcett's child, and to be engaged to Marie Osmond.

Such fixation on multiple celebrities—either in succession or simultaneously—is not uncommon among celebrity stalkers. Another case of simultaneous obsession involved Michael Perry, an escapee from a mental institution. Perry, also obsessed with Olivia Newton-John, was convinced that the actress was able to make dead bodies levitate through the floor of his home. He believed that she could alter the color of her eyes as a signal to him. Perry reportedly carried a list of individuals he was planning to kill, a list that included not only Newton-John but also Justice Sandra Day O'Connor. After being turned away from Newton-John's home by security officers, Perry went on a rampage, fatally shooting five people, including his own parents. In a final act of mutilation, he then shot out his victims' eyes. When Perry was finally apprehended in a Washington,

D.C., hotel near the Supreme Court, police found seven different television sets in his room, broadcasting static signals. On each screen, Perry had drawn a staring eye.

Delusional Disorders

Thought to be relatively rare in the general population, delusional disorders occur when someone who otherwise *appears* psychologically stable holds an unsupportable belief about himself or others. Delusional disorders can be divided into several categories, each with its own predominant type of delusion: persecutory, somatic, jealous, grandiose, erotomanic. An individual suffering from a persecutory delusion, for example, may incorrectly believe herself to be on the run from the Mafia. Someone with a somatic delusion may imagine that some body part is grotesquely large and misshapen, despite the fact that he appears perfectly normal to others. Delusions of grandiosity may lead someone to believe he is the son of God, or that he has supernatural powers to heal the sick with his mind.

In the erotomanic delusional disorder—sometimes referred to as de Clerambault's Syndrome or *psychose passionelle*—the delusion primarily relates to feelings of love given to and received from another. An erotomanic typically believes he or she is loved by someone who is far more powerful or socially prestigious, such as a movie star or politician. Erotomanics idealize the loved person, believing that theirs is a perfect match, even though usually they have never met. Though some erotomanics keep their belief a secret for months or even years, others go to extraordinary lengths to find and make contact with the loved one.

Examples of erotomania in psychiatric literature illustrate this delusion. One of de Clerambault's patients in 1921 was a fifty-three-year-old Frenchwoman who felt herself loved from afar by King George V of England. She believed that all British tourists in France had been sent by the King as evidence of his love. On several occasions she traveled to England to stand outside of Buckingham Palace. Once she saw the curtains moving at a window, and she believed the King to be signaling her.

According to Dr. Michael A. Zona of the USC School of Medicine, erotomania tends to make its first appearance in relatively young individuals. The condition has a rapid onset, often without warning. "Prognosis," writes Zona, "is considered poor for these individuals," though he notes that a few erotomanics have responded positively to the psychiatric medication Pimozide. In one such case, a woman who worked as a clerk at a hospital became convinced that an older male physician was secretly in love with her. She felt the man indicated his love to her through the use of secret signals, such as brief head movements. After she left her job, she believed he continued signaling her through telepathy. On occasion she claimed she could actually feel the presence of the man's hands on her body. These feelings gradually overtook her waking life and interfered with her thinking. According to the woman's psychiatrists, treatment with Pimozide and other medications ultimately helped dispel her erotomanic feelings.

John Lane points out that in many cases, closet erotomanics will not "come out and express their delusional beliefs to other people." Since the individual experiencing the delusions may seem otherwise quite normal, the delusion may never be "discovered," and the sufferer may never receive psychiatric help. Yet for erotomanics who do attempt to make contact with the loved person, often fervently, they increase the likelihood that their harassing behavior will bring them into contact with the police. In the seventy-four cases of stalking in the Los Angeles area that he studied, Michael Zona found that those in the erotomanic group were the most likely to seek out a celebrity at home and to stalk that celebrity. Unfortunately, contact, arrest, and subsequent treatment may not be enough to stop someone whose delusion is strong. Lane notes that in the case of the male game show host, the delusional phone caller continued to attempt to make contact even after undergoing psychiatric counseling.

Personality Disorders

What of the celebrity stalker who neither has an identifiable mental illness nor fits the profile for erotomanic delusional disorder? Some stalkers appear to have personality disorders that may be less extreme than diagnosable mental illness, but may induce them to harbor fantasies of love with the celebrity, to make inappropriate contact, even to commit acts of aggression and violence. For these stalkers, a constellation of behaviors may apply.

Personality—the network of qualities, perceptions, and behaviors that makes up our identity—is thought to be formed throughout an individual's life. *How* individual personalities are formed continues to be the subject of considerable academic debate, but most researchers acknowledge the contribution of both biological and environmental factors. Some researchers speak of one's personality as the sum of *temperament* and *character,* temperament being composed of those aspects of a person which are inborn, biologically and genetically given, and character representing the patterns of behavior a person develops in response to life experiences. Personality is thus a kind of synthesis of the biologically determined and the socially learned.

Constructed by the biological and the social, the genetic and the situational, personality begins to be formed in the earliest months of life. Susceptible to biological, interpersonal, familial, and environmental influences, personality can be nourished and sustained, or it can be stunted and deformed. A child possessing a healthy neurochemical makeup, who is loved and encouraged by supportive adults in a stable environment, can grow into a healthy, well-adjusted individual. If all goes well, his or her personality will be within normal bounds, strong enough to weather life's difficulties yet flexible enough to adapt to changing circumstances.

Other children, however, may be subject to such stress—derived from internal or external sources—that their emerging personalities become weakened or deformed. Growing up with abusive or negligent parents, being subject to severe losses at critical junctures in their lives, growing up in dangerous surroundings—all these forces can lead to psychological instability. Over time, the child's defensive reactions to adversity may harden into what psychologist

Robert Fein describes as a "pattern of maladaptive behavior"—a personality disorder.

Personality disorders are usually divided into distinct types, such as the paranoid, antisocial, borderline, and histrionic, but individuals in each of the forms are likely to share some common characteristics. Because their attitudes and actions have hardened into rigid, unyielding patterns, personality-disordered individuals may have trouble reacting normally to stress and may consequently perform poorly at jobs. Because they are likely to feel that problems reside "with everyone else, not me," they are also apt to have difficult personal relationships. In fact, people suffering from personality disorders have been described as "not so much troubled themselves [as] troublesome to others."

Certain personality-disordered individuals express the characteristics seen in those who repeatedly harass or follow another. Paranoid and antisocial personality-disordered people may have an unswerving hostility toward others, and an inability to empathize with other people's pain. As with some domestic violence stalkers (discussed in Chapter 3), these individuals may feel that social mores do not apply to them, that they are above the law or not responsible for their actions. They may blame the victim for their own attitudes and actions. They may exhibit aggressive behavior, be irrational and destructive, or become violent toward others with little provocation.

According to experts, some personality-disordered stalkers paradoxically at the same time seek acknowledgment and acceptance from their victims, expressing hope for such acceptance even after having committed inconceivable acts. As he sat in prison for murdering Rebecca Schaeffer, Robert Bardo still sought to believe that Schaeffer had wanted contact with him. As proof, he said that his name and phone number were in Schaeffer's date book on the day he murdered her. Such stalkers may also court the media, desiring publicity or fame as a kind of public acceptance for their actions.

The personality-disordered individual may also don elaborate disguises to gain access to his victim. He might, like Arthur Jackson—Teresa Saldana's stalker—pose as a director's assistant, a publicist, a producer, a photographer, and an agent in order to locate his victim. Like Robert Bardo, who hired a private detective to track down Rebecca Schaeffer's address, he may undertake clever and expensive methods to accomplish his task. He may, like Katarina Witt's stalker, travel extraordinary distances in an effort to make face-to-face contact. Such stalkers hope ultimately to meet the star and get the star's validation for their strenuous efforts. Without such acceptance, the stalker may continue to feel less than whole, worthless or empty.

Today, stars are routinely warned against any indiscriminate response to fans. Whatever the psychological motivation, such individuals can pose grave and unpredictable threats to celebrity safety. Sadly, it may not take much to feed an obsessional fantasy. Even the smallest token—an autographed publicity photo, a form letter—can stoke an obsession to dangerous new levels. Before he killed her, Bardo wrote to Schaeffer, offering a few thoughts on spirituality and friendship. She graciously wrote back, saying that his comments had been touching and "real." She signed the letter, "Love, Rebecca." In an interview with Gavin de Becker, Bardo later recalled that those words represented more favorable contact with a woman than he'd ever known in his life. Tragically, Rebecca Schaeffer's talent, success, and friendly kindness to an anonymous fan ended up being qualities that, in Robert Bardo's twisted mind, sentenced the young star to death.

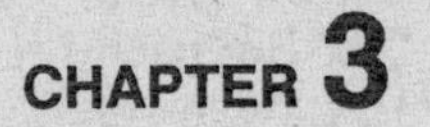

Until Death Do Us Part

Domestic Violence and Stalking

> [People think] you're not being stalked—this is your husband, for Christ's sake! They think of stalking as the Theresa Saldana case or some Freddy Krueger thing.
>
> Julie Owens, battered women's advocate

> I started running. The first bullet hit me in the head. The second bullet hit me in the arm and knocked me down, and I thought he was going to get me then. The third bullet hit me right before I was at the doors and it hit me in the back. I lost control of my body; I couldn't open the doors. . . . It's hard to believe it. I still don't remember hearing the sounds, but I can still remember the smell of the gunpowder.
>
> Stephanie Sund, victim

Few newspaper headlines are as shocking or grim as those that describe the potentially lethal stalking of ex-spouses or intimate partners: "Diary of a Stalker: How I Killed My Wife" (*Chicago Tribune,* 6/26/92); "Despite Ex-Husband's Efforts, Woman Lives" (*Orlando Sentinel,* 6/22/93); "Slaying Suspect's Former

Wives, Girlfriends Tell of Stalking, Terror" (*San-Diego Union-Tribune,* 3/9/93); "Woman Freed After 3½ Hour Ordeal; Ex-Boyfriend Charged" (*Chicago Tribune,* 9/26/92); "Ex-Boyfriend Kills Woman, Self" (*Newsday,* 7/21/93); "Man Gets 2-Year Sentence for Terrorizing Ex-Girlfriend" (*Chicago Tribune,* 11/25/92). According to experts, the majority of stalking offenders—83 percent—are comprised of spouses, ex-spouses, or former "significant others." In a startling statistic, the National Coalition Against Domestic Violence reports that every five years the death toll of persons killed by relatives or acquaintances equals that of the entire Vietnam War.

Domestic violence occurs in American households an average of once every fifteen seconds. In fact, the U.S. Surgeon General found that physical abuse by male social partners accounts for more injuries among American women than auto accidents, muggings, and rape by a stranger *combined.* In 1984 the Surgeon General declared domestic violence as this nation's "number one health problem." Far from being a private or isolated phenomenon, patterns of abuse in battering relationships take predictable and repeated forms, often combining tactics of emotional, psychological, sexual, and economic abuse with actual physical violence.

Common tactics of domestic abuse include intimidation and threats; isolating the victim from friends, family, or the outside world; tormenting the victim psychologically with insults, humiliation, and mind games; keeping the victim economically dependent; controlling every aspect of a victim's life, including who she sees, where she goes, what she is or is not allowed to do. In all cases, the threat of physical violence is never far from a battered woman's mind. A

1992 Senate Judiciary Committee report, *Violence Against Women: A Week in the Life of America,* documents a wrenching account of the range and brutality of domestic violence acts in this country. A single week's logs from police precincts, emergency rooms, and battered women shelters show that victims are pinched, slapped, shoved, kicked, punched, beaten, raped, strangled, choked, and stabbed. They document accounts of women burned by cigarettes, scalded, dragged by the hair, sliced with broken glass, beaten with hammers, broom sticks, gun butts, and metal pipes, and thrown from moving cars. Domestic violence is not just a spontaneous angry outburst or an occasional argument. It reflects a pattern of power, intimidation, and domination—and often systematic surveillance and control have already been established while the victim is still in the home.

One characteristic of batterers is extreme jealousy and suspicion of the victim's behavior. Some abusers are so suspicious, writes psychologist Lenore E. Walker, that they insist that their partner "generally account for every moment of her time." Such abusers keep detailed mental, or even written, records of everything the partner says and does, so that her behavior can be monitored and any imagined "slip" punished.

Such extreme suspicion dominated daily life for one victim, Teresa Bender. Virgil Bender and Teresa Zeleske were married in May 1992. Sometime after that, Teresa began to seek counseling because she so feared her husband's obsessive behavior. A friend who knew them both recalled that Teresa reported having her phone calls monitored, being timed on her way home from work, even being followed to the bathroom. Finally, Teresa left the relationship.

However, as in Teresa's case, it is often *after* victims attempt to leave an abusive relationship that these patterns of surveillance and dominance escalate—sometimes lethally. In May 1993, after a year of terrorizing and actively stalking his ex-wife, Virgil Bender shot and killed Teresa and two co-workers, then killed himself. Such tragedy, moreover, is not an exception. Advocates estimate that victims who leave a battering relationship have a 75 percent higher chance of being killed by their partners—and in the vast majority of cases, stalking precedes the fatal attack. Indeed, experts report that 90 percent of women who were killed by their husbands in 1991 were stalked prior to being murdered.

"If I Can't Have You, Nobody Will"

Domestic violence stalkers, as a category, constitute the most dangerous and potentially lethal group of stalkers. Not only do these individuals have a proven history of violence, they also know their victims intimately—as a result, the threats they make and pose become more pointed and potentially deadly. Abusers often operate out of the mindset that their victims belong to them, are theirs to control or punish for trying to escape, and they often rationalize their violent or invasive behavior by blaming the victim's actions.

According to Julie Owens, a battered women's advocate in Hawaii, the abuser—and the stalker he may become—frantically attempts not to lose control over his wife or girlfriend. "The women I know who have been stalked have been in relationships with people who have power and control issues," she notes. "[What the] stalker and the abuser . . . do is based in their belief systems, and their belief system says, 'I have the right, and maybe even the responsibility, to keep this woman in line . . . to tell her what to do and where to go.'"

Further, says Owens, such a man believes that "'I have the right to enforce this any way I see fit.'" Such a stalker often aims to "teach the victim a lesson"—a lesson fueled by his own fear of abandonment, rage at being rejected, feelings of impotence, or desire for revenge. If he has suffered only insignificant consequences for past domestic violence crimes, moreover, he may believe he is omnipotent or above the law—and subsequently that he has the right to hunt down and reclaim (or eliminate) that which he once "owned."

Kathryn Chaney, Executive Director of the Women's Community Association in Albuquerque, New Mexico, recalls a disturbing case of abuse, pursuit, and attempts to repossess. One woman who came to the attention of WCA's staff was being repeatedly abused at home, with her husband also obsessively monitoring her whereabouts. After weeks of careful planning, she managed to slip away and go into hiding at a women's shelter. Despite the shelter's secret location, early one morning her husband was able to find the shelter, break into it, and confront his wife. When asked how he had found her, his reply was chillingly simple: "I'm a hunter."

The image of the abuser as hunter, the victim as prey, occur again and again in cases of domestic violence stalking. It occurred in the case of Wayne Chaney (no relation to Kathryn Chaney), who battered and sexually abused his wife Connie until she fled their home, filing for a series of protection orders against his violence. But it was Connie's escape that truly escalated Chaney's efforts. According to one entry in a grisly diary Chaney kept, which documented his obsession for control: "I couldn't live with myself thinking or knowing she won, or she got me. No! This is war." Chaney's "war" was outlined with cold-blooded detail in his diary as he planned the way in which he would stalk her and move in for the murder. "I can't wait to see Connie's face when I suddenly appear," he wrote, adding as an afterthought, ". . . oh of course see her sweat it out and die."

Chaney's surveillance of Connie was meticulous: he knew her whereabouts, her schedule, her every move. On one occasion he was prepared to shoot her just after she had left her apartment with her boyfriend David Hansen, but unexpectedly the Chaneys' small son Max was with them that time. "I couldn't kill her and David in front of Max," Chaney wrote. "As I watched I was saying to myself holding that gun, I said, 'So lucky Connie . . . I'll be back.'" Chaney made good on his threat several weeks later. He described the morning of March 17, 1992, as a beautiful, sunny day: "I'm sitting here waiting for the right time to go. I'm not nervous at all. . . ." Like the hunter he was, Wayne Chaney finally closed in on his wife at her office and shot her dead. "I hit my safety off of the gun and shot her square between the shoulder blades . . . she fell like a rock."

Such behavior seems so extreme that it stuns those of us unfamiliar with the patterns of domestic violence. Unable to comprehend the needs or motives of violent partners, we can only ask, "How could that happen?" Experts who study domestic violence may have some answers. Looking at the causes of abuse from a number of perspectives, many agree that abusers share a range of psychological characteristics. Counselors Richard A. Stordeur and Richard Stille, in their book *Ending Men's Violence Against Their Partners,* describe traits of the battering personality that they and other experts seem to find most consistently.

First, batterers have difficulty identifying any of their own emotions other than anger. They may find feelings such as fear, embarrassment, or sadness, to be overwhelming. They may also believe these are unacceptable male emotions, and may go to great lengths to suppress them. Stordeur and Stille describe this suppression and its consequences as a "male emotional funnel." Suppressing real feelings may translate later into anger, then spiral out of control into violent rage. A man trapped in such a spiral may have little awareness that the rage is connected to some other, original feeling like sadness or shame. Others who witness—or feel the effects of—his rage may experience it as impulsive and erratic.

Abusers also seem to have trouble realistically perceiving themselves and others. As a group, batterers report feeling more negative emotions than men who do not abuse, and they respond to these feelings that they are under personal attack by adopting outwardly defensive or hostile postures against the world. They also tend to perceive otherwise neutral interactions as negative; they believe far more often that others are hostile or rejecting them.

Abusers seem to have difficulty expressing ordinary wants and needs through regular interpersonal communication; ironically, they are often described by others—in and out of their immediate families—as being unassertive. Violence thus becomes their sole means of expression. Most dangerously, batterers also tend to deny or minimize their own behavior, including the severity and frequency of their assaults on others, while exaggerating the bad or disobedient behavior of their partners. They frequently refuse to accept responsibility for their violence, instead projecting blame onto other people and external factors, such as alcohol or stress.

Perhaps the most common feature of assaultive men is their jealousy—and the feelings of extreme dependence that give rise to that emotion. Though on the surface he may seem to be in control of his partner's every move, the batterer actually suffers from a profound fear of losing control. Dependent on his partner in the extreme, and terrified that he will lose her, he will go to extraordinary lengths to ensure that she remains near him, submissive, and ready to fulfill his every need. "If his partner makes any autonomous move," write Stordeur and Stille, "the batterer may become violent, homicidal, or even suicidal in an attempt to prevent what he sees as an abandonment."

This extreme fear of abandonment can bring about deadly results. The numbers of homicides and homicide/suicides committed by intimate partners in this country offer a daily reminder that the lethality of the Chaney case is not an isolated one. In 1990 the murders of four women from Orange County, California, helped impel legislators toward passage of the country's first antistalking law (see Chapter 1). Most of these women had requested help from the police and had restraining orders out against ex-partners. One of the women, Patricia Kastle, had her restraining order in her purse when she was shot. Another case in California came to a bloody conclusion in

March 1993 when Daniel John Dorescenzi killed his former girlfriend in the San Diego parking lot of her workplace. Dorescenzi had a long history of assaultive behavior toward female partners and toward his son, whom he is accused of molesting. By the time he finished, Dorescenzi had shot Beverly Mertz over twenty times, once even stopping to reload.

Another widely publicized story, that of Kristen Lardner, illustrates the fact that even those victims who experience a partner's violence once or twice can be at risk. An art student at Boston University, Lardner met and dated Michael Cartier, a twenty-two-year-old bouncer at a Boston nightclub. During a two-and-a-half-month relationship, Cartier assaulted Lardner twice, once knocking her to the sidewalk near her apartment and kicking her repeatedly in the head and legs. After the attack, Lardner told Cartier she would have nothing more to do with him; she applied for a restraining order and was proceeding to press charges against him for assault. Cartier, who was on parole for repeated assaults on other girlfriends, defied the restraining order by calling Lardner. Yet Cartier was neither arrested for violating his restraining order nor for the assault charges. Tragically, the day after the Massachusetts antistalking law was signed into effect, Cartier shot and killed Kristen in broad daylight on a busy street near her apartment, then turned the gun against himself.

Kristen Lardner's story, in addition to pointing out occasional tragic inadequacies of law enforcement and the courts, also highlights one potentially disturbing feature of stalking that stems from domestic violence—the extraordinary desperation of perpetrators that may lead them not only to violence against others, but also against themselves. Of the four Orange County cases mentioned in Chapter 1, for example, two of the murderers immediately shot and killed themselves; one set himself on fire and almost died; and the fourth repeatedly begged sheriff's deputies to shoot him as they led him from the crime scene. Similar tragic outcomes occurred in Chapter 1's three cases of stalking-related violence against men. In each of those cases the perpetrator committed suicide. Such extremity sends up warning flags for victims rights advocates and others, who believe that stalkers obsessed enough to contemplate both murder *and* suicide are unlikely to view the law with any fear whatsoever.

Cycles of Violence

Somewhere between battering and homicide lie the actions and activities of thousands of abusive partners who right now are trying to "get her back." Directors of domestic violence shelters and coalitions across the country confirm the link between stalking behavior and domestic abuse. Linda Van Den Bossche is Victim Advocacy Coordinator of the Rhode Island Coalition Against Domestic Violence, an organization that oversees the work of six member shelters throughout the state. In 1992, Van Den Bossche notes, 4,510 cases of domestic violence were reported through the state's mandatory arrest law. Of those, Van Den Bossche says that "there's really active stalking going on in probably one-half of the cases we deal with." Such cases include "continued contact despite a court order . . . harassing phone calls, bothering [the victim] at work, causing her to lose her job." In many instances, Van

Den Bossche believes the harassment is so great that a woman will "end up going back because he won't leave her alone."

Kathryn Chaney of the Women's Community Association supports these figures. She notes that her organization has encountered literally hundreds of stalking cases among its clients. Julie Owens, founder and former Coordinator of Hawaii's Hospital Outreach Program for Battered Women (HOPE), agrees as well. Owens notes that during the time she worked at her former organization, she saw so many domestic-violence-related stalking cases, they were too numerous to count. Bonnie Gainer, Director of the Rutland County Women's Network and Shelter in Vermont, also comments on the high incidence of stalking among domestic violence victims, claiming that stalking is most prevalent "when the woman first leaves the battering."

Domestic violence stalking—like domestic violence itself—often follows a repeating "cycle" that can become increasingly frequent and severe. Wendy Collier of the Colorado-based Victim Protection Services outlines three hypothetical phases in the cycle of stalking. The first phase, which Collier calls the "Tension Building Phase," may move from relatively innocuous invasions to more dangerous efforts to control the victim. Behaviors such as annoying phone calls, unsolicited letters, and odd gifts may be followed by actual threats, then proceed to surveillance of the victim, following the victim, minor acts of vandalism, and other gradually more serious attempts to control and terrorize the victim. In the second phase, the "Explosive or Acutely Violent Phase," minor acts of violence become major attacks—which can include physical assault, kidnapping, rape, burglary, violence against the victim's family and friends, or the perpetrator's "final act of control": murder, suicide, or both.

A third phase sometimes separates the other two; during this "Hearts and Flowers" phase, the stalker may either switch techniques and ask for forgiveness, or a period of relative silence may leave the victim feeling temporarily safe. Many stalking victims report a period in which the stalking behavior seems inexplicably to taper off. Understandably, they may take this as a sign that the stalking is finally over. However, this phase, Collier points out, is often only a new tactic in the cycle of stalking; she cautions that victims can become complacent about their safety during this seeming lapse in activity, leaving themselves particularly vulnerable when the stalker resurfaces and the terror begins again.

In these ways, stalking can mirror the cycle of domestic violence itself, which Dr. Lenore Walker sees as falling into three similar phases:

- *tension-building,* in which there is a gradual escalation of tension and minor but increasing incidents of physical, sexual or emotional abuse
- *acute battering,* in which violence erupts and may last for hours, days, or longer
- a *loving contrition* (or *honeymoon*) phase, during which the batterer apologizes and begs for forgiveness, claiming remorse and promising change.

Both Walker and Collier emphasize that *not all victims will experience each of these phases,* or each element within a given phase, and there is no guarantee that a cycle will unfold predictably. Every victim must judge her situation individually.

Collier suggests that, in cases where stalking follows

a pattern, these cycles can continue for years. In some cases, the stalker may escalate to murder after the cycle has been repeated often enough that the stalker feels all other attempts at regaining domination have failed. In this case, lethal violence becomes the ultimate act of desperation and control. On the other hand, Collier notes that some perpetrators "abandon their current victim and redirect their fixation to more 'challenging' and vulnerable prey—someone who is not yet alert to their dangerous patterns and treachery."

The ability for stalkers to transfer fixation—or to stalk numerous victims at one time—became graphic to one stalking victim, "Pamela." Pamela recalls a disturbing on-again, off-again relationship she had with a boyfriend. Each time she felt it was time to break off the relationship, he began stepping up his "hearts-and-flowers" gestures: phone calls, notes, gifts, and visits to her home and workplace, trying to keep her with him. Although Pamela was flattered by such gestures, and stayed with him as a result, she began noticing other, more disturbing features of his personality. One evening her curiosity led her to a strange revelation:

> Supposedly he had dated a model for five years, this woman "Ellen." He kept an overnight suitcase in my closet, and one day it got the best of me. I looked in it—and there were all these letters to this Ellen—*to* her, not *from* her—I don't know if he ever mailed them or if they were all sent back to him. And there was this piece of paper that said "Ellen's favorite drink," "Ellen's favorite food." *He kept a log on her.*

Pamela's good instincts led her to break off her relationship for real this time—but her suspicions of his potential stalking fixations were all too quickly borne out. Despite her clear messages that "it was done, it was over," he persisted in visiting her workplace, loitering around her house at odd hours of the day, and sending numerous, insistent notes that now included chilling evidence that he was keeping close surveillance on her. Pamela had to resort to taping her mail slot shut, to keep the deluge of invasive notes and letters at bay. The evidence she had seen in his suitcase, formerly aimed at Ellen, now seemed to have been transferred to her.

After months of harassment, events began to escalate. One night, Pamela was awakened by a noise, and found her stalker in the backyard:

> I said, "What are you doing out here at two in the morning?" . . . He said, "I was just looking for the dog. I wanted to pet the dog." I said, *"At two in the goddamn morning?!* . . . As of tomorrow I'll have a restraining order against you, and if you ever try it again, you'll be behind bars." He looked at me and he said, "People who get restraining orders get destroyed."

Terrified, Pamela did not take out a restraining order. She began to see him everywhere: cruising in his car, walking in her neighbors' yards. His presence seemed inescapable, and she felt it was only a matter of time before his persistence turned more dangerous. She took to sleeping with a baseball bat, hiding in a house whose blinds she kept drawn. At last, for her own safety, she decided to leave her home and move in with her parents, who lived several hours away. "I loved my home," she recalls, "It was wonderful. To give up that home meant a lot. . . . Everybody that meant something to me, I left behind . . . as soon as I got to the outskirts of town I just burst into tears. It was sadness, because I was leaving a life that I loved. But it was also a cry of relief, because I was getting away."

Pamela's ordeal, however, was not yet over. Within two weeks she received a note from her stalker: "Some day, in some way, we'll be together." As with many stalking victims, her stalker was able to find her and again initiate escalating cycles of terror and control, even moving himself to her new city.

Warning Signs

How can you spot a potential stalker, a potentially violent offender, before becoming involved in a relationship? In the words of one victim, "Perpetrators don't wear signs that say, 'Hi, I'm a homicidal maniac, baby.'" However, there may be certain warning signals that can alert you to a potentially dangerous personality. Wendy Collier has compiled the following list of "high risk" traits. According to Collier, individuals who possess these sociopathic traits:

- don't believe their behavior warrants consequences
- are extraordinarily cunning, persuasive, and manipulative
- lack social conscience, empathy, or concern for the welfare of others
- exude charm that is not easily discernible as superficial

- fail to display anxiety and nervousness in situations that would normally produce these feelings
- are unreliable and irresponsible: make no effort to attain long-range goals
- are insincere and untruthful
- display a lack of remorse
- display poor judgment about how to obtain what they want
- have an inability to identify with others or form meaningful and enduring relationships
- consciously decide not to conform to social mores or to obey the law
- chronically refuse to deter gratification, tolerate frustration, or control impulses
- become very irrational and destructive, even if not under the influence of alcohol or drugs (which only serve to remove inhibitions that modify behavior)

Since many abusers go on to become stalkers, many of the warning signs for domestic violence are the same as those for stalking. To repeat, some signs of a potential abuser include partners who exhibit excessive jealousy, or who show an unreasonable need for control in the relationship, which may involve trying to isolate their partners from friends and outside activities. These individuals may exert pressure for quick involvement and commitment from their partners, rushing them into the relationship. They may hold unrealistic expectations of their partners, and may tend to blame others for their problems or for their own growing feelings of anger or insecurity. They may also hold stereotypical views of women and men, often exhibiting macho attitudes and beliefs. They may themselves have been abused as children, or been witnesses to violence in the home. According to studies, many also have substance abuse problems, although drugs and alcohol are not the cause of battering.

Prior to the passage of antistalking laws, police and the courts were unable or unwilling to move against an abuser who continued assaulting and terrorizing his partner once she had left him. In the following story, told at her state's legislative hearings on stalking, Erica describes what it was like in the months following her departure from an intimate relationship.

Erica's Story

During the time that my boyfriend and I were ending our relationship in April of 1992, a number of very frightening things happened. He threatened to kill me by holding a knife to my throat and told me that if I didn't change, he would slit my throat. My cat disappeared, my car engine blew up, and he took all of the money in our savings account. He followed all of this by telling me that the coup de grace was still to come and that he would make it impossible for me to remain living in our city.

I went to the police to tell them that I thought my safety was in danger. The police suggested that I obtain a restraining order against him. That same day, I went to the courthouse and within a few hours had obtained a judge's approval for a restraining order to be served. I told the sheriff's department where they could find him, but it took them five days to get around to serving him, during which time he wasn't even aware that I had filed any complaint, nor was I yet protected by the order.

The restraining order stated that he could not harm, bother, molest, disturb, follow, harass, intimidate, telephone, or threaten me in any way. Violation of the order would be considered a criminal offense. The wording sounded good, and in my naiveté I assumed that once the restraining order had been served, my trouble with him would be over. I have since learned that this is rarely the case with restraining orders, both because of the disregard for the order often felt by those who have the orders served to them—and because of weak interpretation of the orders by law enforcement officials.

Over the next seven months he violated the terms of the restraining order again and again, very often in terrifying ways. The police department became very supportive of me as the weeks and months went past and he continued doing what he had been ordered to stop doing. The police always responded to my calls promptly and with sincere concern, but in essence they acted like a secretarial service for me, logging in incidents and complaints but doing nothing more. Under the city's interpretation of the restraining order, they were unable to do anything to protect me.

I can't count the number of times that I heard a heartfelt "I'm so sorry that this is happening to you. I wish we could do something for you." But the police had their hands tied. As the restraining order was interpreted by the city, the police had to log in each complaint of a violation, make a written report to the city attorney, who in turn had to make a written request to the city judge. (This can be an incredibly slow process. In one instance it took upwards of two weeks for the city attorney to get around to even looking at a complaint, even with persistent calls from me and my personal attorney.) It is then up to the judge (getting the story thirdhand at this point) whether an arrest warrant is justified. Unlike so many other crimes where a suspect is simply identified and arrested—the process for a restraining order is a bureaucratic mess.

Under the city's interpretation of the restraining order, the only exception to this (and I was even told this by the city attorney) is if he were to physically injure me. The restraining order was established to protect me from someone deemed to be a serious potential threat to my safety and welfare, but getting him arrested for a violation of the order seemed to take forever in the few cases that it actually did happen. In most cases even calling the police seemed to be a waste of time.

I'd like to share with you some of the things that I have had to live with this past year. Over the spring and summer a pattern developed. Every time I would see him (for example, if we passed each other in our cars), something creepy would happen within the next few hours. Usually it amounted to something being stolen from my yard or me hearing a crash in the night, which usually turned out to be porch furniture being turned over. Once in the middle of the night I had a stink bomb thrown in through a window. Another time I came home to find that all of my flower beds had been doused with gasoline. On each occasion the police took a report, but did nothing. They were afraid that since there was no "hard evidence" linking these things to him, their approaching him or interrogating him could be viewed by him as harassment, something they didn't want to get charged with.

He also made it a habit to sit in his car near my house, drive up and down the dead-end street that I live on, and watch me as I went about my business downtown. I never went anywhere without looking out for him. I jumped every time I saw a car that looked like his and pretty well came unglued every time it was him. I kept my house and car doors locked at all times. I stopped letting my cat go outside. I wouldn't go to public places with my friends for fear that he would show up. I'd travel as much as possible on the weekend to stay with my sister—just to be out from under his watchful eye—but then I'd worry that something would happen to my house while I was gone. I basically stopped living my life.

Over a period of months I received literally hundreds of hangup phone calls. This began immediately after he moved out. They came at all hours of the day and night. I had my phone number changed, unlisted, and was very careful about who I gave it to, but somehow he got ahold of it almost immediately and the calls continued. The city attorney told me that all I needed was proof that at least three of these calls were coming from his phone and they could prosecute on two counts, violation of the restraining order and violation of the privacy in communications act. I went through the difficult process of getting the phone company to tap my phone, and then for a three week period had to log and report all suspicious calls. During this time I reported about forty calls. Most of the calls turned out to be coming from pay phones on the local university campus where he is a student and from other pay phones around town, but we did get four calls coming from his phone, one more than we needed to prosecute. The police made the necessary report to the city attorney and that's where it ended. The city attorney changed her tone and said that she didn't think we had enough for a case. She did write him a threatening letter, letting him know that she had evidence against him and that she would prosecute him on those charges if he did anything else. We all thought that this would be a great deterrent to further activity, but we were wrong. The letter didn't seem to faze him. A week later he approached me at a bar and tried to talk to me, then when I left the bar, he followed me across town. When this happened I was sure the city would have him arrested *and* prosecuted on the telephone charges. Again—*nothing* happened.

Because I was in such fear of him and his potentially violent reactions, I have been afraid to date other men for most of this last year. On the first date I did have (four and a half months after I had split up with him), he saw and approached me. When I ignored his demands that I tell him the name of the man I was with, he became enraged and yelled obscenities at me. When I arrived home that night I found that some belongings had been stolen from my porch and that my yard had been doused with gasoline again. I made a report to the police and, feeling certain that I wasn't safe in my home, I went to spend the night at a girlfriend's house. When I returned in the morning I saw that more things were missing from my yard. After this incident the police were so fed up that they called him in for questioning (though they felt that they *still* didn't have the evidence to legally interrogate him). Though they did their best to frighten and threaten him, their talk didn't work.

Because the system has been so ineffective in

guarding my safety and in keeping him away from me, I have had to hire both a private investigator and a lawyer. The private investigator has watched me and my house during times that I felt most in danger. This has amounted to quite an expense for me.

Since he and I split up, I have been hearing stories of other women who have also had a terrible time with him. There is an incredibly consistent and frightening pattern from woman to woman. Two of the women never even dated him, but because they thwarted his advances, he began harassing them. Both of them were frightened to the point that they bought guns and kept them loaded. A third woman actually fled the state to get away from him, and she has been very careful to never let him find out where she is.

I have also been hearing through the grapevine that he has gone out of his way to get close to people who know male friends of mine in order to get information about their relationships with me. And he has been asking people he doesn't even know, and who hardly know me, if they know anything about my sex life.

Finally, to my relief, he has been arrested twice in the last few months. The first time was for chasing a friend and myself across town in his car. The second time was for approaching and following me in the grocery store, and then prohibiting me from leaving when I tried to go to my car. He has been charged with four counts of violation of the restraining order. He has pled not guilty to all charges, has requested a jury trial, and has hired a lawyer to represent him. We will probably see a court date in the next month or so, and I look forward to it with a great deal of fear. I will have to testify as a witness, and two of the women who have had similar problems with him have made sworn statements that will be read and used in sentencing if he is convicted. In addition to my own safety I am now nervous for the safety of these two women. I'm told that if he is convicted, he'll probably serve a maximum of a week or two in jail and pay up to a $2,000 fine.

It was ten months ago that this all started, but I still keep a can of mace beside my bed. The two other women think I'm crazy not to have a gun and have warned me that they think my troubles with him are not yet over—especially since I'm having him prosecuted. The bottom line is that I wouldn't have made it this far without the incredible support of my family.

I want to know when I can look forward to feeling safe again. I have really felt all along that he was the one being protected and that he has been allowed more rights than me. I am so sick of hearing the police say that they have to be careful not to harass him.

I want to share a word of advice that I got from two different police officers. These officers, who I appreciated and respected, had come to be very concerned about me. They each told me, on two separate occasions, that based on the current legal system, there was only one thing that could be done to effectively force him into leaving me alone. They suggested that I take the law into my own hands and find someone or someones to beat the daylights out of him and give him the scare of his life. Those are the sentiments of two concerned and frustrated cops. That's a pretty heavy statement about the current system's lack of power when it comes to protecting its citizens.

Asserting Your Rights

Despite the frequency of domestic abuse and domestic-violence-related stalking in this country, a victim's experiences at the hands of an intimate partner are still often minimized. Hounded, harassed, terrified women seeking relief from the police and the courts are all too often given a variety of responses that fall far short of protection. Some claim they have been told that they should expect abuse from "this kind" of husband or boyfriend; that they should have left the relationship far earlier; that the dispute is only domestic or personal; that the violence in the home must be mutual; that they are hysterical, overly imaginative, or lying; that police have far more important real crimes to solve.

Many police and judges, of course, do *not* hold such biased attitudes, and effectively work to use their state's domestic violence and antistalking laws against perpetrators. (See Chapter 6, "Legal Recourse," for a discussion of the roles of law enforcement and the courts.) Nonetheless, if you are being stalked by a former intimate partner, you should be aware that, for a variety of reasons, the police and the courts *may* minimize the crimes being committed against you. They may not understand the cyclical nature of assaultive behavior, that a man who has abused is likely to abuse again. They may be unaware that his violence is likely to escalate, and they may have little or no experience with a woman's repeated efforts to leave a relationship, or with the fact that these efforts may initially place her in great danger. Despite considerable recent publicity about stalking and the passage of antistalking laws, some agencies simply remain unaware of both the problem and the remedy.

Leaving an assaultive relationship requires care in planning and execution. Victim assistance personnel at domestic violence shelters can be of tremendous help in working out the details. The staff of hot lines and women's crisis coalitions are sensitive about the need for privacy and protection. In addition, many states have victim witness services, usually affiliated with the offices of the state's Attorney General and administered through each county prosecutor's office; these services are provided to victims of violent crimes without charge.

If you are a victim, we urge you to remember: you neither deserve to be battered in the home, nor stalked if you choose to leave. Asserting your rights as a citizen will help ensure that all victims of abuse are protected, free to lead productive—and safe—lives.

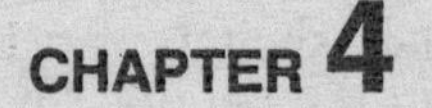

This Can't Be!

Casual Acquaintances and Random Targets

> The loss is more than just time out of your day to fight it. It's your soul, it's your privacy, it's your being, it's your emotions—everything is taken away from you. You are robbed of everything.
>
> "Jodi," stalking victim

> It's my option to make your life miserable.
>
> stalker Richard Wade Farley
> to his victim, co-worker Laura Black

According to Robert Fein, consulting psychologist to the U.S. Secret Service and visiting fellow to the National Institute of Justice, celebrity stalking and intimate partner stalking represent just two ends of the stalking continuum. In between fall two other types of stalking: those stemming from casual connections, and those apparently random targets in which no prior interaction exists. In these latter cases, Fein adds, the pursuer may simply have glimpsed the targeted person once, or perhaps may just know *about* her. In either case, the fear and stress provoked by these random encounters—which may escalate from annoyance to harassment and finally to criminal stalking behavior—can make for an experience of nightmarish proportions.

Out of the Blue

For Beverly Hannon, stalking wasn't a word commonly used when her harassment began in the late 1950s, but the anxiety and panic she experienced due to the attentions of a mysterious stranger were very real. Hannon, who was later to become an Iowa state senator, remembers the events surrounding her stalking by a man who identified himself as "John":

> I was working as a secretary at the IBM office in Cedar Rapids . . . and my desk was right in front of a big plate-glass window that bordered the sidewalk. I had my name on a name card on the front of my desk. A man who lived in Cedar Rapids who had been injured in the Korean War used to walk by there; he fixed on my name and me and started imagining that I had been engaged to him at one time and that I broke off our engagement and wrote him a "Dear John" letter in Korea. He was trying to "win me back."

John tried to win back this person he had never met by mailing romantic cards and letters to Hannon, and by sending her flowers at her workplace. He began to phone her repeatedly, entreating her to remember him and let him back into her life. "He would call me at all hours of the night and day, and at my work. . . . It really spooked me. He would always say, 'Don't you remember me?' and I would say, 'No, I'm sorry, I think you have the wrong person, no, I don't remember you, no, I don't remember any of that.' He knew so many things about me, that in his mind he knew me, and figured, well, I knew him, too."

Hannon began to realize John had her under constant surveillance, shadowing her to and from work and to restaurants. "The man would call me continually and tell me where he had seen me and what I was wearing and who I was with and what time I had left and that sort of thing—and I had no idea who he was. I didn't know what he looked like at all." Her fear increased when her local pastor reported that someone had stopped by to talk about her; the visitor had wanted the pastor to intercede for him with Hannon. When she asked what this man looked like, the pastor's response chilled her: "He said, 'Well, the way I'd describe him is, I'd never want to meet him in an alley at night.'" Hannon was particularly unnerved because she often worked late hours and would travel to and from her workplace alone. Though she reported this man's behavior to the police, they were unwilling to intervene, allegedly claiming, "If he's not threatening you or anything, there's nothing we can do, unless he does something to you.'"

One night, after several months of being followed and harassed, Hannon did meet her stalker face to face:

> I was working late one night at the office. The office manager was way back in the back of the office. I was up in front, typing. The front door was unlocked. I was busy doing what I was doing, and you know how

> you can feel when somebody's there, watching, and I stopped typing. I turned and saw this guy standing there. He had a black leather jacket—a real tall fellow with sandy hair, and it was kind of stringy, hanging down over his eyes. He startled me at first, because I hadn't heard anyone come in. He'd come in the office and come right to my desk. I knew the office manager probably hadn't heard him either, so I spoke extra loud, and I said, "Could I help you?" And he just looked at me and he said, "Don't you remember me?" I said, "Are you John?" and he said, "Yes." I said, "No, I'm sorry, I think you have the wrong person." . . . That was the one and only time I ever saw him.

Suspicious that John might go over the edge, Hannon found herself experiencing "more than low-level anxiety." Even ordinary events began to cause her alarm. "One night after I was married and I was pregnant, I was sitting in our living room. My husband had gone out for a meeting. This guy had just contacted me within that week. The phone rang a few times while my husband was gone, and my heart would start thumping every time I'd go to answer the phone. It was the wintertime, and apparently the ice and snow had thawed and it went "Kerwhump" off the porch while I was sitting there. I jumped straight out of the chair, absolutely terrified, because I thought, 'It's this guy. He's out there.'"

John's behavior continued for ten years. Like many other stalking victims who live with the daily reminder that their tormentor may be just a phone call away, Hannon remained constantly alert for signs of his presence, fearful of the possibility that he might approach her again. It was only in the late 1970s—nearly twenty years after the events began—that she was able finally to feel safe. "I never stopped thinking about the possibility that that guy was around, someplace—until I saw his obituary."

Another victim of random stalking also illustrates how relentless such behavior can be. Jane McAllister, founder of Citizens Against Stalking (see Chapter 5), recalls her own experience with a casual encounter that was to devolve into a nightmare. In the early 1980s, as manager of her corporation's employee assistance program, Jane was an active public speaker on mental health issues. One day, during a coffee break at one of her lectures, she bumped into a man she assumed had been an audience member, and they exchanged some small talk. Within days the man was sending Jane love letters and making passionate declarations on her answering machine. In a flash, she said, "he went from 'Hi, my name is' . . . to 'I want to marry you.'"

After four months of behavior that escalated from childish or mildly strange to seriously annoying, Jane confronted the man and insisted he stop. To her relief, he complied, and Jane believed the harassment was finally over. Nine years after their first encounter, however, she ran into him again in a local convenience store. "I didn't even recognize him," she recalled; unfortunately, *he* remembered *her*. Just as in 1981, he began again to pepper Jane with letters and three or four phone messages per day. When his persistence became too annoying to shrug off, Jane decided once more to confront him. This time, however, the confrontation seemed to take a frightening turn.

> He acted like a little, little child would do. He started mimicking everything I was saying. I was really

> unnerved by it, but I let him run down, and then I said, "You need to hear this. I'm going to say it again and I really want you to listen to me. . . . I want to be real clear that the letters, phone calls, the attention that you're giving me have to stop right now. No more. I'm not interested in you. Is that clear?" His demeanor changed to that of a somewhat older child but nevertheless a child who had been scolded. He was very apologetic, he said, "I'm so sorry. I didn't mean to hurt or scare you and I won't ever do it again, I promise. I didn't mean anything by it." . . . And with that [the stalking] escalated and became very hostile.

Jane contacted friends in the mental health community and described her situation. They warned her that the man, a former client, was mentally unstable and that she should be very careful. By this time Jane had changed her phone number. The strategy, unfortunately, proved problematic. No longer able to maintain contact through the phone, Jane's stalker began to step up his efforts through other, more personal, intrusions. He began to drive by her home, passing back and forth "constantly, day and night." When her neighbor's house was put up for sale, he called the realtor to discuss making an offer, visited the house several times, then approached Jane to tell her he planned to buy the house, and, she recalls, "there was nothing I could do to stop him." When the homeowners traveled out of town, her stalker even broke into their house, presumably to watch her.

He also began to follow her when she left home, tailing her throughout the city. He discovered that she was training for her pilot's license at a local airport, and so he signed up for lessons himself, going to the considerable expense of taking a flight physical exam merely to shadow her activities. He approached Jane's neighbors, posing as a friend to extract information on her whereabouts and activities. Once he appeared at her gym, entered the workout room and simply stood before her silently, as if to demonstrate that he could find her anywhere. On another occasion, he followed her on foot to deliver a whispered threat: "I have something for you, Jane, and the police won't be here when I decide to give it to you."

Much of the fear experienced by both Jane McAllister and Beverly Hannon stems in part from barely knowing the person who began stalking them. Some victims, however, are *never* able to learn the identity of the stranger pursuing them. Consider the situation of "Lori," a twenty-five-year-old who today lives in a mid-sized southern city. Lori's ordeal began when she was fifteen, working at a clothing store on weekends:

> One day when I answered the phone there was a man taking a survey. He said he was going to try marketing different sizes and absorbency of tampons in one box to match the ebb and flow of women's cycles. I started answering questions—that is, what brand tampon I used, where I bought them, etcetera. Then things started getting more personal and I realized it was not a random survey.

Over the next few months, Lori received many more "disguised" calls, where she would realize, after a few minutes' conversation, that she was speaking with her harasser. Her parents also began receiving silent calls at their home.

Like Jane McAllister, Lori experienced a series of escalations in the contact. In college she met and began dating the man who would become her husband. Soon the anonymous caller phoned again, clearly agitated about her new relationship, and graphically threatened to slit Lori's throat. As she continued to date her boyfriend, the frequency and the intensity of the calls increased, with the caller even threatening her boyfriend's life. His surveillance during this time was constant. On several occasions he would phone to tell her what she had done the previous day, whom she had visited, even detailed accounts of what she and her friends had been wearing. Some of those friends, too, began receiving harassing calls.

The threats and the fear intensified, spiraling in on Lori and those closest to her. On three different occasions Lori was followed at night in her car and nearly run off the road. Lori and her boyfriend eventually married; however, the terrorism did not let up. She, her parents, and even her in-laws found copper roofing nails in their cars' tires. One morning at their home, Lori and her husband brought their new puppy inside—only to watch in horror as it tracked blood across the floor from a cross that had been cut into its paws. Shortly thereafter her stalker called again, taunting, "Did you think I couldn't get to your dog, babe?"

Despite all efforts, the police were unable to discover the caller's identity. For Lori, that missing piece of information continues to be frustrating—and terrifying: "I don't know who my stalker is. It could be any man who passes me. On my day off from work I stay locked in the house, afraid to go out on my own."

Lori's ordeal has gone on for ten years and continues to this day. Due to the accumulation of details over the years, she and her family suspect they may now have narrowed down the identity of her stalker, but they have no hard proof. The police, subsequently, have not been able to make any arrests. Meanwhile, for Lori, the harassment has almost become a way of life. "There's no real definite pattern, but my birthday is in September, and he usually calls me to wish me a happy birthday, not on the exact day, because I could trace [his call then] and that would be too easy. Things pick up from there; they're usually pretty slow in the summertime, and in January, February, and March, when it's really cold, there's really not much activity." But, Lori observes, she'll always get a few random calls, "just as a reminder that he's there."

Casual Acquaintances and Would-Be Friends

Some victims are harassed and pursued by people they know—or thought they knew. Stemming from an acquaintance or casual social relationship, their situations fall somewhere between intimate partner stalkings and those in which only a random encounter or two has taken place. "Carolyn," a thirty-four-year-old woman living in a small town in the Southwest, remembers a stalking that began when she was in high school. "We were all pals," she remembers of her schoolmates, but one young man in the group seemed to have expected more. "I had no inkling of an idea that this guy may have been in love with me. I ended up going out with one of his best friends, and this is when it all started."

"It" began with taunts, curses, and obscenities shouted at the couple on the school grounds. Carolyn found the boy's behavior perplexing, then disturbing, then downright frightening. "In school he would follow me around and tell me he loved me, and then the next thing, that he was going to kill me." One day his mother appeared; she, too, seemed as obsessed as her son: "[She] would wait at the [school] door and tell me that I was going to marry their son . . . she would say, 'You love him. You know you love him.' "

Carolyn soon was being followed off school grounds as well. "The car chases were the big thing," she recalls. She would be driving, only to find herself sandwiched between two cars, the driver in front repeatedly slamming on his brakes, the car behind ramming her. Twice she was run completely off the road. Once she and her boyfriend pulled into the parking lot of a fast food restaurant. Her harasser was parked nearby. While Carolyn waited in the passenger's seat, her boyfriend walked over to speak with him. Suddenly her harasser threw his truck into gear and rammed Carolyn's boyfriend's car from behind. In panic, Carolyn clambered into the driver's seat and drove out of the parking lot, with her harasser in pursuit. Within a few miles she came screeching to a halt, aware of the danger of a high-speed car chase. Then, she recalls, "He grabbed me . . . got me out . . . put me in the truck, took me to his mother's house, and they would not let me leave. They basically kidnapped me." Carolyn was only finally rescued by her boyfriend the following day.

After eighteen years Carolyn continues to feel the impact of this high school pal who could not let go. She and her boyfriend married, and for several years afterward, the couple was visited repeatedly, usually during the evenings. Sometimes her stalker would show up alone, sometimes he would be accompanied by other family members or by unknown companions. Their car's tires were repeatedly slashed, its finish gouged with a screwdriver, the windows of their home smashed with bricks. On one particularly terrifying occasion, she and her husband had guns drawn on them in their front yard by a group that included her stalker's father, who announced, "We're gonna blow your brains out." Altogether Carolyn estimates she has filed over a hundred reports with the police, who have refused—for a variety of reasons—to make an arrest.

These assaults threw Carolyn's life into chaos. Within months after the start of her ordeal, while still in high school, she began to suffer migraine headaches and would alternate between periods of hyperactivity and depression. Two months before graduation, Carolyn dropped out, due to what she now considers a nervous breakdown. Her first marriage failed, she believes in part due to the terrorism they were forced to endure. "It ruined our lives," she says. Now remarried, she allows few people apart from immediate family and close friends to know her whereabouts, and she rarely leaves her home.

To Hell with the Consequences: The Stalking of Co-workers

As one victim, "Erin," was to discover, even the person who sits next to you at work can engage in harassing and frightening behavior. In the early 1980s, Erin was a twenty-three-year old college graduate working as a computer operator in her father's company. Shortly after she started, she was assigned to a project with a co-worker, a man in his forties.

They shared a cubicle, where it quickly became apparent he was not going to confine his hands to the computer keyboard:

> If he had something to say to me, it involved a hand on the shoulder, a hand on the knee, always prefaced by, "Well now, Miss Erin," because he knew I hated that . . . and there was always this annoying physical contact. And because my father owned the business, I really never said anything to anybody but to [this co-worker]. I asked him repeatedly to stop it, or not do it, or to leave me alone. He always laughed me off, or shrugged me off, like, "You don't really mean it."

In addition to the sexual harassment, Erin's co-worker exhibited other strange behavior. Erin recalls him speaking strangely about "twenty-five to thirty different jobs he'd held," jobs too numerous for his age and too complex given his current position. "He had no social life that anybody knew of, no friends. His entire life surrounded his work, and . . . he very rarely entered into a lot of conversation about anything other than work."

Erin was growing increasingly anxious about the unwanted contact, but felt she couldn't report it. As the daughter of the company's owner, she didn't want anyone to think she was receiving special treatment. Then, eight months after they began working together, and much to her relief, Erin's co-worker left to work for a competitor:

> I really didn't think he was anything to worry about, and I was glad he was gone. Then the mail started coming to my house . . . brochures, books, pam-

> phlets, newspaper articles, a lot of them dealing with women executives because he saw me as taking over my father's business, which was a possibility, it wasn't a secret. Everything was hand-addressed; I knew the handwriting. I got a lot of religious pamphlets . . . this . . . continued for over a year.

By the middle of that year, Erin began receiving silent calls and hang-up calls. She changed her number twice, but the calls continued. Erin's boyfriend grew frustrated with the stacks of material coming through the mail, and at one point took a pile of it to the police, who suggested that the phone company place a tap on their phone. Suspiciously, for the month the tap was on, she didn't get one call; two days after the tap went off, the calls began again. Erin estimates that at the height of her harassment she was receiving four or five calls a night between ten P.M. and one A.M. On two occasions she and her boyfriend observed her harasser sitting in front of her apartment in his car. She began feeling anxious about being home alone, yet most of all she worried that if he were to harm someone else, she would feel responsible.

Mysteriously, the harassment ended after Erin and her boyfriend married. She believes that a co-worker who knew about her situation may have confronted her harasser and intimidated him. Nonetheless, like Beverly Hannon, she remembers how unpredictable her harassment felt and what it suggested about her former co-worker: "That's what worried me . . . You don't know what's going to put somebody over the edge."

Given the increasing climate of violence in the American workplace, Erin's situation—and her fear—is sadly no longer a rare occurrence. The term "job security"—whether you'll keep your job—has become increasingly overshadowed by "workplace security"—whether you're safe from others, including co-workers, between nine and five. According to a 1992 Bureau of Labor Statistics report, on-the-job murder has become a bona fide occupational hazard: "Life-threatening risks in the workplace were common in colonial times, when many earned their living from the sea, wild animals were hunted for food and clothing, farmers walked behind horse-drawn plows . . . Today, [though] the number of total workplace fatalities has declined over the past decade, *intentional killings* in the workplace have gained prominence." (Italics added) In 1992, workplace homicides took the lives of 1,004 employees, a number second only to work-related motor vehicle accidents. More chillingly, homicide on the job was, in 1992, the leading cause of death for American *women* in the workplace.

The workplace is neither exempt from violence nor from other criminal behavior like stalking. In cases of intimate partner or domestic violence stalking, the workplace is often targeted because the victim must be there daily; it's one sure place the stalker knows he can find her. As in Erin's case, the workplace also can be the perfect place for harassment and pursuit *to begin,* as people who would otherwise never meet come together on a regular basis, sometimes with unexpected—and deadly—results.

Perhaps the most highly publicized case of one co-worker stalking another was the story of Laura Black. In 1984, Laura, a twenty-two-year-old engineer, began work for ESL, Inc., a high-tech firm in California. Shortly after she was hired, Richard Farley, another engineer at the firm, asked her out on a date. She declined the invitation, but it was soon followed by others. Though Black refused each request, Farley persisted, until, exasperated, Black angrily told him she would not date him if he were the last man on earth. With twisted logic, Farley was later to say, "I had the right to ask her out. She had the right to refuse. When she did not refuse in a cordial way, I felt I had the right to bother her."

Farley's idea of "bothering" Laura was to shift from requests for dates to letters—some two hundred over a four-year period—then gifts, then breaking into confidential personnel records at work and tracing outlines of her home and office keys, and following her to and from work, her health club, her softball games. Black moved three times in an effort to escape him. Each time he found her, and the harassment and pursuit began anew.

Farley was fired from ESL in 1986 for his continual harassment of Black. But after he was fired, his letters became increasingly threatening. "I feel capable of killing to protect myself," he wrote, "and to hell with the consequences." On February 16, 1988, Farley, carrying almost a hundred pounds of guns and ammunition, drove to ESL in a rented motor home, eager to show Black "the end result of what I felt she had done to me." There he murdered seven of his former co-workers and seriously injured four others, including Black herself. After a five and a half hour standoff with police, Farley was talked into surrendering. He is now on death row in California.

Laura's story was dramatized in the television film "The Stalking of Laura Black," but more revealing than the violence of her case was the response the movie drew from viewers across the country. Within hours of the film's airing on national television, the National Victim Center received three thousand calls from other victims who had also suffered or were themselves suffering the threatening obsessions of stalkers. The ordeal of one California woman, it seemed, was less publicly echoed in the lives of thousands of others.

"When He Gets Me, Mom"

Perhaps no other aspect of this crime inflames more public outrage and fear than the stalking of children. Our desire to protect our children, natural under any circumstances, becomes strongest in situations where they are at risk of being harmed by a stranger. Highlighting the worst dangers of the crime, recent cases of the harassing, terrorizing—and even murder—of children and teens has helped underscore the need for legislation and greater public involvement against stalkers.

In one highly publicized case in 1992, eleven-year-old Crystal Peterson of Oregon was stalked by Robert Thomas Coker, a disturbed twenty-four-year-old who lived across the street from the girl and her family. Coker harassed the girl for months, sending her numerous inappropriate gifts and odd, rambling letters in which he described Crystal as cute and talked about her effect on him: "When I looked at you, my heart felt funny, like it was melting. And I had trouble breathing." At the same time, in other letters Coker would accuse Crystal of consorting with boys and would abuse her, calling her names like "slut." Coker—who was ultimately arrested for trespassing on the Petersons' property, then rearrested in violation of the ensuing restraining order when he refused to cease the stalking—protested that he didn't know he was doing anything wrong. He explained to police that he wrote to Crystal because he hoped to marry her when she was of age and "wanted to get [his] foot in the door early."

Another case in 1993 involved a fifty-six-year-old New York tennis coach named Gary Wilensky. Obsessively attached to a young girl whom he was instructing, Wilensky was fired by the girl's mother, who became disturbed at the depth of his interest. Three months later, Wilensky attempted to abduct the girl and her mother following an upstate tennis tournament, injuring both of them severely. It could, however, have been far worse. When police investigated a nearby cabin Wilensky had rented, they found a veritable torture chamber, stocked with chains, handcuffs, high-powered night telescopes and video equipment. They also found in Wilensky's Manhattan apartment a variety of stalker-type videos depicting young children. Wilensky, who committed suicide as police closed in on him, had apparently been following children for a number of years and appeared ready to move beyond mere observation.

Young children are clearly at special risk in stalking situations. Less attuned than adults to signs of danger such as odd or menacing behavior, children may be easily seduced into the confidence of a stranger. The ease with which this happens can be astonishing. In an informal study conducted by a New York TV station in the fall of 1993, a reporter posed as a friendly stranger in a neighborhood playground to test the reactions of several toddlers and small children. As each child's parents watched from afar, the reporter casually approached the child playing in the sandbox or climbing on the monkey bars, and engaged him or her in small talk. Then he asked if the child would care to accompany him as he walked away. The results were startling even to the parents themselves, who watched as the reporter easily lured the children away, one after another. Moreover, this study took place in the middle of the country's largest city, where parents are likely to encourage their children to be particularly wary of strangers.

The case of Caty Richards stands as an enduring reminder to the special terrors posed by stalkers of children. Caty, a cheerful, athletic child living in Springfield, Vermont, was "not an adult . . . not streetwise. She was a child who played with her dolls," remembers her mother, RoseAlyce Thayer. "She was a Girl Scout, she sold her cookies, she was vice-president of her 4-H group, she was a cross-country skiier, she was on the town swim team." The youngest of RoseAlyce's four children by a previous marriage, Caty was RoseAlyce and Charlie Thayer's only girl. "She was," RoseAlyce recalls fondly, "a great treasure to us, a much-appreciated person." Now a national spokesperson for victims' and children's rights, RoseAlyce remembers Caty's tragedy "as if it was yesterday."

Caty's is actually the story of two stalkings—one she survived and one she did not. The first began at the start of the school year of 1981, when the bus schedule, according to RoseAlyce, "hadn't yet gelled." One afternoon, the bus brought ten-year-old Caty home a half hour earlier than scheduled. When Caty didn't see her mother, who would normally meet her at the bus stop, she began the tiring trek up the steep hill leading to their home. Suddenly, a man in a Jeep drove up and swerved toward the girl, apparently trying to frighten her. Caty ran to a neighbor's barn to hide. When she thought the Jeep had disappeared, she started home again, only to meet the Jeep farther up the road. The man who then jumped out of the Jeep and chased her was a twenty-eight-year old Springfield resident. This time Caty ran into the woods, and because she knew them by heart, she managed to elude the man. Terrified, Caty made her way home, arriving just as RoseAlyce was leaving to meet her. RoseAlyce remembers asking, "'What are you doing here?' And [Caty] started to cry. She was just about hysterical. She held on until she saw me. . . . That night, she crawled into bed with Charlie and myself. It was the first time she'd done that since she was about three. . . . She was frightened. She was a child."

The Thayers complained to the police; RoseAlyce recalls that they refused to take action, saying there was no law against harassing a child. That harassment, which included repeatedly driving by the family's isolated home, was to continue for the next nineteen months. Unsatisfied with the police response, the Thayers ultimately were able to get the state attorney's office to hire an outside investigator to talk with the perpetrator and his mother. According to the investigator, the man's mother thought her son was just pulling boyish pranks; the perpetrator himself claimed he was merely "yucking around." Caty began having nightmares, and the Thayers took her to a child psychologist. Years later, RoseAlyce told legislators about the kind of fear her child had been forced to live with:

> [That] child [made] preparations for her funeral. . . . I had to go to the Superintendent of Schools and say, look, Caty is so terrified of strange men, I want her to have just women teachers next year.

It was not this man, however, but another Springfield resident, Gary Lee Schaefer, who would pick up where the original stalking left off. RoseAlyce was accustomed to standing with Caty at the bus stop in the mornings. On a couple of occasions she had noticed another man sitting nearby in his car. "He [Schaefer] would wait in the morning, I had the feeling, before he went to work, while Caty waited for the bus. And he would just sit on the corner and watch her. I saw the man every day. I imagine he was thinking either my husband or I would not [walk up] with her."

For RoseAlyce, though, a man sitting in his car was nothing special. "This is an isolated area. I figured he was up there waiting for a girlfriend, or maybe checking out the deer herd, because it is a deer crossing right there, and it was hunting season." One morning, as she stood waiting for the bus with her mother, Caty noticed the man as well:

> Caty was crabbing, because I'd wait at the corner and she didn't like that. . . . "Mother, why don't you go hide in the woods?" [and] "I don't see why you have to wait with me. The other kids see you there and it's babyish," and so forth. Finally, I got disgusted and I said, "Look, do you see that man sitting in that car over there?" "Yes," [Caty said]. I said, "You don't know him." "No." And she looked at me. "Do you know him?" And I said, "No, I don't know him." I said, "He might be after you." And she moved very close to me, and she looked at me and she said, "Well, I guess I can stand you waiting with me."

For a couple of times a week over the next six months, Schaefer continued his observations of Caty.

The child, already worn down by repeated intrusions into her life, became further traumatized. On one particularly disturbing occasion, RoseAlyce found the child arranging her dolls in orderly rows on her bed. When RoseAlyce asked her if she was playing school, the child looked up sadly and said, "No, I'm deciding which of my friends gets my dolls and books when the man who's been following me gets me."

On April 9, 1983, as Caty played with a friend in North Springfield, Gary Lee Schaefer pulled up beside the girls in his car. "I don't think she recognized him when he asked for directions," says RoseAlyce. "But then he got out of the car and he said, 'What would you say if I told you I have a gun and will shoot and kill you if you don't get in the car?' Rachel said Caty gasped and began to cry." Rachel turned and ran to a neighbor's house, and Schaeffer grabbed Caty. RoseAlyce believes that the long ordeal Caty had suffered with the original stalking had worn her down, dulling her normally alert defenses, so that by the time Schaeffer accosted her, the child simply could not fight him off or run away in time.

RoseAlyce speaks of this sense of wearing down that child-stalking victims experience:

> The difference between an adult and a child as far as that sort of thing goes—and it's a huge difference, but adults never think of it—[is that] when you're an adult you know that no matter how horrible a situation is, one way or another there will be some resolution, and you'll go on to the next thing. But with a child, the horror itself is so overwhelming, they can't see beyond it. And that is why it is so ghastly.

Late the next day, Caty's body was found in an isolated field in North Springfield. She had been repeatedly sexually assaulted, mutilated, and beaten to death.

"I Just Never Let Her Out of My Sight"

Teenagers, poised on the brink of adulthood, also face the danger and emotional damage of stalking. Christy Crawford was seventeen years old at the time her stalking began. Her mother, Beverly, remembers clearly the first night of their ordeal:

> I came home from work. It was dark outside. I came into the kitchen through the garage door and all the lights in the house were on, all the shades were drawn, the curtains, and Christy was sitting at the desk in the kitchen near the telephone and I knew something was terribly wrong. She was clutching a butcher knife in her hand and just shaking. It took me at least five minutes to get the knife out of her hand.

Christy had arrived home to find an envelope on her bed. In it were two Polaroid shots of a man's body, from his neck to his knees. The man had an erection. On the photos' white borders were written obscene comments addressed to Christy.

The next morning, she and her mother became further alarmed when Beverly opened the door and found that a second letter had been placed on their doorstep during the night, this time accompanied by three more photos. Beverly contacted the police and spoke with Detective Lisa Racz of the North Brunswick, New Jersey, Police Department, who would work closely with them until the case was solved. "And what we did from that moment on," recalls Beverly, "[was] I just never let her out of my sight." Because Christy usually was the first to arrive at her job at a quick-print shop, Beverly would drive her to work, then wait while Christy unlocked the shop and looked around inside. Only when Christy gave her the okay sign and locked the door behind her would Beverly leave, confident Christy wouldn't open it again until her boss arrived. "Everyone at [my] work knew—if I went out to get a soda—they knew where I was going so they could contact me instantly in case anything happened."

Things did happen. As in so many similar cases, the Crawfords began receiving silent phone calls, which they attempted to monitor with Call Trace. A few days after they'd received the second set of photos, Beverly went outside to get the paper. She noticed a strange substance on the front screen door. At first she thought it was bird droppings, then realized to her horror it was semen. By the middle of the following week, the third letter was found, taped to the garage door. The sender again used foul language; this time he also asked Christy if she'd "figured out who I am yet," and he asked her to join him at the local fast food restaurant on the following Saturday.

Though she was petrified by the thought of meeting him, Christy, working with the police, agreed to appear at the restaurant at the specified time. Two undercover detectives sat near her as she pretended to eat. Another set of plainclothes officers watched the parking lot outside the restaurant, while others waited outside her home. They all turned up emptyhanded. In the next several days, however, Christy received another letter and two cassette tapes of music mixed with moaning sounds. Each of these items was added to the growing stack of evidence, useful for fingerprint identification and handwriting analysis.

Finally, the case broke. Late one Friday evening, three months after the letters began arriving, Beverly heard the doorbell ringing. At the door was an old acquaintance of Christy's, casually asking if he might have Christy's number at work. Tired because it was late, and exhausted by her daughter's ordeal, Beverly gave him the number. It was to prove the perfect slip. On the following Monday, for the first and only time, Christy's stalker phoned her at work. Call Trace on that call and one she received the same day at home revealed the telephone number of Christy's friend, the one who had visited Beverly three days earlier.

Christy Crawford's stalker was arrested and charged with thirteen counts of terroristic threats, harassment, and passing obscene materials through the mail to a minor. Though she was emotionally drained by the ordeal, Christy was able to recover and get on with her life. For others, particularly young children, the outcome may not be so assured.

How can children and teenagers be protected—and protect themselves from such crimes? The answer is likely to lie with a combination of increased personal vigilance and awareness, strict enforcement of antistalking laws, and evolving social alertness to the causes and consequences of such crimes. In recent years, growing awareness of the sexual abuse of children has led to a number of innovative programs designed to help children spot dangerous adults and resist their advances. One such program is Kid Power, developed as a parallel program to the Model Mugging self-defense course for women described in

Chapter 10. Kid Power is a program that helps children aged six to fourteen identify personal boundaries, and teaches them age-appropriate self-defense tactics to use if those boundaries are crossed. Kid Power instructors teach children that they should be the ones to decide whether or not an adult may approach or touch them. By helping children realize that they control their own bodies and by teaching them that some adults may act inappropriately—even dangerously—Kid Power helps children stay alert and safe.

Another program, Child Lures Community Plan, stresses a similar theme of "heads-up" awareness. Run by child safety advocate and writer Kenneth Wooden, CLCP teaches children that while most adults are trustworthy, some adults may not act in their best interests. "If there was a lightning storm and you were outside playing," Wooden will ask a group of children, "would you come in? Of course. Is it safe to go outside most days? Of course it is." Ultimately, of course, for children and teens it will only become truly safe to go outside if stalking and other crimes committed against them could be eradicated. Until then, "People are like the weather," Wooden says. "Most people are safe, but some are like lightning storms."

CHAPTER 5

Support and Survival

Personal Responses to Stalking

Some psychologists believe that stalking is a throwback to the instinctive predatory behavior of prehistoric man. Others explain it as a form of psychiatric illness. Still others describe it as the action of an emotionally and spiritually bankrupt person. Whatever theory you choose to accept, one thing is certain. It is devastating to the victim.

Jane McAllister, President,
Citizens Against Stalking

Try to close your eyes and picture yourself in the same position. What does it feel like? Be there to listen, to support, give shelter, give hope. . . . Don't pity us, support us.

"Carol," stalking victim

It is an average Sunday in Richmond, Virginia. The sun is warm and the weather is mild. Joggers are out and couples are strolling along the paths of the city park. At a picnic table eight people have gathered around a cooler of soft drinks. They seem to come from very different walks of life—a young couple, a middle-aged executive, a social worker, a housewife, a psychologist. Yet they are close in a unique way. These are the members of Citizens Against Stalking, one of the first support groups for stalking victims in the country.

Citizens Against Stalking was founded by Jane McAllister, whose own ordeal as the target of a stalker led her to understand firsthand the extraordinary fears, frustrations, and stresses that stalking victims feel. The group has been active in lobbying for legislative change, educating law enforcement officials and the public about stalking, and creating helpful documents for victims of this crime (see "Stalking: How to Strike Back," at end of chapter). But most important, members are available to each other to talk out the personal and emotional impact this devastating experience has had on their lives—and to help each other to heal.

How do you cope if you become a victim of stalking? How can you help others who may find themselves the target of relentless attention, harassment, or threats? Understanding the real impact of this crime involves understanding the personal responses victims experience, the human costs of fear and prolonged invasion of one's life. In many ways, the unpredictability and long-term nature of this crime make it one of the most life-altering and emotionally scarring ordeals an individual can face. Stalking is not just a statistical event; it is a daily reality in the lives of thousands of individuals—and a crime that may at any time impact your own life or the life of someone you know. Hearing some of the common phases victims go through can help you learn to support—or to survive.

Learning the Boundaries

Stalking has been called an elusive and subtle crime, one that in its early stages at least seems to blur the boundaries between "normal" persistence and obsessive behavior. Although virtually every stalking victim can identify with precision the moment he or she became aware that unwanted attentions had crossed the line from mere annoyance to a dangerous intrusion, often those around the victim—family, friends, co-workers, law enforcement officials—have trouble seeing the problem for what it is. "Oh, he's just in love with you," victims have been told; "Ignore it," or "It's just a lover's spat," or "You should be flattered by all that attention," are common ways that victims' experience of invasion and fear are minimized.

Indeed, we are socialized into defining interpersonal contacts and intimate relationships in ways that often help blur the boundaries between persistence and predation, between courtship and crime. How often have we heard the lyrics of popular songs define relationships in terms of pursuit, ownership, self-validation? Yet phrases like "You belong to me," "I'm nothing without you," "I'm going to make you mine," take on sinister overtones when the context of attraction becomes dangerously obsessive, when passion becomes predatory and "love" is laced with threats. Even beyond the arena of intimate relationships, the roles we play in society demand various levels of accessibility to and influence over others, channels that are forever open to being distorted or abused. The role of teacher to student, therapist to client, celebrity to fan—all are potentially subject to distortion in which boundaries of normal interaction give way to obsessive fantasies and potentially criminal invasions.

And yet we have to live and function in the world; we have to manage occasional unwanted or unpleasant interactions with others, deal with relationships that fail, wrestle with the stress of inevitable human miscommunication or misunderstanding. One way to do this is to minimize events that upset us, to downplay or explain away unpleasant or annoying experiences—and in many cases this is an effective and realistic approach to the normal frictions of social life. Your co-worker snapping at you over the coffee machine may indeed stem from a bad mood that has nothing to do with you; the cabbie shaking his fist at you in traffic can be written off as an isolated irritation; the person you met at that party last week whose invitation for dinner you've declined twice will probably understand that you are not interested and stop calling.

At what point, however, is the boundary crossed between insignificant, if annoying, contact and dangerous behavior? Stalking can start out small, and many stalking victims remember an early phase of downplaying unpleasant contacts or events that later escalated into a pattern of full-scale harassment and even violence. The impulse is strong to ignore or deny potentially frightening behavior: "He's just upset; he'll get over it," or "She's just hung up on me; if I ignore her she will go away," are common forms of explaining away early stalking behavior. One victim speaks for many when she recalls thinking, "This is just a phase. It will stop." Still terrorized years later, she realizes that she was wrong. Another victim, harassed throughout her teen years, clung to the belief "that he would lose interest as I grew up and changed." After more than ten years, her anonymous stalker continues to torment her and her family on a nearly daily basis.

If you find yourself on the receiving end of repeated, unwanted contact—particularly if it seems abnormal, inappropriate, or threatening—you must trust your instincts concerning the nature of the situation. Be alert to your own feelings of discomfort, and where appropriate, set clear boundaries about unwanted contacts or behaviors. Setting limits early will not only help you define for yourself what is acceptable and what is invasive—remember that you set the terms on which you feel comfortable with others—it can also establish a firm foundation on which future judgments by law enforcement and other professionals are based. One victim, harassed for months by obsessive, subtly threatening "love letters" from a former client, arranged for her attorney to send a cease and desist letter to that individual, spelling out with absolute clarity that any further contact by telephone, mail, or in person would result in criminal prosecution. When several weeks later the stalker left a telephone message deriding the letter and announcing his intentions to ignore its terms, the police had all they needed to establish his intent and the certainty of the behavior continuing. The limits set were reasonable and clear; his violation of those limits was invasive and deliberate. He was arrested and arraigned two days later.

Clearly, not all victims know their stalkers, and in some cases the behavior is so extreme or threatening that it needs no boundary setting to be seen as unwanted. The important thing is for the victim to be alert and clear in her own mind, and understand that irrational behaviors do not always just go away.

Friends and family, moreover, should know that minimizing intrusive events or trying to "talk away" a victim's discomfort and fear does not help, but instead can leave a victim feeling that her experience is invalid or crazy. Virtually every victim we have spoken to has experienced some form of disbelief or minimizing by those around them, and their pleas to the families and friends of other victims are eloquent:

> "Listen to the person. Don't tell them they are imagining things or are paranoid."
>
> "The fear is real. Please don't belittle or try to lessen that reaction to the circumstances."
>
> "No one would make anything like this up. Listen to us!"
>
> "Listen. Really listen to the victim. Please don't dismiss these fears as foolish."
>
> "The most valuable support I got was validation of my fear—an empathy about why the actions of the stalker were frightening. Most damaging were those who minimized by saying 'He hasn't really done anything. . . .' "
>
> "Friends and co-workers don't understand the seriousness of it. My mom can't comprehend it. My dad says ignore it. I've had people say 'He just really loves you.' My own boss told me at one point . . . that he didn't know who was the liar, [my stalker] or me! . . . I was fuming mad."

Believing victims, and resisting the impulse to minimize potentially dangerous events, is the first step in providing victims with the support they need and deserve.

A Stalker Loves Silence and Secrecy

Few experiences can feel as isolating as being the victim of a crime. With stalking in particular, the pattern of emotional violence involves singling out an individual, targeting her personally, invading her privacy in unpredictable, frightening, and often humiliating ways. When victims try to put words to their feelings, the metaphors they use are those of being hunted down, separated out, isolated:

> "The stalker is a predator. Predators look for the weak one, isolate that one. . . . The rest of the herd (so to speak) is afraid to intervene."
>
> "A stalker loves silence and secrecy; it makes it easy to get you alone. The more people who are aware and alert, the more eyes you have helping you. . . ."

Unanimously, victims urge others to "Talk, talk, talk about it!"—to make the behavior public, keep records of all the stalker's activities, reach out to create the networks of personal and professional support you need. Being targeted by a stalker can bring with it a feeling of stigma or shame, but it is important to remember three things: (1) you are not to blame, (2) you deserve support, and (3) you are not alone. Remember, your stalker is banking on your silence—don't do him that favor!

Telling others is important, not only for your emotional well-being, but to break through the secret terrorism on which stalkers depend, and to maximize your own safety as well as the safety of those around you. We understand that it may be difficult to speak out about your situation—our world is less than ideal, and belief and acceptance are not always guaranteed. Families may feel threatened or targeted themselves and, responding from their own sense of helplessness, may inadvertently place blame on the victim. Friends may not always respond with understanding or sensitivity; and employers are only gradually learning their responsibilities in supporting and protecting their workers against harassment and violence at the workplace. But despite the difficulties, the more people you talk to, the greater your chances of finding effective help and solid support.

When you approach others, be ready to tell them exactly what you need and what you would like them to do for you. Sympathy is short-term; real help and support are quite different levels of involvement and need to be discussed with clarity and openness. You may ask one friend simply to be available to talk. You may ask a neighbor to keep alert for suspicious activity around your home. You might set up a safety routine with family members whereby they telephone you at a prearranged time. You might ask a co-worker to escort you to your car, or insist that your workplace security department be appraised of your situation. Discussing practical options can yield positive results, and can give those around you tangible, concrete ways in which they can help.

Ironically, what frustrates family and friends of victims most often are their own feelings of helplessness, particularly if the stalking continues over an extended period of months or even years. If you are supporting a victim, watch out for the "rescue syndrome"—the desire to erase or solve the situation quickly. Most stalking behavior is unpredictable and ongoing; often, events will taper off for a period of time, only to resurface weeks or months later. Providing steady, long-term encouragement to a victim can be draining to even the most supportive circle, and ever more frustrating in proportion to their desire to see the problem end. One victim speaks from the heart when she states, "It's such a burden to ask someone else to listen, because there is nothing they or anyone else can do, and they seem to get tired of listening. Eventually they stop asking how things are." This same victim advises, "Don't give up on the person because you cannot solve their problem. Just being there and being a friend keeps them from feeling so alone."

Outside of friends and family, victims are encouraged to seek professional support—via counseling, support groups, victims organizations, or women's advocacy centers. The input and advice of professionals can be invaluable in helping one deal with the stress and isolation of this crime. Support groups for victims of stalking are springing up across the country, an acknowledgment of how pervasive this crime is, and a forceful movement on the part of victims to fight back. You might consider starting a support group in your own area if none exists, either on your own or by approaching possible sponsoring organizations, such as women's crisis centers, victim advocacy organizations, or mental health clinics. The sense of purpose and power in taking action, uniting with others to provide personal support and fight back on a political level, can be invaluable ways of reclaiming control.

The most important step in fighting the silence and secrecy in which stalking thrives is to *keep records of all stalking behavior.* Document all contacts made or attempted by the stalker; keep copies of letters, "gifts," messages left on answering machines, and the like, and be sure to record accurate dates, times, and locations where events took place or items were received. Start a file or a journal in which to keep records of everything, and make a copy of all evidence to keep in a safe place—either with police, with your attorney, or in a safe deposit box. Stalkers have been known to steal evidence against them in order to eradicate any legal case the victim may have. Our next chapter deals with legal recourse, and outlines the avenues of assistance provided by law enforcement and the courts. But it is crucial to remember, as Jane McAllister warns, "Without evidence and documentation, there is *no* possibility of legal help with the problem."

As unpleasant as it may be to save disturbing messages or threatening letters, keeping good records can be a way of reclaiming power in the midst of what feels like a helpless situation. Think of each incident you record, each contact you document, as another bar on your stalker's jail cell. In a very real way, you are turning from victim to strategist by collecting the evidence that will build a strong case.

You Are Not to Blame

As important as it is to speak out about this crime, it can still be a difficult step for victims to take. Two feelings that compound the trauma victim's experience are shame and guilt. Both are unwarranted feelings—yet both are very common, very natural, and in all cases painfully real.

Perhaps because of the public's misunderstanding of the nature of this crime, or perhaps simply by virtue of everyday insensitivity, victims are frequently subject to subtle (or not so subtle) blame for somehow bringing the terrorism on themselves. "What did you do to attract him?" "Why did you speak to him in the first place?" "Why didn't you simply . . . ?" or "Why couldn't you just . . . ?"—all are ways in which victims are made to feel "responsible" in some way for being the targets of this crime.

Even unspoken questions and comments can create a devastating climate, and victims who have had the courage to speak about their situation feel keenly when others react to them as odd or stigmatized. "People at work treated me as though I was a leper," recalls one victim; "I felt that some of them lost respect for me. . . ." Another claims, "I still experience feelings of embarrassment and fear that others in the community feel I've overreacted to the problem." "I haven't told my family. I can't talk at work, even though that is where so much of the activity has taken place." "I have always felt embarrassed."

Just as damaging is when victims internalize these issues in the form of guilt or self-blame. One young woman recalls her outrage at being told casually by a police officer that, since she was so attractive, she should "expect this kind of attention"—attention that included the stalker wounding her dog, graphically threatening to slit her throat, vowing to murder members of her family, and several times attempting to run her off the road! The impact of such insensitive remarks runs deep. She states that even today "I still have really bad guilt feelings. I feel if I dress a certain way or attract any kind of attention from men, it is my fault and I am asking for the stalker to stalk me. . . . I constantly blame myself. If I wasn't so friendly or sending out the wrong messages this wouldn't be happening to me." At the same time, she is justifiably angry at this twisted equation that blames the victim: "What about my rights to thank God for being an attractive woman and not curse it and try to hide it or feel guilty about it?"

It is not unnatural for any victim to experience a phase of guilt, or for victims to engage in a process of searching for ways in which they themselves might have better warded off or prevented a crime. Guilt can be a type of internal "balancing mechanism"—the mind's way of trying to make meaning out of seemingly random events, of trying to gain control in what feels like a senseless, uncontrollable situation. Asking "What did I do . . . ?" or "What could I have done differently . . . ?" can be ways of trying to reclaim inner power and control. If a traumatic experience was brought on by something one did, then by changing one's behavior, one can logically make the experience stop, or prevent it from happening again.

The reality, however, is that there are no proper actions by which to safeguard against the criminal attentions of an individual obsessed with establishing contact. Victims of stalkers *are not to blame,* any more than the victim of a carjacking is to blame for driving on public roads, or the victim of a burglary is to blame for owning a VCR. Stalking is a crime that can strike anyone, at any time. As a society, we must focus on the causes within the perpetrator, not the victim. As individuals, we must be sensitive to how blame and guilt can compound the feelings of isolation and trauma that every victim experiences.

Anger and Fear

Their voices may be weary or harsh; their statements may be laced with expletives or apologies—but at some point nearly every victim expresses a feeling of anger against her stalker, rage at the injustice of constant terrorism and a backlash against the relentless personal and emotional violence they are suffering. Anger is a natural response to the stress of invasion and the helplessness most stalking victims feel. And yet, as with most powerful emotions, anger can either heal or harm.

How can victims deal with the rage they feel at times against their perpetrators? How can one channel such explosive emotions as "I want to kill [my stalker] with my bare hands, I want to tie him up and slice him to pieces!" Or deal with anger directed inward, as in the case of the following victim: "I have yet to feel rage against my stalker. I should but I don't. I think I am internalizing. I have a nervous stomach and I go through whole days where all I do is throw up and no medicine helps. . . ." Jane McAllister remembers her own feelings of rage as "one of the most difficult aspects of the experience for me because I didn't know how to expel the anger." What Jane found helpful in the end was using vehicles by which to help channel and dispel the rage: "I used many tools for this—physical exercise, counseling, and continuing to fight for protection by advocating for myself—and ultimately by starting a support group."

Anger can be an empowering step to asserting one's sense of self and validating one's rights. At the same time, you must be aware of the ways that anger can be misdirected or can become self-destructive.

- Don't let your anger debilitate you, whether it is directed against your stalker, insensitive individuals, or at a system that seems at first to fail in protecting you. Keeping your rights clearly in mind can keep you strong and persistent in your demands for protection, and focused and determined as you articulate your needs. Think of your anger as a laser beam that can keep you directed, not as a packet of dynamite that explodes at everything around you.
- Don't let your anger become directed inward, blurring with guilt and becoming aimed against yourself or your own actions. For many people, anger toward others is extremely difficult to express; interpersonal conflict is stressful, to the point that at times we elect to get angry at ourselves rather than break the social taboo of confronting others in rage. Yet feeling angry in your situation is appropriate and natural. Remember that *you are not to blame* for being the target of this crime. Anger turned inward can do nothing but emotional and physical damage.
- Don't let your anger become aggression in ways that might jeopardize your safety or escalate a situation into violence. By no means should you try to take the law into your own hands by attempting to return the harassment, following, pursuing, or assaulting your stalker. Not only do you risk escalating the contact into a potentially lethal encounter, you also risk arming your stalker with countercharges against you, muddying the situation for law enforcement officials and judges in the future.
- Don't let your anger create a false sense of courage or security. That chip on your shoulder or cocky attitude of "Just let him *try!*" could make you foolishly unalert to the real risks of your situation, lower your guard, and put you in needless danger. Your task is to balance the positive ways in which anger can clarify limits, strengthen your resolve, and sharpen your sense of self-preservation—without

letting that anger run away with your reason or become yet another weapon in the stalker's arsenal against you.

Even more pervasive than the anger are the ongoing feelings of shock and fear that permeate the experience of stalking victims. Few people understand what intense and prolonged fear actually feels like—and victims themselves are often overwhelmed by their own reactions. One of the grimmest, most devastating aspects of stalking is its unpredictability: at any time, anywhere, the stalker may approach, try to make contact, attempt to close in. All that is certain is that there is an individual out there obsessed with the life and activities of the victim. Where he may be—or even *who* he may be—are often terrifying unknowns. No experiences in our lives—short of war or repeated natural disasters—prepare us for the impact of such ongoing, extreme fear. Of all personal responses, terror can be the most exhausting and difficult for a victim to deal with.

Stalking victims report nightmares and anxiety attacks as common occurrences. Sleeplessness and panic, or drastic alterations in lifestyle, are not unusual. Imagine the daily experience of the following victim, who writes, "I cannot look strangers in the eyes . . . especially since I don't know exactly who my stalker is, it could be any man who passes me. On my days off from work I stay locked in the house, afraid to go out on my own." Another writes, "I slept with a baseball bat. I must've gotten up out of bed a hundred times some nights, looking outside because I heard something. At times I just crawled in bed and refused to eat, speak, or move for hours at a time."

There are no easy solutions to managing the long-term fear that accompanies the trauma of being stalked. A program of counseling or the help of a support group are invaluable first steps, and we believe taking personal measures toward self-defense, discussed in Chapters 8–10, can also go far in helping a victim reclaim strength and reestablish a sense of safety. In times of panic, try to *stay present:* focus on your breathing, and *allow* yourself to fear. Nearly every victim reports having had moments of paralysis: seeing the stalker in person, receiving a death threat in the mail, needing to find safety fast, yet seeming unable to react. Prepare for these moments by anticipating them; some tips include preparing a "safety kit" or preprogramming emergency automatic dial numbers, as discussed in Chapter 8. Above all, be kind to yourself if you do experience moments when fear seems to overwhelm you. Courage is not the *absence* of fear, but a realistic acceptance and channeling of our bodies' natural alarm device.

Most importantly, learn to distinguish for yourself the difference between being tough and being strong. Being *tough*—trying to "tough it out" by repressing your emotions, numbing your responses, or being overly self-reliant—can damage your stamina and delay your eventual recovery from the stress of the experience. Being *strong,* on the other hand, means staying alert and realistic, being expressive and patient with yourself when you experience natural responses such as fear and anger, and committing yourself to active self-protection. Overcoming the trauma of stalking involves reclaiming power—personally, psychologically, and legally. Fear and anger are natural emotions that can work *for* you, by keeping you determined to fight back and win.

Stress and Survival

We all know that stress is a part of everyday life—interviewing for a job, taking a final examination, even meeting new people, are examples of everyday stressors we are called on to deal with. Indeed, psychologists note that without some stress, our lives would be relentlessly dull and our personal growth minimized. Moderate levels of stress stimulate and keep us mentally alert; we learn best and react most sharply to events when a limited amount of stress is involved. Watch someone playing a video game, for instance. Part of the pleasure and excitement of the activity comes from the tension of scoring, competing, and winning. Or think of a lively classroom discussion, in which the energy of exchange keeps everyone awake and motivated. Just as physical activity improves our bodies' stamina, so too do such moderate stressors exercise and stimulate our inner resources, keeping us sharp, interested, and mentally fit.

Traumatic stress, on the other hand—the shock and disorientation of major, life-changing crises, ongoing exhaustion, extreme fear, or prolonged frustration—carries far different consequences. These are stressors that shake our worlds and overwhelm our resources, making it difficult at times even to deal with the everyday occurrences in our lives. The very energies we normally call on to respond to ordinary events become overtaxed and depleted in times of traumatic stress, leaving us feeling unable to manage even the smallest details. Trauma is *injury*—and, just as the body tries to heal itself, so too does the mind.

A number of psychologists have created models to explain the impact of stress on the body and mind. In the 1930s, Walter B. Cannon formulated a theory of "emergency reactions" we undergo in response to stressful events, in which we diverge from our normal state of "homeostasis" or inner balance. Our brains, in a sense, are hard-wired to produce certain survival responses—the old concept of fight or flight when faced with a sudden or potentially life-threatening situation. The brain triggers in the body a burst of adrenaline, for instance, which energizes our physical capacities; recent research has shown that stressful events can also temporarily alter the flow of blood to the brain and the brain's production of neurotransmitters, chemicals that regulate moods and responses.

These cerebral events are not only normal, but at moderate levels are highly adaptive as warning systems and reflexive survival reactions. Think of what happens when a car pulls out suddenly in front of you in traffic. Often even before you have a chance to think about what has happened, your brain's emergency mechanism has kicked into gear, triggering reflexes that help you orient and respond. Your muscles automatically tighten; your heart pounds; your eyes open wider; you gasp; your foot jumps to the brake pedal. These emergency reactions all happen in a split second, and after the crisis is over, you gradually return to a calm, balanced state: your heartbeat slows, your muscles deadrenalize and relax, your breathing regulates—often with the classic "Whew!" that signals the event is over.

But what of stressful events that do not simply end, or are of such a magnitude that they overtax the brain's natural emergency responses? Hans Selye, a student of Cannon's, identified a pattern of mental and physical changes in response to *ongoing* stress, which he termed General Adaptation Syndrome. Psychologist Elizabeth Waites, in her study on *Trauma and Survival,* explains Selye's model as follows:

> . . . General Adaptation Syndrome (G.A.S.), evolves through three phases: an alarm reaction, which energizes the body for action; a stage of resistance, which is in many respects the opposite of the alarm reaction and may represent an attempt to reinstate homeostasis; and a state of exhaustion, the end point when energy reserves are depleted and breakdown occurs.

Under extreme or prolonged stress, the mind is increasingly unable to restore the balance it needs to remain healthy, and the mental resources we normally have in reserve are simply worn out.

Kathryn D. Cramer, in her book *Staying on Top When Your World Turns Upside Down,* details some of the personal energies that traumatic stress can deplete in us. These resources include:

1. physical stamina and resistance to disease
2. mental clarity, flexibility and creativity; self-confidence and optimism; a sense of control and responsibility for one's self
3. emotional vitality, ease of expression, the ability to give and receive love
4. spiritual groundedness and reflection; a sense of hope and fairness in life; strong commitment to our goals

As anyone knows who has suffered from long-term stress, it can wear you down physically and mentally, seem to rob you of confidence and hope, erode your energy toward others and yourself, freeze and tighten your normal responses to the world.

Stalking victims, however, face an even greater form of trauma than the pain of a single major crisis like the death of a loved one, or a prolonged but relatively common stressor like an unsatisfying job or an unhappy relationship. Psychologists have identified the most severe types of stress as those that are *repeated, unpredictable, extreme,* and *seemingly unavoidable.* They have termed this type of stressful pattern as "inescapable shock" (I.S.) and have shown it to be the most potentially damaging to an individual's resources and response capacities. Mice in a cage subject to random electrical shocks that are unpredictable and inescapable, yet which after a while are expected to happen, rapidly reach a state of chronic distress and breakdown. In humans, severe stressors from which the individual can see no means of escape, yet which happen over and over at unexpected times or in unpredictable ways, constitute the same kind of severe I.S. trauma. It should come as no surprise that the ordeal of being stalked qualifies as just such a pattern—the shock and fear of repeated harassment, threat, or even violence that inflicts an unpredictable, endless, and seemingly inescapable net of anxiety.

According to Elizabeth Waites, I.S. trauma can deeply impact an individual's psychological and physical energies, including the ability to process information, memory, resistance to addiction and diseases, tolerance for other stressors, even one's long-term identity and self-image. Knowing some of the ways such extreme stress can affect victims can help others provide understanding and support, and help victims themselves know they are not crazy or alone if they experience some of the following symptoms of I.S. trauma.

One potential outcome of severe, repeated stress is the mind's attempt to desensitize itself by regulating the flow of traumatic realities. This can involve a growing difficulty to focus on negative events, an increasing impulse to avoid or deny painful incidents. One begins to have difficulty concentrating on or processing painful information in an attempt to ease the stress of constant vigilance. According to Waites, however, "a cocoon can eventually prove dangerously maladaptive" by reducing the individual's alertness and control of negative situations and heightening vulnerability if danger is a part of the scenario.

Another change in the mind's ability to respond can take the form of a hypersensitivity to any other forms of stress, even those once considered fairly mild or normal. Individuals suffering from the fallout of I.S. may find themselves avoiding even slight stressors such as facing new challenges or pursuing new interests, meeting new people or engaging in activities that once were pleasurably stimulating. Everything begins to feel like too much to handle, since one's normal resources have been exhausted. This, of course, can tend to compound a victim's sense of isolation and unhappiness; it is important to keep engaging in outside interests and activities for the mind to stay healthy.

Memory is another function that can be affected by extreme stress. The most severe example is amnesia, whereby the mind blocks or cannot recall extremely painful incidents or information. Yet nearly everyone has experienced some of the milder forms of memory impairment that stress can bring about. Think of how difficult it is for people who have been in a car accident to accurately recall the events that took place—for most of us, stress tends to blur and jumble the facts, and insurance claim reports are filled with nearly nonsensical accounts of how accidents unfolded.

For victims of stalking, however, who may be asked to recall and report in minute detail the events surrounding extremely frightening or stressful incidents, these normal lapses in memory can bear painful consequences. Victims who have trouble recalling exact sequences of events or who revise their narratives when they have double-checked or better recalled incidents have been accused of lying or overdramatizing their situations. Some victims begin to lose confidence in their own abilities, especially when others deny or minimize the facts, and the subsequent loss of support and self-esteem, not to mention the feeling of unreality or craziness, can be devastating. It is important to understand how stress can temporarily slow down the memory process—patience in helping a victim recall highly stressful events, and good record-keeping, are vital.

Extreme stress also has an impact on physical functions, such as our resistance to illness and even our susceptibility to addiction. Under severe stress or grief, the brain naturally produces analgesic chemicals. These powerful natural tranquilizers help moderate pain and allow a measure of temporary relief. If you have ever seen a small child begin to yawn and grow sleepy after a hard crying fit, you have probably seen these natural analgesics at work. Yet often people suffering from repeated, severe stress are tempted to supplement the mind's chemicals with external numbing agents, such as drugs or alcohol. The exhaustion of stress can leave an individual especially vulnerable to the dangers of addictive substances—and part of a strong program of support involves helping the individual avoid these substances and recognize that their situation makes them particularly susceptible to becoming dependent.

Similarly, prolonged stress can impact the individual's immune system, leaving them far less resistant to illness and disease. Numerous studies have reported a high degree of illness after major crises or life-altering stresses. Again, it is important to remember that during this vulnerable time special attention should be paid to rest, diet, and exercise that maximize one's chances to stay healthy.

In some cases severe, ongoing trauma can influence one's sense of identity and self-image. Waites states that, on one level, "being a victim defines who one is," particularly when trauma is frequent or occurs during formative years. And yet she strongly points out that the detrimental effects of trauma are largely erased when victims feel their experience is recognized and acknowledged by society, when the dangers are shared through support and through the victim's knowledge that she is not alone. It is one of the driving forces behind this book itself—to help victims see that their experience is not an isolated one, to help others recognize and take a stand against the crime of stalking. Being a "victim" is not a permanent state—indeed, when victims join forces, take action, and speak out, they are victims no more.

Recovery from the impact of long-term stress involves restoring one's personal resources and sense of wholeness. Kathryn Cramer outlines the pattern of crisis and recovery, as it involves gradually exercising greater amounts of control, thereby beginning to manage the depleting effects of stress. The first phase of trauma involves the crisis itself, after which we experience a sense of disorientation and helplessness. Our world seems to have been shattered; the "rules of the game" have changed; we feel unable to deal with the situation. However, the first step in reclaiming control involves an appraisal of the situation, beginning to define and understand it. If you are a victim of stalking, *this is precisely the step you are taking at this moment, by reading this book,* taking action to learn more about your situation and possible avenues for help. Next comes a stage of forming strategies—clear, objective, and reasonable plans of action by which you can maximize your safety and fight for change. Working with others to achieve your goals constitutes the final phase of reaching out and claiming control. Knowing the patterns that stress can take, and the particular challenges it poses for your mental and physical well-being, can help you be prepared and sensitive to your own responses and, we hope, can inspire ways to manage its impact on your life.

Depression

There are times when the mind cannot fight back, when stress and exhaustion seem to have reached their limit, and our emotions and responses seem essentially to shut down. The combination of ongoing fear, shock, anger, helplessness, and disruption of life that is a part of stalking presents the perfect recipe for depression and other major stress-related disorders. What is important to remember, however, is that these disorders are treatable—and beatable.

Clinical depression involves two or more of the

following symptoms, experienced over a period of time:

- depressed mood—feeling "rotten" or "blue" for extended periods, crying spells
- diminished interest or pleasure in activities one normally enjoys (anhedonia)
- decreased appetite, significant weight gain or weight loss
- insomnia (inability to sleep or sleep interruptions) or hypersomnia (sleeping too much)
- either abnormal restlessness or a drop in physical activity
- fatigue
- feelings of worthlessness or guilt
- diminished ability to concentrate or make decisions
- recurring thoughts of death or suicide

When several of these symptoms are taken together, they can be the signs of a clinical depression—and can be a signal that you should seek help to break out of the spiral. Depression can feel like the final burden in an already exhausting situation—however, there are a few things to know and remember to help you cope.

First, depression is not an unnatural response to a stressful situation, and it can have physical as well as psychological bases. Often people who suffer depression feel guilty, as if it is their own negative attitude or some weakness on their part that has brought it on. But clinical depression is in some ways merely an extension of the "resource depletion" discussed in our section on stress, a phenomenon brought on through one's natural reactions to extreme or long-term trauma. Sleep disorders, changes in appetite, lethargy, and suppression of pleasure are ways in which the mind announces that its reactions are out of sync, that its balancing mechanism has been overtaxed. One mental health professional notes that blaming yourself for feeling depressed is like blaming yourself for having trouble catching a bus after you've just run a marathon race—your resources are temporarily spent, but it doesn't mean you will never catch that bus again!

Depression can be treated—with dramatically successful results—both psychologically and medically. Psychological counseling addresses the initial stressors, the causes of the depression, and seeks to provide coping strategies and support. Medication can rectify the chemical imbalances that result in the blue moods or feelings of worthlessness and fatigue that depression causes individuals to suffer. Recall our earlier discussion on the physiological changes in the levels of neurotransmitters, chemicals in the brain that regulate moods, that high levels of stress can bring about. Antidepressant medication temporarily restores the balance of these chemicals, until the brain can resume producing its own needed amounts. Once restored, patients can be taken off the medication; it is not an addictive or lifelong treatment.

There are many ways to be kind to yourself if you are feeling the symptoms of depression. Understand that it can be a natural response to your situation, and that you are not at fault for bringing it on or somehow weak if it persists. Know that depression should be discussed with a professional—a counselor, psychiatrist, or your family doctor—and that treatment is available. Thousands of people in far less demanding circumstances than yours have experienced and managed depression. It is not something you have to live with forever.

Post-Traumatic Stress Disorder

Psychologists have noted that the experience of victims of an ongoing crime like stalking bears striking parallels to the experience of soldiers in battle. Both involve unexpected dangers, the need for constant vigilance, surprise attacks, and fear that is both intense and prolonged. Not surprisingly, therapists have found an increasing occurrence of the syndrome called Post-Traumatic Stress Disorder (PTSD), originally diagnosed as a severe stress response in soldiers, in victims of crimes like stalking.

Symptoms of PTSD can take a long time—months or, in some cases, years—to manifest themselves. Yet their impact is unquestionable and disabling. These symptoms include:

1. Persistent re-experiencing the traumatic events in one or more of the following ways:

- distressing, intrusive, and recurring recollections of the event for no explainable reason
- upsetting recurrent dreams of the event
- suddenly feeling as if the event were happening again, which includes a strong sense of reliving the experience, hallucinations, illusions, and "flashbacks"
- intense distress in response to things that symbolize the traumatic event or recall it, such as driving by a place in which an incident occurred, or seeing an object that recalls the event

2. Persistent avoidance of anything associated with the trauma, or a type of numbing of emotion and response, including:

- deliberately avoiding any thoughts or feelings associated with the trauma
- deliberately avoiding any activities or situations that might bring up recollections of the trauma
- being unable to recall important aspects of the trauma
- significant loss of interest in outside activities
- feeling of detachment or estrangement from others
- feelings of emotional numbness or inability to love
- sense that the future will not be long, productive, or normal

3. Persistent symptoms of increased arousal that weren't present before the trauma occurred, including at least two of the following:

- difficulty falling or staying asleep
- irritability or outbursts
- difficulty concentrating
- being hypervigilant or excessively alert
- physiological reactions to events or things that remind one of the trauma—breaking out in a sweat, for instance, or beginning to shake

For a clinical diagnosis of PTSD, symptoms in all three of these areas must be present at the same time for a period of at least a month. However, if you experience any of these symptoms, we urge you to consult a professional.

Therapy for PTSD varies widely, but often includes a program of working through the traumatic event with the guidance of a caring professional. A therapist can help the victim reopen channels of feeling that have been repressed, and learn to manage the impact of distressing, invasive thoughts or flashbacks. Most recently, researchers have been experimenting with physiological therapy, such as Eye Movement Desensitization Reprocessing (EMDR), in which a supervised course of intensive lateral eye movements seems to afford relief for PTSD symptoms. It is not yet known why or how this works, but initial results seem encouraging, in some cases dramatically so.

Recovery

Dan Kohler, a Virginia counselor who has treated victims of stalking, says that at some point in therapy he asks his patients how they think they will feel after the stalking is over. Unanimously, his patients paint gushing accounts of how blissful life will be, how free from worry, how joyful and productive once again. Dan acknowledges that these are normal reactions, but he persists with his question until his patients begin to achieve a more realistic view of the process of healing and recovery that follows a major traumatic event. The degree of trauma, of course, affects the length of time it will take for a survivor to fully recover—but in all cases, victims must be prepared for the work it will take for them to readjust their lives.

One aspect of stalking that can present an obstacle to recovery is the difficulty knowing when the stalking is actually over. Stalking often takes place as a *cycle* of behavior, which can taper off or cease for months at a time, only to resurface unpredictably into a fresh series of events. Victims who have not experienced any harassment for a long period are realistically hesitant to believe the ordeal is really over, to allow the process of healing to begin. Time and support are valuable commodities in helping victims gradually regain equilibrium and feel safe again; patience and encouragement are priceless in helping to restore confidence and begin recovery.

Even after victims feel assured that the stalking has ended, many find themselves having trouble learning to trust again—both others and themselves. A phase of overcompensating can take place, in which survivors of stalking tend to mistrust their own judgment in meeting people, or feel intensely suspicious of others, resulting in potential difficulties forming new relationships, whether personal or professional, intimate or casual. Existing relationships may also be affected; survivors may find themselves reacting with far greater caution and vigilance around others than is normal for them.

Processing the overall impact of the traumatic event on one's life is another phase in the progress of recovery, and that might include needing to grieve over other relationships that have been damaged or lost as a result of the ordeal. In a more general sense, survivors need to assign some meaning to what they have been through, in order to understand it and be able to move on. Charles R. Figley, an expert on traumatic stress and recovery, claims that, after a period of feeling safe, survivors seek to answer five basic questions that will help locate and make some sense of the traumatic event:

1. What happened to me?
2. How did it happen?
3. Why me?
4. Why did I act as I did?
5. What will I do in another catastrophe?

Family and friends, along with professionals, can guide the survivor's efforts by helping them find insights, correct misperceptions, avoid self-blame, and prepare for the future.

Healing from trauma can be a gradual and demanding process—but it can also be a positive challenge, an avenue for new learning and growth. It can be a time for rethinking boundaries, reestablishing a sense of self that includes pride in the achievement of survival, newfound strength and purpose. Jane McAllister speaks of her own journey toward recovery, which for her involved reaffirming the role of empathy for others in her life, a stronger sense of community and spirituality, and a powerful commitment to political activism and social change. Each step in this journey of healing can bring about lasting insights and valuable affirmations. We believe, in the end, that the old saying holds true: things that have been broken often mend even stronger than before.

Stalking: How to Strike Back

by Jane McAllister
President, Citizens Against Stalking

Stunned and angered by the inability of the police to put a stop to the man who had stalked me for eighteen months, I decided that, to save my own sanity and to survive the emotional ordeal of stalking, I needed to take matters into my own hands. Using local media, I formed a support group for people who were being stalked. Together we began to look for solutions to the problem that we shared. Through our own experiences, we developed a number of actions that we could take. Putting these things into practice helped us reclaim our personal power and accomplish something tangible, despite the indifference and impotence of law enforcement.

Here they are, for those who are suffering the truly soul-destroying experience of being stalked.

Actions to Take Against the Stalker

- *Document everything.* Include date, time, and a description of each incident, names of witnesses, and any action taken by you. Even though a single incident alone may not be serious, the documentation will show a pattern of behavior that may help you legally later on.
- *Talk to the witnesses* to determine whether they will testify in court if necessary.
- *Notify law enforcement* of each incident. Keep police informed even if the stalker's action is not illegal, and even if the police seem uninterested. When you report each incident, tell the police to log your call. This may serve as important documentation later.
- *Explore the legal remedies* available in your state. Most states now have antistalking laws. If your state has such a law, find an attorney who is familiar with it and who is sympathetic to your situation.
- *Have your attorney send a registered letter* telling the stalker he must stop the behavior immediately, and that you are working closely with the police to secure his arrest if he continues to stalk you.
- *Approach local newspaper, magazine, and broadcast media* who have public service features or public advocacy programs. Make yourself available for an interview and

encourage media to do a feature on the stalking problem. You can remain anonymous for purposes of safety, but still raise public awareness.

- *Talk to local politicians.* Ask for their support in getting the police to intervene. Tell them you are working with the media.
- *Get a restraining order* if the stalker trespasses on your property.
- *Inform all of your neighbors,* co-workers, and the receptionist and security staff where you live or work. Prepare them for the possibility that the stalker may look for you there, and ask them to support you. Do the same with the key people in the organizations to which you belong. The moment that the stalker shows up in a work or social setting is not the time to explain the situation. All too often the stalker will adopt his most friendly demeanor, thus discrediting the victim.
- *Get a free home security review* from your local police. Many police departments now provide this through their community relations departments. Then follow their recommendations about upgrading the locks and lighting of your home where possible.
- *Give a description or a photograph of the stalker,* if you have one, to anyone who might ever see him.
- *Write down the license number and description of the stalker's vehicle.* Give this to your family, friends, neighbors, co-workers, and police.
- *Keep a camera handy,* so that if the stalker comes near you, you can take a picture which will serve as proof that he was in your vicinity.
- *Consider purchasing or renting a surveillance camera.* These can be placed strategically inside your home or apartment to film the areas around your doors and car, where stalkers are likely to leave "gifts" or letters.

A filmed record of such activities will help with legal action.

- *If you are thinking about buying a gun,* weigh your decision carefully in view of these cautions:
  - —an intruder may use it against you
  - —most people hesitate to shoot an intruder
  - —there is the potential for a tragic accident with a gun in the home, particularly if children are present.
- *Carry a mace canister or small air horn with you.* In many cases these have proven more effective against assailants than a gun.
- *Consider getting a car phone* if your stalker typically follows you while you are driving. This is especially important if your job requires you to drive alone at night.
- *Consider installing a home security alarm system.*

Things to Do for Yourself

- *Join a support group.* If none exists, start one. The media can help. Local domestic violence groups or the state's attorney general's office can refer you to others who have called seeking help with a stalker.
- *Keep nothing to yourself* about the stalker or his activities. Report every encounter to someone immediately.
- *Seek support* from people who understand. Avoid people who minimize the problem and tell you that you are overreacting.
- *Seek therapy* if any of the following symptoms begin to cause you trouble:
  - rage
  - severe depression

restlessness
fear
sleeplessness
inability to concentrate
suspicion of others
cynicism
unwillingness to trust anyone
extreme fatigue
the wish to withdraw
significant increase or decrease in food intake
use of sedatives or alcohol to cope with the stress
hypervigilance
irritability

- *Know that the longer this trauma lasts, the deeper the emotional wound to you.*
- *Know that the situation is potentially dangerous.* Stalkers have been known to murder their victims.
- *Reject the notion that since you have not been physically assaulted you have not been harmed.* The emotional assault that stalking victims experience can be just as harmful—if not more harmful—than physical assault.
- Know that regardless of a past relationship with the stalker, if any, *you have every right to insist that the stalking stop.*
- *Refrain from retaliation of any kind,* such as vandalism to the stalker's car or home. Though you may be tempted to lash out in this way, any action of this type could place you in physical danger, may have emotional repercussions for you, and could later be used against you if you take legal action against the stalker.
- *Don't joke with others about wanting to kill the stalker.* This could be misconstrued and could be used against you later in a court of law.

- If possible, *be sure that someone knows where you are at all times,* and when you are expected to arrive home.
- *Consider getting a dog* if this is practical for you.
- If you jog or belong to a health club, *do your workouts with a buddy*—preferably someone who knows your situation. This will make you feel safer and also provide a witness if your stalker approaches you at that time.
- *Never, never walk or jog alone at night.* This is not a good idea under the best of circumstances, but for a stalking victim it is out of the question.
- *When going to your car, ask someone to walk with you,* or at least to watch you until you are safely in it.
- *Understand that stalking is disordered, sick, and abnormal.* It is essentially violent, abusive, antisocial behavior not acceptable or justifiable under any circumstance.
- *Know that what is happening to you is not okay, not your fault, and not caused by anything you did.*
- *Care for yourself* by eating well, and getting plenty of rest, exercise, and companionship. Remember, you are undergoing tremendous stress.
- *As much as possible, let neither the stalker nor fear of him rule your life.* Take action, and fill your days with the people, places, and things that give you comfort and joy.

CHAPTER 6

Legal Recourse

> If only I hadn't been so naive about the system and how it works . . . I would have contacted the police more frequently and stood my ground, refusing to run.
>
> "Debbie," stalking victim

> The laws need to be stronger against stalking, and lawmakers need to stop worrying so much about the stalker's rights. What about my rights to be a normal teenager and grow up not worrying about being followed or killed?
>
> "Lori," stalking victim

> I think we're undoing thousands and thousands of years of human history. . . . Women's voices are just beginning to be heard in the law, and the law is very recalcitrant, whether it's judges or lawyers or the police.
>
> Sheila Kuehl, attorney,
> California Women's Law Center

Before the passage of antistalking laws, police and prosecutors had few legal avenues available by which they could apprehend stalkers or effectively put an end to their activities. At times, police had to resort to pressing minor secondary charges—such as littering, trespassing, traffic violations, harassment, or disorderly conduct—in an effort to address individual events. The fit, however, was far from perfect, and many law enforcement officials were relieved when laws were passed that identified and made stalking itself a crime. In the words of one law enforcement official, "It's much easier now to go after somebody. We've got a law with some teeth in it now that can be used."

But even with antistalking laws on the books in most states, those laws are only as effective as the determination to recognize and implement them. Sadly, stories still exist of victims who have been repeatedly frustrated by the seeming inability of police to intervene, or the unwillingness of prosecutors to pursue their cases. Even in the event of arrest, light sentences and early releases have placed victims back in danger all too soon.

As with any new legislation, a process of education and training for law enforcement is imperative, particularly in the case of a crime that takes as many forms as stalking and that can at times be notoriously secretive or elusive. One of the difficulties of identifying and judging stalking is that some of the behaviors, taken out of context or alone, do not seem to be criminal. Driving by someone's house or sending flowers, by themselves, appear to be innocent activities, even "flattering attentions," to observers unaware of a pattern of ongoing, unwanted, or threatening contact. How could a love letter or a seemingly benign gift be perceived as a criminal approach? How does one prosecute an ex-spouse who simply seems brokenhearted, or a suitor who is merely being persistent? Understanding the importance of context and the pattern of repeated activities—an understanding fostered through experience and training—helps police, prosecutors, and judges recognize the very real dangers of this crime.

Moreover, some public attitudes about this crime may need adjustment, as we begin to learn more about its prevalence and its severity. The history of change surrounding our public understanding of domestic violence might set a precedent for challenging old viewpoints about other hidden crimes such as stalking. The misguided "sanctity of the home"—the idea that what went on between spouses was somehow private and beyond the law—has had to undergo radical revision, as we begin as a society to understand that physical or sexual assault in the home and between spouses is no different than violent crimes on our streets. Old views about the rights of husbands to discipline or abuse their wives has had to give way to the recognition of the rights of all citizens to safety both within and outside the home. In the same way, attitudes about stalking, both as a component of domestic violence and as an invasion of the safety and privacy of any individual, must take into account the vast difference between normal human contact and the move into criminal pursuit and potentially deadly persistence represented by stalking.

Societal attitudes do not only take the form of how we interpret and evaluate this crime. They also play a part in how we penalize it, the weight of the sentences our courts place on perpetrators, and the acknowledgment of the potential danger the offender poses. As we'll see in the next chapter, antistalking laws are now undergoing a process of evaluation, and in some cases revision, as we learn the ineffectual nature of light sentences and early, unsupervised release of stalkers back into the community. Yet according to one expert, many existing laws still only offer little tools by which to chip away at this growing crime.

Nonetheless, the law is your most powerful weapon if you find yourself the target of a stalker, and it is worth knowing your rights and how to secure them under the law. Since processes and procedures will vary from state to state, district to district, and even case by case, you should thoroughly research the laws in your area and seek the services of a competent legal advisor. This chapter offers a general overview and basic tips on negotiating what often seems to be a perplexing or intimidating criminal justice system, in an effort to help you feel more comfortable and knowledgeable in working with law enforcement and the courts.

Police

Your first line of defense if you find yourself the victim of a stalker is your local police department. Law enforcement officials urge victims to be alert to the nature of the crime, and to help their efforts as much as possible by keeping accurate and reliable records of activities. This is where keeping a journal of events and copies of evidence such as letters, telephone messages, or gifts becomes crucial. If you telephone police, be ready to explain your situation clearly, giving as much detail as needed at the time. If you are in a crisis, dial 911 and ask for immediate assistance.

In either case, you will most likely be asked to file a police report so that the police can begin their investigations and open the case. In their report, police will take down information about you, about the nature and duration of the events, and any information you can provide about the perpetrator or suspect. They may try to identify what type of stalking this is, whether this is a first-time offense or part of a pattern of repeated contact, whether you already hold a restraining or no-contact order against the perpetrator, and particularly whether any threats were made or implied. It is a good idea to have your evidence with you at the time, and many victims have found it extremely helpful to come prepared with a typed narrative of events as they unfolded. The muddle and stress of trying to tell your story clearly and accurately in a busy police station, relying solely on memory, can be frustrating to you and confusing to the officer taking the report. Important details can be left out or vital dates jumbled—and returning to amend or correct your report later might weaken your credibility. On the other hand, being prepared with clear documentation provides the police with a reliable chronology of events, and impresses the fact that you are willing to work with them as a team.

Some victims feel more comfortable having a supportive family member, friend, or a professional such as a victim's advocate or attorney be with them when they go in to file the report. We recommend, however, that you avoid bringing someone who will want to speak *for* you, or who may dive in with a jumble of their own perceptions and details as you tell your story, or who may become overly emotional or angry during the taking of the report. Friends and family are understandably upset whenever a crime touches someone close to them, and often they wish to jump in and rescue that person. Remember that *you* are the one standing up for your rights; you are the one responsible for seeing that the police have all the accurate information pertinent to your case.

It goes without saying that you need to be open and thorough in explaining all the relevant details of your case. If your stalker is someone you were intimately involved with, tell the police the nature and extent of your relationship. While victims are sometimes nervous that this will undermine the seriousness of their case or open them up to the suspicion that they have somehow brought on this behavior, it is always in your best interest to tell the truth. If you do feel the police react inappropriately to this information, minimizing or dismissing the seriousness of your charges, stand your ground. Ask to speak with someone higher up if you feel you are not receiving the service and protection you deserve.

At times the police may feel they need to ask for more information, and even neutrally phrased questions might seem, given the stress of having to tell your story, as if you are not being believed or are yourself somehow on trial. The tip is to remain calm, understand that the police are there to work with you and find out all the facts of the case, and give straightforward answers. One victim recalls having brought the police evidence of her stalking, which included cassettes of recorded messages left on her answering machine. In those messages her stalker, a former co-worker, made references to fictional romantic encounters the two had had, and to fantasized cards and letters that *she* had allegedly sent to *him.* When the police asked routinely whether the stalker's references were true, the victim recalls feeling furious at being put on trial. However, she soon realized that the police were simply sorting out the facts—and indeed, the stalker's veering into obsessional fantasies gave them valuable information about his mental state and the level of threat he actually posed.

Finally, you should be aware that in most cases you are entitled to a copy of your police report. This is a right generally protected under the Freedom of Information Act passed by Congress in 1966, which allows individuals access to information held by government bodies such as law enforcement agencies. Each state government, however, has its own regulations concerning the disclosure of records held by local agencies, and you should ask about the particular laws governing your area. If the report is available to you, it is a good idea to request a copy for your own files. In either case, you will be given a case referral number, through which you can identify your case whenever you contact police or investigators. You might also want to take down the reporting officer's name and badge number for your files.

It is worth mentioning at this point that each state also has guidelines that specify your rights as a victim of crime. These rights cover a wide variety of areas and concerns, including your right to receiving certain information promptly, your right to be present or absent at future trials, your right to confidentiality and to notification of the progress of your case. We urge you to insist on receiving a copy of victims rights for your own state, and on having those rights explained to you if you have questions. Most police departments carry brochures and pamphlets explaining your rights as a matter of course, and many prosecutors' offices have a specific individual who acts as a "victims rights contact person" to answer your concerns. The bottom line is to be *informed* from the start.

From Investigation to Arrest

After you have filed your police report, it may remain with the initial officer, or it may be passed on to an investigator for handling. It is the investigating officer's job to sort out, discover, and confirm the facts of the case, in preparation for further legal action. He or she may phone you or others involved to discuss your case and may, in this initial stage, explore various strategies outside of arrest to end the behavior. Some investigators report that milder cases of harassment have responded to mediation—in the case of one angry ex-boyfriend who was pestering his victim by telephone, a call by the investigator informing the young man that a report had been filed and that any further contact would result in a warrant for his arrest was enough to stop the behavior immediately. Other investigators may choose to send a cease-and-desist letter to the suspect in hopes of achieving the same ends.

Not all perpetrators, however, will respond to the mere fact of police intervention or to third-party mediation. Investigators have a difficult job to do in assessing the severity of a crime and the potential danger to a victim, particularly in a "new" crime such as stalking. Some networks are being developed that can help law enforcement assess the dangerousness of suspected criminals; the computerized MOSAIC system currently offers profile data on stalkers and seeks to estimate the level of threat posed in particular scenarios. However, the technology is relatively new and not yet available in many districts, and investigators still need to rely on experience and personal judgment.

One officer, seasoned in handling stalking cases,

reflects that each case is unique and must be evaluated based on "what is said, what is done. If it's a deal where an ex-boyfriend calls up and says, 'Oh, honey, I love you, don't leave me'—this type of thing—well, that in itself doesn't show that he is going to do something wrong. But if it's 'Honey, if you leave me I'm going to kill you,' then we're going a little bit overboard. If things are left, like paintings on garages, or if they do damage—flatten tires, put sugar in gas tanks—when they take violent action, then of course the threat escalates . . . or if it's a stranger who also has these fantasies, then I'd say you've got a definite mental problem there—it's not just anger." When asked about the percentage of "false" reports or instances where the behaviors reported were clearly not stalking, his response is grave: "Most of it is legitimate. Some of it is very serious. *Very* serious."

If the investigator feels the case presents enough "probable cause" that a crime has been committed, he or she will request the prosecutor to authorize a warrant for arrest. In some cases, however, there may be the perception that not enough evidence exists, or that the pattern of behavior is not sufficiently "criminal" to result in prosecution. If the investigating officer assigned to your case does not seek a warrant, yet you feel that an arrest should be made, you have the right to contact the prosecutor directly to discuss your situation and request that a warrant be issued. Note that in cases of certain crimes, such as domestic assault or kidnapping, arrest may take place without a warrant, on the officer's own initiative.

The task of the prosecutor is to assess each case, to decide whether an individual should be charged with a crime, and to determine what that crime should be. If and when the warrant is issued, the complainant may be called in to swear to and sign it—a rather rapid formal procedure—after which the arrest can take place. If the perpetrator cannot be located, the police place the information on their LEIN system—the Law Enforcement Information Network—so that if the perpetrator is found, or apprehended on any other charge like a traffic violation, or if he shows up at the victim's residence, he can be arrested on the spot. LEIN systems are generally statewide networks, and for felony crimes, can extend across state lines as well. The system—and some of its gaps—are discussed later in this chapter.

From Booking to Sentencing

Once arrested, the suspect is brought to the police station for the process known as booking. He is fingerprinted and photographed, and his name, arrival time, and offense are recorded. He may either be released before his arraignment, by promising to appear before the magistrate at a specific date and time, or he may be held until the time of arraignment, which is usually at most a matter of days. This preliminary arraignment takes place at the lowest level of the court system, known by varying names in different jurisdictions: district court, magistrate court, municipal court, justice of the peace court, police court, or recorder's court. For misdemeanor charges, this is the only court in which the suspect will be arraigned; for felony offenses, the suspect will later be arraigned again in circuit court—also called trial court or superior court—which then takes over the proceedings for the felony charges.

As the complainant, often you will be notified that the arraignment will be taking place, although you will not be required to be present. During an arraignment, the individual is informed of the charges being brought against him or her, and the terms and conditions of bail are set. In the case of felony charges—which include aggravated or second-offense stalking, or cases in which stalking was combined with a felony offense such as kidnapping or assault with a weapon—the date is also determined at this time for the subjects' pretrial examination or preliminary hearing, discussed later.

Most first-time stalking offenses are currently charged as misdemeanors, and it is not infrequent that perpetrators are released after the arraignment "on their own recognizance"—also known as "personal bond"—without financial bail, that is, the posting of cash or a secured (monetary) bond. In the cases where financial bond is set, often the amounts seem extraordinarily high, yet perpetrators seem able to come up with the money and obtain release. An option in many jurisdictions is that the arrestee is allowed to obtain release by posting the cash equivalent of 10 percent of the bond set by the magistrate. This was the case for Illinois stalker Wayne Chaney, who was able to secure his release at a fraction of his set bond—and subsequently used his liberty to track down and murder his wife, Connie.

Senator Ed Royce, one of the original authors of the California antistalking law, has advised victims of stalkers to be an active part of the bail-setting process, particularly given the dangers of perpetrators remaining at large. If possible, victims should speak with the prosecuting attorney at the time of arraignment and insist that high bail be set. In addition, at the time of arraignment, courts will often append a "no-contact" order as a condition of pretrial release, which specifies that the suspect is to have no contact whatsoever with the complainant—whether by telephone, via letter, or in person—until the time of trial. Of all injunctive orders—such as restraining orders, "stay away" orders, or conditions of probation or parole imposed by court order, which will be discussed later in this chapter—these "bond condition" orders can be the victim's strongest temporary protection. Violations of bond conditions, unlike other injunctions, can result in the suspect being jailed *without release until the date of trial,* since his violation proves that he cannot be trusted to comply with the terms set by the court.

In any event, many states mandate, particularly in felony cases, that the victim be provided, within twenty-four hours, with vital information emerging from the arraignment, such as the availability and terms of pretrial release, information about whether or not the defendant has been released from custody, and procedures to follow to revoke the bond if you experience further harassment or if you can present evidence of intimidation or threat that were not available at the time of the arraignment. Check with your local prosecutor's office or crime victims rights advocate for information about your rights and responsibilities at this stage.

Felony offenders at this point generally move to a Preliminary Examination, which is a pretrial hearing held before a judge. It is what is called a "contested" hearing, during which the attorneys representing each side present evidence and may cross-examine witnesses, in order to convince the judge that a crime has or has not been committed. If the judge sees enough "probable cause" that the felony was committed, the defendant is sent to circuit court for a second arraignment—at which time he is asked to enter a plea—and for subsequent trial proceedings. Defendants may waive the right to a preliminary examination, particularly if they intend to plead guilty. Misdemeanors are not given preliminary hearings, and they remain in district court for trial.

In both cases, what follow are Pretrial Proceedings, during which many things can take place. This is the phase of the process in which the defense attorney and prosecutor may meet to plea-bargain or determine what charges the defendant will plead guilty to. One of the most common bargains struck is an agreement to reduce the charges in exchange for a plea of guilty to the lesser offense. For instance, an individual arrested for stalking may agree to plead guilty to a lesser offense of harassment or trespassing. At this time too the court may hear motions on what evidence may or may not be admitted in the trial, or whether there is some reason that a trial should not take place. The victim does not need to be present at these proceedings but can elect to be involved. Even if she decides not to be present, she has the right to be informed of the procedure, of a schedule of the proceedings and any changes, and of any plea bargaining arrangements decided on during pretrial discussions. If the case proceeds to trial, the victim also has the right to meet and confer with the prosecutor before jury selection and before the trial itself.

Most felony and misdemeanor cases do not actually reach trial; by this stage of the process many have either been disposed of by a guilty plea (even if to a lesser sentence) or by dismissal (due to lack of evidence or a host of other legal and interpretive concerns). Only a small percentage of felony cases that reach circuit court will actually go to trial, and the percentage is even lower for misdemeanor cases. The criminal justice system has been described as a kind of funnel or sieve—as the caseload moves through the process, more and more cases are sifted out or handled outside of trial proceedings. To some extent, this system of seemingly endless checks and cross-checks, investigations and reinvestigations, hearings and examinations, are designed to protect all of our rights, by guaranteeing that only legitimate cases proceed all the way to trial. For victims, however, this aspect of the justice system sometimes seems unnecessarily roundabout. The same procedures that ensure controls on one level can seem from a different perspective like cracks through which criminals can slip with light charges, minimal penalties, or outright dismissal. While understanding the need for a system of checks and balances, we urge victims to keep alert and informed at all levels of the process, to make sure their interests are being served.

Trials, whether by a lone judge (a "bench trial") or by jury (a "jury trial"), are conducted as "adversary proceedings"—that being, the counsel for the prosecution attempts to present enough evidence by which to convict the defendant, who is represented by his own attorney. Witnesses are called to testify and are cross-examined, and formal evidence is laid before the court. If the defendant is found guilty of a crime, or has previously pleaded guilty, the judge sets a date for sentencing, giving enough time for the probation officer assigned to the case to prepare a report which reexamines the details of the crime, takes into account the defendant's past criminal history and background, and makes a recommendation of the type and length of sentence to be imposed.

At the sentencing, the judge considers the information contained in this "presentence investigation report," along with other guidelines for establishing appropriate sentences, and comes to a decision. *In the case of misdemeanor crimes, however, a presentencing report is not always prepared.* Moreover, in a majority of misdemeanor cases, sentences involve a fine or probation rather than imprisonment, or the defendant may receive a suspended sentence. If you feel that your case requires special consideration, and you believe a presentencing investigation would be valuable in helping the judge determine the severity or extent of the sentence, you might consult the prosecuting attorney to arrange for such an investigation to take place between the trial and sentencing. This may be particularly important if the original charge was a felony that was reduced to a misdemeanor as part of a plea-bargain arrangement.

Civil Suits

In some states, victims of stalkers also have the right to pursue restitution against their stalker in civil court—in other words, to sue for emotional, physical, or financial damages incurred as a result of the stalking and/or file suit to obtain a restraining order against the stalker. On the one hand, this allows victims to take action if they do not receive satisfaction through the criminal justice system—if, for instance, the county prosecutor is unwilling to take on a stalking case, or the case is dismissed for a legal technicality. But civil action is not only meant as a last resort for justice; victims may also file suit *in addition* to criminal proceedings, in order to recover damages or strengthen their protection.

There are a number of benefits and drawbacks to pursuing a civil course of action. On the benefit side, the victim may be able to be reimbursed for damage to property, for medical expenses or the cost of therapy to deal with the emotional distress that so often accompanies stalking. In a legal sense, the benefit of a civil suit lies in the fact that the victim is more in control of her own case; she chooses her own attorney and is not dependent on the county prosecutor assigned to the case in a criminal proceeding. In theory, also, the "burden of proof" is lower in civil court cases—the victim needs only to demonstrate a "preponderance of proof" that the crime has taken place, whereas in a criminal trial that proof must be "beyond a reasonable doubt." In practice, however, some lawyers warn that the difference of standards in the two courts may actually be minimal.

The drawbacks to filing a civil suit largely revolve around cost. Although individuals are allowed to file suits "pro se" or by themselves, without the aid of an attorney, most professionals absolutely advise a victim to retain the services of a lawyer, whose advantages are that he or she knows the system, is trained in proper procedures, and may be more articulate and objective than the victim in presenting the case. This, however, raises the problem of lawyer fees. An affluent individual might choose to retain a private attorney through an hourly fee, but the cost involved in this arrangement may be prohibitive to most.

A more common arrangement—particularly in "fee-generating" suits such as those seeking to recover damages—is to find an attorney who will work on a "contingent fee" basis, in which the lawyer agrees to take on the case and recover payment from the monies collected as a result of the suit. Some sources nickname this arrangement the "Riverboat Gamble"—that is, the attorney agrees to go into a gamble with the client, in the hopes of winning and then sharing the money recovered.

Not all lawyers, however, are willing to enter into such an arrangement, and their decision may rest on a number of variables. First and most important is the question of whether the defendant is "collectible"—in other words, whether the perpetrator actually has money that can be recovered. Second, some attorneys may be hesitant to take on a relatively "new" type of suit such as stalking, the evidence for which can sometimes be difficult to document or argue. Lawyers obviously want "winnable" cases—both for their clients and for themselves—and victims should not be surprised if they find some resistance to taking on civil stalking suits that have few precedents.

In choosing an attorney who may be open to taking on your case, you might look through your local phone book for the names of personal injury lawyers. These lawyers usually operate on a contingent fee basis, are experienced in recovering damages for personal suffering and emotional distress, and may be willing to take on the risk of a suit such as stalking. Another avenue might be to call legal aid services—particularly organizations that deal with women's issues, sexual assault or harassment—to inquire whether low-cost, experienced legal help is available. Not all legal aid services will take on "fee-generating" cases, however, as they are often overwhelmed with other cases that take priority over those seeking monetary rewards; however, each organization may have different guidelines and practices, and it is worth informing yourself of all your options if you choose to pursue a civil cause of action.

Restraining Orders

You may use civil court as well to file for a restraining order or injunction against a stalker. "No contact" orders can also generate from the criminal court at various stages of the judicial process, in the form of court-imposed conditions that aim to protect the safety of the victim. We have seen one such "stay away" order, in the form of a "condition of bail" at the time of arraignment, at which a judge mandates that the defendant have no contact whatsoever with the victim until the time of trial. Court orders may also be issued between arrest and arraignment, or as a condition of probation or of parole at the time of sentencing if the defendant is convicted. However, if your case is not proceeding through criminal court, or if you have chosen to pursue civil action rather than criminal prosecution, you can file for your own restraining order in civil court.

What are the differences between restraining orders, "no contact" or "stay away" orders, or (in some states) the new "antistalking order"? Essentially, "no contact" or "stay away" orders are generated by judges as either conditions of bond (before conviction) or conditions of probation (after conviction) or conditions of parole (after conviction and after prison time has been served). Violations of such orders can carry stiff penalties—although the extent of those penalties, within the given bounds, are at the discretion of the courts. As seen earlier, violation of a condition of bond can result in imprisonment until the time of trial. Alternately, a judge could increase the bond previously set. Violations of probation or parole no-contact orders can result in the offender serving prison time up to the original term of the sentence. At least one state now also provides judges with the option of an antistalking order for cases of convicted stalkers, which increases the length of probation to five years and automatically restricts all stalking behaviors—such as surveillance or appearing on the victim's property when she is absent—in addition to general no-contact limitations.

Restraining orders (or "injunctions") are orders generated by the victim and filed for in civil court—usually as a result of divorce proceedings, domestic violence assaults, or other activity such as stalking. The victim presents evidence that some prior event has taken place, such as assault, then requests an injunction mandating that the perpetrator abide by certain limitations, such as staying 150 feet away from her or her children, having no contact by telephone, and so on. The language on restraining orders presents a fairly standard list of limitations, but individuals filing for restraining orders can request more specific behaviors to be appended, provided evidence can be provided that these behaviors have occurred in the past.

In stalking cases, for instance, in which a victim has been followed or put under surveillance as part of the pattern of harassment, she might consider requesting that these behaviors be added to the restraining order. If you are filing for a restraining order, we suggest that you attempt to have your order cover any or all of the following behaviors:

- placing you under surveillance or following you
- approaching or confronting you in a public place or on private property
- appearing at your workplace or residence
- entering onto or remaining on property owned, leased, or occupied by you, *even when you are not on the premises*
- contacting you by telephone
- sending mail or electronic communications to you
- placing an object on, or delivering an object to, property owned, leased, or occupied by you

These, of course, should be in addition to the usual restraining order prohibitions against assault and other specified invasions.

Filing for a restraining order usually involves a fee. In addition, the costs of a civil protection order can include the lawyer's fee, and the cost of having the perpetrator "served" with the order. There are some lower-cost avenues for avoiding legal fees by filing one's own forms (see "Issues on Restraining Orders," end of chapter). We urge you to inform yourself of the forms and fees required in your own district when deciding on this process.

Violation of a restraining order incurs a penalty for "criminal contempt," which varies in different jurisdictions but is often a maximum of ninety days in jail and/or a limited fine. Part of the "clumsiness" of restraining orders in the past has been the burden placed on the victim after the violation has occurred: she must call her attorney and have a hearing set up (which could be weeks away) in order to charge the individual with the violation. Some states are attempting to streamline this process, with new legislation that allows police to arrest violators without a warrant and on "probable cause." The case will still have to go to court, but meanwhile the offender can be taken into custody immediately.

Debate is ongoing about the effectiveness, or even the wisdom, of taking out restraining orders. Gavin de Becker believes that restraining orders may be as likely to provoke an obsessed individual as to restrain him. According to de Becker, the very fact of an injunction might serve as a type of challenge—and the many women in possession of restraining orders whose cases have ended in violence seems at best to cast doubt on the effectiveness of such documents, at worst to suggest they might have been a final "line" begging to be crossed.

Speaking of his own review of violent cases, De Becker warns:

> Cases which escalated to violence have one factor in common alarmingly often: INTERVENTION (usually in the form of police warnings and restraining orders).
>
> It is common that TRO's precede violence in stalking cases; this fact alone calls for the greatest caution when making the intervention decision. Study the cases, work back from the murder, and you'll find police interventions or TRO's, or both.

In cases that have not escalated to acts of violence or other crimes, de Becker advocates a policy of "aggressive nonintervention"—the deliberate and steadfast breaking of all contact with the perpetrator, including the contact represented by legal interventions such as restraining orders. De Becker calls this strategy one of "detach and watch," where the victim makes one unequivocal communication—and one only—that breaks contact and serves notice to the stalker that his actions are unwanted. De Becker, who describes in "Rejection 101" (Chapter 11) how such contact can be broken, believes that such a "detach and watch" attitude may keep many cases from escalating, with the perpetrator ultimately backing off and ceasing his invasive activities. (Keep in mind that before he does, he may continue to harass and frighten you; for a time—perhaps a long period of time—detaching and watching may require tremendous patience, strength, and courage on your part.)

Restraining orders *can* provoke a perpetrator to greater acts of violence, but there are also numerous arguments for the benefits of restraining orders, particularly as tools that hypothetically help put muscle behind law enforcement efforts. Although it must be realized that restraining orders are simply pieces of paper, their existence is entered on police information networks, allowing police to take action when the conditions of the order have been violated. In addition, violations of restraining orders can in some cases increase the stalking charges from misdemeanors to felonies, allowing for stiffer penalties and a cogent record of criminal behavior. Finally, the existence of a restraining order speaks *for* you in a case where your stalker may try to deceive police or undermine your story by claiming you invited him onto the premises, or that the situation is simply a "lover's quarrel." In this event, presenting your restraining order should end any argument that this was *unconsented contact,* and should clarify the situation for the police immediately.

At the same time, any injunctions are only as powerful as the willingness to enforce them, and victims relate stories of numerous violations that were either discredited by law enforcement officers or were recognized but not effectively punished. In theory, witnesses to a violation of an order *are not required* for an arrest to be made; however, victims still report cases in which they were "simply not believed" or where it became "a case of my word against his—and *his* won out." Indeed, some victims are not lucky enough to complain after the first violation; often the first contact is the fatal one. In the cases of the four Orange County, California, women whose stories helped impel the passage of the country's first antistalking law, three were armed with restraining orders at the time of their deaths.

Moreover, computerized records of orders and/or of prior violations of orders have only recently been part of reforms in law enforcement information systems. In the case of Kristen Lardner, her assailant was already on probation for attacking a previous girlfriend, and there was a warrant out for his arrest at the time Lardner filed for two civil court restraining orders. The courts were unaware of the details of his criminal history, however, and the resulting orders were light and tragically ineffective. Kristen's stalker subsequently followed her and shot her to death in the middle of the day on a busy Boston street.

Ineffective monitoring of stalkers seems another prevalent complaint of victims who feel the system has failed them. In the case of Mark David Bleakley, arrested and convicted for stalking his former girlfriend Leslie Wein, Bleakley was put on probation and sentenced to serve time in a rehabilitation facility—where at one point he was left unsupervised enough to simply walk away. He was apprehended waiting for his victim outside her gym and, fortunately, taken into custody before he could do her more harm.

Other stories abound of the vagaries of light sentences, early and unsupervised release, and the general sense on the part of dissatisfied victims that the courts have a poor understanding of the potential danger of stalkers. Illinois victim Dawn Wilson, stalked and attacked by her ex-husband, was nonetheless horrified to learn of his release after he had accrued *223* technical violations of the electronic monitoring system he had been placed on to ensure that he stay away from her. Such stories clearly underscore the need for greater education in our courts, and for far more committed enforcement of no-contact orders against stalkers.

Fighting Back

Stalking as a crime is complex, often overlapping with other crimes such as domestic violence or workplace sexual harassment, or containing elements of other crimes—kidnapping, trespassing, assault, criminal menace, conspiracy to commit a crime. Stalking targets may find themselves victims of more than one crime—and sometimes may find themselves experiencing tangential forms of harassment or discrimination as well. More than once we have heard of victims fired from their employment, or not hired at new jobs, when employers learned they were being stalked. While employers seldom specified this as a reason for termination or not hiring, often the case has seemed a clear situation of employers not wanting to get involved with a "high risk" employee. If you find yourself experiencing similar forms of discrimination because of your situation as a stalking victim, we urge you to contact your local victims rights organization, women's advocacy program, or legal aid society to find out what recourse is available to you.

Although the tone of this chapter may seem to be one of "you against the world," it is not at all our intention to suggest that you will be alone in fighting back against this crime or in securing your right to live in safety. If the profile of legal recourse begins to look like a frustrating, time-consuming, and sometimes ineffectual process, our interests are in realistically presenting some of the areas that may need change and education, not in implying that the system will always fail. Indeed, the speed of legal and legislative responses to the crime of stalking has been encouraging, despite the fact that improvements are still needed.

The words of Suzanne Schultz, an advocate working in the field of domestic violence, may sum up our attitude toward the legal system, and stalking as well. She states, "I will continue to work with [victims] and say, 'Yes, the system sometimes has some flaws.' However, you know, after all the years that patriarchy has been in place, and we've had rules and systems that haven't worked for us, it is changing. It is changing. It's slowly but surely changing. And we have to stick with it, because that system can be successful. I've seen it." We urge you to reach out and secure your rights—by understanding the process, being aware of your role in it, and standing firm for the service and safety that you deserve.

Issues on Restraining Orders

by William R. Kordenbrock
Legislative Specialist

There exist two schools of thought regarding the wisdom of using restraining orders against stalkers. One view holds that the filing of a restraining order aggravates the stalker and will potentially cause the stalker to escalate his efforts—or in the worst case scenario, resort to violence. This theory is based on the belief that restraining orders are pieces of paper that offer little to no protection. The second school of thought holds that restraining orders are effective both as a deterrent and an enforcement tool against stalkers.

The belief that restraining orders are not effective—to the point of posing a potential threat to the victim by exciting the stalker—has some historical credibility. Before antistalking laws, restraining orders often were not aggressively enforced. When they were enforced, the orders offered little protection. The victim was left with a false sense of security, and the stalker was further antagonized.

Nevertheless, the use of restraining orders should not be discouraged in states that have adopted comprehensive antistalking laws. In many of those states a violation of a restraining order can lead to warrantless arrest of the stalker, increased penalties, and lifetime stay away orders. Under laws similar to those adopted in Michigan, the antistalking restraining order specifically prohibits any conduct outlawed by the general antistalking law. This makes the orders more readily enforceable, and when violated, may subject the stalker to felony rather than misdemeanor charges.

Although there has been a marked increase in the number of legal tools such as restraining orders to assist victims, many victims believe they do not have access to these tools. A restraining order can appear out of reach to an individual who cannot afford an attorney. However, many state laws provide for individuals to appear "pro se"—or without representation—in court. Pro se appearances provide an inexpensive means to obtain the protection of a restraining order. As an example, a new law in Michigan requires the State Court Administrator's Office to develop a "plain English" form that will assist victims in appearing pro se before the court. The law also requires that the courts provide nonlegal staff assistance to victims who desire to represent themselves.

In states that have not developed a program for assisting individuals in representing themselves, there are still resources available for victims. Domestic violence shelters can be a source of information and assistance in obtaining a restraining order. Another potential source of legal help can be nonprofit legal aid organizations. These groups often provide legal assistance for individuals who otherwise cannot afford an attorney. Victims can also look to their State Bar Associations. Attorneys are encouraged by the Bar Association to provide a certain amount of "pro bono"—basically free—legal assistance each year. Within the State Bar there are often special purpose groups organized around specific interests, such as the Women Lawyer Association or a Domestic Violence Bar Association. A victim without adequate resources may be able to find an attorney within these interest groups who would be willing to assist them on a reduced fee or pro bono basis.

Another possible source of legal help is through law school clinics. Many law schools have programs that allow students to gain experience by assisting individuals who otherwise could not afford an attorney. The students are supervised by a licensed attorney. Victims living near a law school can contact the public relations office to see if the school offers legal aid clinics that cover domestic violence or stalking issues.

Many states also have state-funded offices such as state women's commissions, domestic violence prevention and treatment boards, and court administrator's offices. A victim who needs assistance in obtaining a restraining order can check with these organizations. Often they can be a source of referral, and in the case of a court administrator's office, may be able to provide the necessary forms and nonlegal assistance that victims need to proceed on their own.

A restraining order can be a useful and powerful tool in protecting a victim from a stalker. However, for the restraining order to be effective, it must be properly filed. If victims choose to represent themselves, great care should be taken that all instructions are closely followed and all required materials are filed with the court. The stalker must be served with a copy of the order, and the law enforcement community must be made aware of the order. A faulty restraining order can be dangerous. Whenever possible, victims should seek the advice and assistance of a lawyer. If that is not an option—and as a last resort victims decide to represent themselves—they should use as many resources as are available to ensure that they completely understand the requirements and the necessary procedures.

As more states adopt programs to assist victims in the pro se process, the access to restraining orders should no longer be an impassable cause of concern for financially challenged victims of stalkers.

CHAPTER 7

The Law Is Here to Serve Us

Applying the Laws and Constitutional Issues

The stalker . . . is a law unto himself.

Stanton Samenow, author,
Inside the Criminal Mind

Instead of describing the prohibited behaviors, which is virtually impossible because it's so broad, I . . . instead [drafted] a law to describe the effect on its victims, which is easy to describe and is very similar in most cases: the terror, the fear . . . and what I call the loss of the quality of life.

Superior Court Judge John Watson,
co-author of California's antistalking law

At the time of this writing, the story of antistalking legislation is a story of change—of laws formed and challenged, of the vagaries of education and enforcement, of a balancing act between protection for victims and protection of civil liberties in the population at large. The rapid passage of antistalking laws across the country represented a massive response to this crime by lawmakers and the public. Now this sense of emergency has given way to a process of fine-tuning those laws and to researching and debating anti-stalking legislation on a federal level.

In taking a second look at the laws, legislators are grappling with a number of issues. Are the laws written too restrictively; that is, do they require that stalking occur in a certain way, thereby excluding many stalking victims from protection under the law? Or are the laws written too broadly, and might they be subject to constitutional challenge? In the examples that follow, we look at several examples of anti-stalking laws and how the wording of these laws *as they are currently written* could affect your ability to use them.

Course of Conduct

As we saw in Chapter 1, stalking is defined as a "course of conduct" in which harassment or following occurs on two or more occasions. But in some states—Kansas and West Virginia are examples—in order for a victim to charge that she is being stalked, she must be harassed *and* followed. In these states, a perpetrator who repeatedly follows his victim around town but never harasses her otherwise could not be charged with stalking, and by the same token, neither could someone who leaves repeated, harassing phone messages or sends harassing letters.

Some states disregard the incidents of harassment altogether, instead focusing only on the element of pursuit. Washington State, for example, prohibits repeated *following,* Maryland prohibits *approaching or following,* North Carolina prohibits *following or being in the presence of another person without legal purpose,* and Connecticut prohibits *following or lying in wait.*

Other variations on the basic model exist. West Virginia's first antistalking law, for instance, narrowed the definition of stalking considerably by requiring that *a prior intimate relationship* between perpetrator and victim exist in order for a claim of stalking to be made. (The state deleted this requirement in 1993.) In North Carolina a victim must herself request—or request through another person—that the stalker cease his behavior before she can press antistalking charges. Texas law imposes yet another restriction. In that state, a victim may only begin to count the acts that make up a "course of conduct" *after* she has reported any one act to the police. Her stalker may have followed or harassed and threatened her on numerous occasions, but until she contacts the police, it is as if these prior acts "don't count" as evidence by which to press stalking charges.

On the other end of the spectrum lie states whose legislators recognize that the crime must be defined broadly enough to encompass the full range of intrusive behaviors. For instance, legislators in some states acknowledge that some stalkers also threaten to harm a victim's family members or damage a victim's property. California amended its law in 1992 to reflect this observation; now, a person who targets a family member can be charged with the crime. In Washington State a charge of stalking can be made if a victim fears that her (or another's) property will be damaged. Michigan has written its law even more inclusively, listing a host of activities that might fall under the umbrella of "unconsented contact." As defined by this law:

> "Unconsented contact" means any contact with another individual that is initiated or continued without that individual's consent, or in disregard of that individual's expressed desire that the contact be avoided or discontinued. Unconsented contact includes, but is not limited to, any of the following:
>
> (i) Following or appearing within the sight of that individual
> (ii) Approaching or confronting that individual in a public place or on private property
> (iii) Entering onto or remaining on property owned, leased, or occupied by that individual
> (iv) Contacting that individual by telephone
> (v) Sending mail or electronic communications to that individual
> (vi) Placing an object on, or delivering an object to, property owned, leased, or occupied by that individual.

According to attorney David Cahill, "This definition of 'unconsented contact' makes legally enforceable the traditional idea of privacy as 'the right to be let alone.' "

Your state's attorney general's office or Legislative Services office can provide you with a copy of your state's antistalking law. Local battered women's shelters and district attorneys' offices can also be excellent sources of assistance as you investigate the particular provisions of your state's law.

Threats Made or Implied

Laws that narrowly define threats or the manner in which they are made may be limiting the ways they serve and protect victims. In Illinois, for example, lawmakers require *two* acts of harassment or following after a threat has been made for the conduct to be considered stalking. Critics of that law contend that by the time a threat *does* occur, it may be too late to avert a physical assault or murder. "In real life," says Lake County Chief Deputy State's Attorney Steven P. McCollum, "the threat is the *last thing* that happens before the person is harmed." (Italics added)

You should also know that your state may require that a threat be of "great bodily injury or death." "Great bodily injury" has a relatively narrow definition; a victim must fear she will be maimed or disfigured, or that she will die as a result of her injuries. In these states, victims who have not been threatened with maiming, disfiguring, or life-threatening injuries are not protected. Some victims rights advocates have charged that such a requirement is unduly strict. Why, they ask, should a threat of such extreme violence be required before a victim can be protected? In some cases lawmakers have agreed by redefining the threat provisions in the law. In Rhode Island, for example, the law originally required such a threat, but in 1993 lawmakers struck both the "credible threat" and the "threat to cause great bodily injury" sections of that law.

Victims rights advocates are further troubled by some laws that require threats to be *made* in an explicit written or verbal form. This makes invisible the wide range of nonverbal behaviors that can *pose* a threat to the victim. As numerous stalking victims can attest, a stance on the street, a gesture, a pattern of surveillance, or symbolic gifts—dead roses, animal parts, drawings of weapons or blood—can all signify menacing hostility to a victim without constituting "direct" verbal threats. (Recall, for example, how Kimberly Poland, discussed in Chapter 1, received drawings of dripping blood and an arrow embedded in one of her family's trees.) Sometimes these cues are subtle, but nonetheless powerfully suggestive, particularly if the victim knows her stalker. It may take nothing more than a quick private gesture to suggest harm to a victim of prior domestic violence, for example, and the gesture may not even be recognizable as a threat by any outsider. A battering spouse may whisper to his wife, "Remember your birthday last year?" To a casual listener, this could be interpreted in a number of innocuous ways: "Remember our dinner out that night?" "Remember the gift I gave you?" Only the victim would be able to understand its real meaning: "Remember the beating you got on that day?"

But regardless of a couple's past relationship, context is everything in the interpretation of interpersonal threats and their credibility. Context can make many gestures appear quite credible, suggestive of real violence. Lawmakers are just now beginning to realize how frequently the *victim's* perception of possible violence is the most accurate indicator of whether such violence will occur. Stalking expert Gavin de Becker addressed the importance of interpretive context at the Senate Judiciary Hearings on stalking:

> A viable law will take into account that the perception of the victim is a key element of threats and unwanted pursuit. The CONTEXT is an important

part of the victim's perception. If I say to you in this testimony, "I will shoot you tomorrow as you walk to your car," not one of you is alarmed, because in this context, it is not a threat. On the other hand, if a person your daughter dated once three years ago shows up in the parking lot near her car and stares at her ominously, if he follows her on campus, if he sends her dead flowers, leaves bizarre messages on her answering machine, shows up at a family event and points his finger at her with a trigger-pulling gesture, well, that is threatening conduct—even though he may never have spoken a threatening word.

Intent

According to some victims rights advocates, requiring intent creates a loophole that excludes the behavior of one category of stalkers. A love-obsessed stalker (see Chapter 2 for discussions of erotomania and other delusional disorders) may well believe that he is acting merely to show a person "how much he loves her"—despite the fact that his attentions are clearly unwanted and intrusive. Such stalking scenarios may present problems for prosecutors trying to establish guilt by way of intent.

Some legislators have responded to this concern by striking general intent requirements in the case of a crime like stalking. Michigan's law, for instance, requires only:

> a willful course of conduct involving repeated or continuing harassment of another individual that *would* cause a reasonable person to feel terrorized,

> frightened, intimidated, threatened, harassed, or molested, and that *actually* causes the victim to feel terrorized, frightened, intimidated, threatened, harassed, or molested. (Italics added)

Under such a law, the perpetrator *may* intend to produce any of the above effects in his victim, but the state is under no obligation to prove such intent. As long as a victim feels as she does—and as long as the fear she feels is considered reasonable by a court of law—then the stalker's guilt has been established.

Constitutional Challenges: The Wording of Antistalking Laws

But what of the viewpoint that antistalking laws, rather than being too narrow in scope, in fact pose broad and dangerous infringements on our civil liberties? Some critics contend that these new laws have gone too far in their attempts to protect victims of repeated harassment and threats. Others question whether these laws trample on constitutional protections, such as the First Amendment right to speak freely and openly on any subject of one's choosing. Courts are beginning to debate whether some existing antistalking laws abridge the Due Process clause of the Fourteenth Amendment, which requires both that laws be written clearly and that they be enforced uniformly and fairly. Do antistalking laws infringe on the right to travel wherever one chooses or to associate with others as one pleases? Do aspects of some states' laws—such as warrantless arrest and no-bail provisions—restrict the civil liberties of defendants?

Might any of the laws be used to oppress and silence people whose views are unpopular with the police or elected officials? How can antistalking legislation be written so as to avoid infringing constitutional guarantees—and at the same time protect the victims they were designed to serve?

The answers to these questions are just beginning to be debated. Some laws have been attacked as unconstitutional and challenged in court, with some judges in the lower courts affirming that the laws withstand constitutional muster and others disagreeing. These disputed cases are now being appealed to the higher courts. And the situation is likely to become more, rather than less, complicated in the coming years, as courts are asked to put many elements of the laws to the constitutional test. Below, attorney Silvija Strikis reviews the major constitutional issues most likely to arise in the debates over antistalking laws.

Of concern to anyone who believes the laws are useful in protecting victims, these constitutional challenges are likely to be resolved on a state-by-state basis. Your state's attorney general's office or local prosecutor's victim witness program can keep you up-to-date on the legal challenges antistalking legislation may be facing in your state.

Constitutional Issues in Antistalking Legislation

by Silvija A. Strikis

Effective control of stalking requires consideration of many aspects of stalking behavior and how it can be controlled. The starting point for many states, and the focus of Congressional mandate in 1993, has been the development of statutory provisions to control stalking. Although such codes cannot eliminate stalking, they are an important step in the process, and therefore must be carefully drafted to ensure their usefulness.

To someone unfamiliar with the legislative or legal process, it may seem strange how carefully the language in antistalking legislation needs to be considered. It would seem that the definition of stalking could be broad enough to cover all the behaviors that most people would recognize as stalking. However, legislation, particularly a criminal statute, must be drafted with special care to ensure the protection of important constitutional rights.

The Fourteenth Amendment of the United States guarantees due process. In the context of a criminal charge, this has been interpreted by the Supreme Court to require that the alleged criminal offense be defined "with sufficient definiteness that ordinary people can understand what conduct is prohibited and in a manner that does not encourage arbitrary and discriminatory enforcement." A statute that does not meet these criteria can be considered entirely void because it is overly vague.

The first aspect of this interpretation can be called the "notice" element: Does the statute provide adequate notice of the types of activities that will be considered illegal? This is particularly relevant to statutes that criminalize stalking, because in many cases such statutes are blazing through new legal territory. A criminal statute that sets forth a new offense must be especially explicit, so that persons are adequately informed of conduct that will make them liable for the statute's penalties. Therefore, all elements of antistalking legislation must be carefully drafted, so that each definition sets forth the proscribed activity as clearly as possible.

The second aspect of the Supreme Court's interpretation of due process in criminal statutes involves enforcement of the statute: Does the statute provide minimal guidelines to effect fair standards for law enforcement? This concern also subjects antistalking statutes to scrutiny, because the statutes must define the crime in such a way that not only are citizens informed of the elements of the crime, but law enforcement officers are also provided with objective criteria by which to determine if the statute has been violated.

Often, concerns about vagueness in a statute go hand in hand with the protection of other constitutional rights. Any statute that acts to control behavior may impact other rights, such as the freedoms of expression, movement, and association found in the First Amendment. A statute that impinges too much on such constitutionally protected freedoms is generally termed "overbroad" or overly vague. Antistalking statutes do limit a variety of activities; therefore, it is important that the definitions they contain be well-considered from the standpoint of the broadness of the statute's potential impact.

Fortunately, there is some flexibility in how courts can assess the overbreadth or vagueness of a statute. First, in determining the impact of an antistalking statute on protected expression, courts may consider that not all forms of speech are constitutionally protected, and even "free" expression may be prohibited if the government has a sufficiently valid interest in doing so. For example, an Indiana public indecency statute prohibiting nude dancing was upheld by the Supreme Court because of that state's interest in protecting public order and morality, despite the fact that the dancing was arguably constitutionally protected expression. Stalking activities that constitute harassment can be similarly limited by virtue of the state's interest in shielding society from such conduct.

Antistalking statutes can also be drafted to set forth limits on the application of the statute to particular types of protected expression. Many antistalking statutes specifically state that the provisions will not apply to labor picketing or lawful demonstrations, and others exempt activities taking place during the legitimate conduct of a business, such as a private detective agency. In this way, explicit statutory language limiting the scope of an antistalking statute can provide a touchstone by which the courts can assess the intended breadth of the statute.

In assessing whether the scope of an antistalking statute is unconstitutionally vague, courts have significant leeway in interpreting the statute. Although considerations of fairness require that no person "be held criminally responsible for conduct which he could not reasonably understand to be proscribed," practical considerations demand that criminal statutes be "general enough to take into account a variety of human conduct." These concerns have often been balanced by the courts such that a criminal statute will not be thrown out entirely unless it impacts a constitutional right set forth in the First Amendment. If the statute does not impact such a right, the court will consider the application to each particular defendant.

When determining whether the terms of a statute are vague, the court considers all possible meanings of the statute, both as commonly understood and as set forth in the statute or by reference to legislative history or judicial interpretation. With knowledge of this process, legislators can draft criminal statutes to withstand challenges of vagueness. For example, the definition of harassment found in many antistalking statutes is similar to the definition found in the longstanding federal statute that criminalizes harassment of witnesses. The history of this term, as interpreted in the context of other valid criminal statutes, gives assurance that an antistalking statute using the same language will be valid. By contrast, the use of a potentially vague term, such as "following," in an antistalking statute may be more problematic. If "following" alone is an offense under the statute, and there is no separate definition of what constitutes criminal "following," then the statute could be strongly attacked as being overly vague.

Even if a statute is potentially vague, language requiring a particular level of criminal intent may work to salvage its provisions. Because the "fundamental predicate" for criminal liability is that the defendant be guilty of conduct for which he is responsible, it is generally preferred that criminal statutes be based upon the defendant acting "purposely, knowingly, recklessly or negligently . . . with respect to each material element of the offense." The Supreme Court has found that, where a statute is potentially vague in some applications, a requirement of intent can help validate the statute. Therefore, even if an anti-stalking statute were to set forth "following" as criminal conduct, the fact that the statute requires that the "following" be associated with purposeful, knowing, reckless, or negligent conduct could limit the success of a constitutional challenge to the statute.

The final, and possibly most important, concern with a criminal statute's vagueness involves the notice the statute provides to law enforcement officers. Under the U.S. Constitution, the determination of whether a person has committed a crime is not to be left to an arresting police officer. There must be some identifiable conduct that violates a statute before a police officer can make an arrest. This avoids the possibility that police will arrest persons on a random or personalized basis. At the same time, a police officer often must act quickly, and is not required to weigh all of the evidence; it is up to the jury to determine if a crime has actually been committed. Antistalking statutes must be drafted so that the proscribed activity can reasonably be identified by law enforcement officials. As is the case with judicial application of antistalking statutes, use of well-defined terms and a requirement of criminal intent can help protect an antistalking statute if it is challenged.

Antiabortion Activists

One of the most publicized challenges to the constitutionality of antistalking laws centers on the concept of freedom of speech, particularly when the law is applied to organized protest or perceived harassment arising from such protest. Recent publicity over the activities of antiabortion activists highlights both an unanticipated use of antistalking laws and the potential constitutional challenges to and limitations of such use.

Antiabortion groups have for years staged protests at doctors' offices, clinics, and other medical facilities where abortions are performed. Whether in small groups or in crowds of several hundred, members of such groups have sought to prevent abortions by disrupting clinic practices. Some of their means of protest—picketing, leafleting, and sidewalk "counseling" of patients—have been wholly legal, legitimate exercises of constitutionally protected free speech rights.

In the last several years, however, some antiabortion activists have extended the scope of their activities into a "gray area" beyond the strictly legal. Activists have blockaded free access to clinics, jammed clinic phone lines, and thrown themselves in front of patients' cars. Simultaneously, acts of physical violence and vandalism at clinics have risen sharply. In 1988, 52 incidents of physical violence at clinics—such as firebombings, chemical releases, and drive-by shootings—were reported. By 1993—the year in which Dr. David Gunn, an abortion provider, was murdered outside a clinic in Pensacola, Florida—that number had climbed to 434.

At this time, acts of harassment, pursuit, and threats of violence against clinic staff and patients continue. Clinic doctors and staff report being followed by car and on foot, often to their private homes, and being photographed and videotaped without their consent. They describe being verbally harassed on the streets, in shopping malls and other public places. Some report that their children have been harassed by telephone at home or approached and verbally accosted by antiabortion activists as they walked to school, derided for being the offspring of "baby killers." Some claim they have received threats of violence or death threats by phone and mail; others have been verbally threatened in person. Patients, too, have been followed and harassed, their license plate numbers traced for identifying information, and their families and employers telephoned.

The National Abortion Federation monitors acts of disruption, clinic blockades, and violence against abortion providers. In 1993 the group began to monitor acts of stalking against staff and doctors. Defining stalking as "the persistent following, threatening, and harassing of an abortion provider, staff member or family member, or patient *away from* the clinic," the NAF logged 188 reported acts of stalking in 1993.

Harassment, pursuit, and threats are precisely the activities that antistalking statutes were written to address. Some legislators, under lobbyists' pressure to prevent the new laws penalizing antiabortion activists' behavior, moved to exempt such activists from the law. Though these exemptions occasionally passed in committee, they were struck from final bills.

Have antistalking laws been successful in keeping at bay acts of personal intrusion that step over the line of constitutional rights, even though they stem from public protest? The answer is yes—and no. At the time of this writing, very few antiabortion activists have been penalized under antistalking laws. At the same time, antistalking legislation gives law enforcement new guidelines with which to deal with the potentially criminal invasions that may evolve from protected speech. One arrest and prosecution came in the spring of 1993, in a case brought forward by

Lorraine Maguire, director of the Charleston Women's Medical Clinic in Charleston, South Carolina.

According to Maguire, a woman named Cathy Anne Rider began protesting at the clinic at the end of 1990. By mid-1991, Rider had begun to target Maguire in particular because, Maguire believes, none of the clinic doctors lived in the area. "It started out [with my] receiving a lot of mail," Maguire says—mail that grew to include five or six mail-ordered packages daily which Maguire had to return at her own expense, and unrequested deliveries from local restaurants. Maguire also received numerous harassing telephone calls; on some she would hear tape-recordings of crying babies. Rider also leafletted Maguire's neighbors, "introducing [Maguire] to the neighborhood," and she would phone clinic employees trying to gain further background information on the director. According to Maguire, staff members told her that Rider had said such things as, " 'You've worked for Lorraine for a long time, you'd better tell me the things you know about her . . . If you don't, you'd better watch out when you go out.' " To impress clinic staff that she was serious, she would refer to *their* family members. "She'd say things like, 'You sure do have a pretty little blond-headed girl,' " Maguire recalls.

Rider seemed to know intimate details about Maguire's past, her children, the contents of her home, even her pet, and she freely shouted this information while standing in front of the clinic. "She's got a daughter," Maguire recalls Rider saying once to the angry boyfriend of a woman being treated at the clinic. According to Maguire, Rider then wrote down Maguire's address and phone number and handed it to the young man, allegedly shouting, "Why don't you go there and kill her daughter and let her know how it feels to have your child killed?" However, Maguire reports, police who were called to the clinic said that this conduct did not cross the line into an actual threat, because Rider *herself* had not threatened to commit murder.

In the spring of 1993, following the murder of Dr. David Gunn, all of that changed. Police warned Maguire that Gunn's death might perhaps embolden Rider, and they counseled Maguire to take extra precautions for her own safety. Two weeks after Gunn's death, Rider approached Maguire at the clinic's entrance and warned her that she should get a bulletproof vest, stating, "I think you're gonna be next." Captured on a clinic videotape, her comments were construed as imminently threatening; Rider was arrested for stalking in 1993 and tried in February 1994. At sentencing, prosecutors worked out a deal allowing Rider's release into the community on five years of supervised probation. A restraining order prohibits her from coming within five hundred feet of Maguire or her family or any clinic staff person and his or her family. At the time of this writing, Rider has been arrested subsequently for picketing without a permit at another women's clinic and for trespassing at a store next to that clinic.

Unlike Lorraine Maguire, who faced a single persistent harasser, others who press for antistalking arrests may have to contend with the group nature of many antiabortion activities. Current antistalking laws have been written to prevent *one* person from repeatedly targeting a victim. If a *group* of people repeatedly target one person, police may have greater than usual difficulty in bringing a stalking charge to bear. To circumvent that problem, prosecutors in the future may combine antistalking charges with a charge such as conspiracy to commit a crime, which covers more broadly the criminal activities of a group.

In the meantime, abortion providers may still refer to antistalking laws as they petition the court for injunctions against antiabortion activists. Such injunctions, often used to create a "safety zone" around a clinic or a doctor's home, have proven effective in specific cases of intense targeting and harassment. By invoking antistalking statutes in their testimony, providers may be able to identify for the courts those patterns of activity that lawmakers have agreed to criminalize. As Lorraine Maguire points out, it is the ongoing *pattern* of invasive activity that is so damaging. "Her attorney kept saying, 'Most of this [harassment] was done in [the] context of protesting abortion.' That was the little veil [over] her defense . . . so therefore anything she said was okay . . . but this doesn't have *anything* to do with abortion."

Other Uses of Antistalking Laws

In the months following passage of the antistalking laws, other unexpected uses have suggested themselves to victims rights advocates and others. Organized groups such as gangs and cults often require of its members a high degree of loyalty to the group and its practices. Members who choose to drop out may find themselves being pressed to rejoin—or else. Though ex-gang members may distrust the police and courts, they may nonetheless find the law to be particularly helpful in ending behavior that can escalate from harassing overtures or surveillance to physical violence.

Councilman Ben Reyes of Houston introduced a citywide stalking ordinance for just that purpose in December 1992. Though Reyes thinks that "the number-one reason for an antistalking ordinance would be the whole issue of domestic violence," he also believes that the laws would assist young gang members attempting to resist their peers. "There are a number of young kids that try to get out of gangs, but they can't because they are stalked," says Reyes. "Gang leaders chase them around, and it's really difficult for the police to protect them." John Lane of the LAPD reflects that practical considerations—such as a gang member's credibility as a victim and his or her prior brushes with the law—would likely prevent some ex-member use of the law. Nonetheless, Lane observes, "If stalking is something that can be legitimately applied and you've got a legitimate victim, no matter what their background, then they should avail themselves of [the law]."

Ex-cult members, too, may consider using the law to press for an end to harassment and abuse. Such abuse can be lengthy and sustained, with cult members often crossing state lines in an attempt to track down and regain control of a lost member. Often complicated by family ties and secrecy, such cases of harassment and intimidation nonetheless constitute stalking, and these victims also deserve the fullest protection of the police and the courts. Such laws could be particularly useful in protecting the children of families attempting to elude old cult acquaintances. Like cases involving ex-gang members, such cases may be complicated by secrecy and efforts to avoid law enforcement. Nonetheless, victims of harassment and intimidation in these cases deserve the fullest protection of the police and the courts.

Existing antistalking laws may also be used tangentially against other criminals who repeatedly engage in menacing, violent behavior. Offenders such as serial rapists, child molesters, and serial killers frequently stalk their victims prior to attacking them. Men who repeatedly rape may hunt for victims over a period of time, often placing any given target under surveillance before an attack. Serial child molesters likewise may disclose their intentions through repeated following and observation. Though such "trolling" usually occurs surreptitiously, in other cases the victim may become aware she's being followed, information that can impel action under the antistalking laws.

Joel Norris, a psychologist who has studied serial killers, writes that they, like many serial rapists, operate under cover of extreme secrecy, making it hard for law enforcement to apprehend them *before* a crime is committed. Nonetheless, Norris points out that "the vast majority of serial murderers were sexual offenders," having begun "their careers with chronic abuse and sexual assault crimes." Norris believes that required therapy programs for sexual offenders during incarceration may help stop the formation of a killer. "There are convicted rapists in jail at this moment who are asking for medical attention, but they are not receiving it. Some of these people, all of whom will sooner or later be released from prison, are human time bombs who will eventually become tomorrow's lurid newspaper headlines." If Norris's hypothesis is true, antistalking statutes that penalize the stalking and abuse of ex-spouses and the following of children hypothetically may help reduce serial killing statistics.

Federal Legislation

Efforts at the federal level to understand the extent and nature of this crime and to legislate remedies for it focus on a number of possible solutions. U.S. Representatives Edward Royce (Rep. CA) and Joseph Kennedy (Dem. MA) have sponsored legislation that would make stalking a federal crime, subject to prosecution in federal courts and the imposition of federal penalties. Senators Barbara Boxer (Dem. CA) and Bob Krueger (Dem. TX) have sponsored similar legislation; Boxer and Krueger's legislation federalizes the crime if the perpetrator commits the crime on federal property—such as military bases or reservations—or uses the telephone or postal service to harass his victim. Such a law would fill gaps in existing state laws and, its sponsors contend, impress upon the public the seriousness of the crime. Yet critics claim that such efforts to federalize, though they underscore growing public understanding of the crime, could potentially crowd the federal court system and result in unnecessary duplication of state laws and procedures.

Other federal efforts have focused on assisting states as they write or amend laws; these efforts are likely to have a greater influence on helping to define and manage the crime. The National Institute of Justice, after being commissioned by Congress in 1992 to study and assess existing laws with the goal of drafting a model antistalking law for states to follow, made its recommendations in the fall of 1993. The NIJ's "Project to Develop a Model Antistalking Code for States" made several major recommendations, many of which are now showing up in state amendments. Among them, the NIJ recommended that states offer a "continuum of charges" against stalking defendants, which would allow police and the courts to intervene progressively as crimes of increasing severity were committed. The NIJ also recommended that states define stalking as that conduct which places a person *or that person's family* in fear of great bodily injury or death. Conduct that does not place anyone in fear of such injury or death, the NIJ observed, could continue to be prosecuted under existing harassment statutes. The NIJ further recommended that the model code include *no credible threat requirement,* noting that conduct which results in a victim's feeling fear should be sufficient for an arrest and prosecution.

By far the most important and far-reaching of the NIJ's recommendations concerned the way in which stalking cases are managed. Noting that "stalking is a complex social problem," the task force calls on police, the judiciary, victims groups, correctional and social service agencies, and other community organizations to work together in a multidisciplinary approach to begin to address that problem. The task force argues that such an approach could stem behavior before it rises to criminal levels, and it would help foster greater public awareness of the problem's complicated roots. One such agency in this approach would be each state's Uniform Crime Bureau, which reports annually on the number and types of crimes committed in individual regions across the country. As stalking is criminalized and categorized, presumably these agencies will be collecting data on the frequency and demographics of stalking crimes.

Federal efforts are also under way to stop crimes that affect women generally. Senator Joseph Biden, Chairman of the Senate Judiciary Committee, has pressed legislators to enact SAFVE, the Stalker and Family Violence Enforcement Act. Among other things, the act would provide access to federal criminal history records for all judges in courts handling stalking and domestic violence crimes. Currently available only to judges at the state level, such records are critical in ensuring that those who are in the position to make probation, sentencing, and parole decisions about stalkers will be able to get crucial information about their criminal histories.

In a broad move both to prevent crimes against women and to stiffen penalties against those who commit such crimes, Senators Biden and Boxer also sponsored the Violence Against Women Act of 1993, enacted as a section of the 1994 crime bill. Seeking to prevent violence before it occurs, the act funds model education programs about domestic violence and sexual assault for students at all levels. The act also speaks directly to domestic violence stalking. In the first legislation of its kind, the act subjects to federal penalties those spouses who cross state lines to harass or continue their abuse of former partners, and it requires that each state honor protective orders issued by courts in other states. Acting on the recognition that violence against women is widespread, this legislation triples existing federal funds for battered women's shelters, and it allows crime victims to sue for civil damages in federal court if they can prove that they were targeted specifically due to their gender.

Legislative remedies—whether enacted at the state or federal levels—are one solution to this invasive, potentially life-threatening crime. As we have seen, however, the laws do not provide blanket protection against all forms of the crime; depending on your state's law, you will be protected, or not protected, depending on the wording of the legislation. Further, your state's law may be subject to revision following constitutional challenges to it. Given that the laws are not necessarily the panacea we might like, how can victims remain as safe and secure as possible? In the next three chapters we explore the devices, skills and services, that you can employ for personal protection. Availing yourself of the best of today's self-defense options can help provide you with additional measures of safety, security, and stability as you face this crime.

Self-Defense I

Home Security and Privacy

> The stalking problem belongs to the victim . . . all these different agencies within government are there to help that person manage the problem, but it's their problem. Many times it's a long-term problem.
>
> Lt. John Lane,
> LAPD Threat Management Unit

> How do you live if you think you're going to die? How do you live day to day if you think you're going to die?
>
> Kathleen Baty, stalking victim

Self-defense is not just a set of techniques or tips, a repertoire of skills or an arsenal of personal protection items. It is a complete mental attitude toward yourself, your rights, and the integrity of your personal space. It is not, as we sometimes think, a matter of running scared, becoming paranoid, or barricading yourself inside a fortress; self-defense means asserting your boundaries, taking charge of your environment, empowering yourself to deflect or deal with adverse circumstances. It is tempting to add the disclaimer "to the best of your ability"—but in a very real way, conscientious steps toward self-defense work to *expand* your abilities, making your best invariably better. At the same time, a false sense of security can be as bad as no security at all. You must be smart in selecting your methods of personal protection, diligent and determined in using them, and realistic about your situation and your options.

Too many people wait until after they have become victims of crime to think about personal protection or take steps to secure their homes and belongings. Despite the burgeoning statistics on crimes against property and persons today, as a populace we still tend to live in a state of denial: *it won't happen to me.* For victims of stalkers, the issue of personal protection is forced, but sometimes avoidance still exists. Out of immediate fear, we may find ourselves practicing simple self-protective moves—screening phone calls, checking the backseats of cars before entering—yet may still procrastinate on taking more complicated or committed steps to improve personal safety.

As a victim of an ongoing crime like stalking, moreover, you may feel you've been thrust against your will into having to be hypervigilant, always alert and on the defensive. The changes in lifestyle or habits your situation makes necessary may feel like one more injustice, yet another in a long line of invasions of your life by a hostile individual. Your first step toward adopting a positive self-defense attitude is to turn that equation around. By making choices about your life and taking active measures to protect yourself, you are reclaiming control of a frightening situation—*you are fighting back.*

Most important, you can begin to make—and act on—many of those choices *today.* This chapter will cover some of the basic aspects of personal defense, looking at options from home security to personal protection devices, from car phones to combat skills. No one chapter in a book can cover each item completely, but we will attempt to guide you—through references to other publications and an appendix of contact numbers—to sources where you can learn more.

Home Security

For Kathleen Baty, wife of Miami Dolphins football player Greg Baty, her nightmare began in 1982, when she received a call from an ex-high-school classmate, Larry Stagner. For the next several years Stagner conducted a systematic campaign of stalking and harassing Kathleen, culminating in one final, terrifying encounter. Late one afternoon Kathleen came home from work, walked into her home and began listening to the messages on her answering machine. She turned around to find Stagner standing behind her, armed with a knife.

Kathleen Baty was lucky. As she tried to keep control of the situation by reasoning with Stagner, the telephone rang. It was her mother, and by deliberately giving irrelevant responses to her questions, Kathleen was able to signal her mother that she was in trouble. After the call, Stagner took Kathleen into the garage, tied her hands, then pulled out a gun and began to lead her toward her car. By that time, responding to her mother's emergency call, the police had arrived and were able to apprehend Stagner at gunpoint. Kathleen jumped for safety, and what followed was an eleven-hour standoff between Stagner and police

SWAT teams. Stagner was finally taken into custody and eventually convicted of attempted kidnapping.

It is every victim's worst fear—turning around to find the stalker in her own home, the final invasion of a private space where one expects to feel secure. For victims and ordinary citizens alike, there is no such thing as a completely intruder-proof dwelling. But numerous safety measures exist by which you can evaluate and improve the security of your own residence—and a complete plan of self-defense should begin here.

Many police departments across the country have special "Crime Prevention Units" whose task it is to help citizens become more crime-aware and more knowledgeable about safety measures they can practice at home and in public. Often these units will provide a free (and confidential) home security inspection on request. We strongly urge that you contact your local police department to see if such a service is available in your area, and if not, to request that one be created. This section will discuss some of the points of basic home security emphasized by those in the business of crime prevention in and around the home.

Landscaping

The first thing a crime prevention specialist will look for in inspecting a home for safety is the nature of the landscaping around the residence. While trees and bushes can provide beauty and privacy for the homeowner, they can also provide excellent means of concealment for intruders. A general rule is that landscaping should be open, allowing for clear vision of the home from the street so that police or neighbors can easily see any suspicious activity on the premises. Whenever possible, trees and bushes should be trimmed from the bottom up, and decorative hedges should be kept under four feet high. In addition, house and building numbers should be clearly visible from the street and well-lit. If the police are called to an emergency at your residence, the last thing they need is to be roaming up and down your street, unable to locate your address.

Lighting

It has been said that good outdoor lighting is the single most deterring factor to any would-be intruder. Security specialists recommend that homes be equipped with outdoor motion-detector lighting, or photocell lighting that remains on from dusk to dawn. Motion-detector lighting operates by means of an electronic sensor that responds to movement within a given radius by flooding the area with light. For the best illumination, experts recommend bulbs that provide color-accurate light, and motion-sensitive lighting can be adjusted to detect movement above three feet from the ground, so roaming pets or wildlife will not illuminate your yard with numerous false alarms during the night. Photocell lighting responds to dimming daylight and turns on automatically at dusk, off at dawn. Special "Energy Source" bulbs made of mercury vapor or high pressure sodium use less energy, and have longer life and clearer color accuracy than incandescent bulbs. But even regular bulbs provide an inexpensive deterrent—the estimated cost of burning one 100-watt light bulb for ten hours per night for thirty days is $2.50, definitely a low-cost investment for security.

Indoor lighting should not be overlooked as a safety measure either. Timers are relatively inexpensive, and attaching four or five to different lamps—and even a stereo tuned to a talk-radio station—can create the illusion that someone is in the home, even when you are gone. Home security specialists recommend creating a flow through your house that replicates the normal movement from room to room when the house is inhabited: at five P.M. you may have the kitchen light go on, at seven P.M. a light in a family room or den, at ten P.M. the bedroom light, and so on. The illusion that a house is inhabited can deter a stalker who may be waiting for an opportunity to break and enter, or deflect him if he is trying to establish your nightly routines.

Doors and Windows, Hinges and Locks

One grim side of a home security inspection is that it will show you—graphically—how easy it is for an intruder to enter your home. Even dead-bolted doors can be kicked in if the frame is unstable or the strike plate not properly secured; exterior hinges can be removed with common pliers; ordinary windowpanes can be broken in an instant; air conditioners can be detached and provide smooth access to your home. In the words of Helen Maxwell, author of *Home Safe Home,* if your dwelling lacks proper security measures, "Get ready for company."

Maxwell, herself a past victim of a stalker, offers a number of tips for safer doors and windows, hinges and locks—and your local crime prevention unit can provide detailed suggestions for improving the security of existing entries to your home. These can include installing dowels or safety pins in double-hung window frames, key-operated window locks, "Charlie bars" or casement locks for sliding glass doors and windows, Mylar or fiberglass replacements for decorative glass panels on doors, nonremovable pins for exterior door hinges, extra-long screws to secure locks into wall studs, and many more. Few alterations are expensive, and most can be completed by anyone handy with a screwdriver or pair of pliers.

We urge you to pick up any good manual on home security, such as Maxwell's, or contact your local police department for recommendations. Be sure to know the codes for your area—fire departments require that doors of egress (escape routes) be kept clear and accessible in case of a fire. Some safety improvements may inadvertently leave you *un*safe if you need to exit the home quickly.

Garages

The area in and around garages and carports provides ideal concealment for intruders or stalkers. For garages, electric garage door openers are recommended, along with good lighting (both inside and around the garage), and securing any doors and windows leading into the garage, whether or not it is attached to the house. Some recommend establishing a routine to alert neighbors and family when you are pulling in—honk your horn briefly before opening the garage. From your car, check the inside of the garage carefully before pulling in—if your garages look like ours, you might consider a good clean-up to eliminate potential hiding places like cluttered corners—and once you're safely inside, use your remote control to close the garage door behind you before you get out of the car. If your garage is not attached to your house, the horn-honking routine can be a prearranged signal for a neighbor, roommate or family member to watch you move safely from your car to your door. In the event that you are alone, you might consider carrying a personal protection item like mace or pepper spray or a personal alarm, discussed in a later section of this chapter. Your own particular situation will dictate your options—overall wisdom is to be alert, think ahead, and trust your instincts if you see anything suspicious in the vicinity.

Alarm Systems for the Home

Home alarm systems come in two general types—central station monitored alarms, or local alarms. The first notifies the police and fire departments, and often a third party designated by the homeowner, in case of an emergency. When the alarm is triggered, a silent signal is sent from your home to the company's central station, either over existing telephone lines—the digital dialer system—over special leased telephone multiplex lines, or over existing phone lines enhanced by an add-on security line. The central station notifies the police, who are dispatched to your home. Local alarms do not include automatic notification of police and fire departments. They usually trigger a siren that may frighten off an intruder, or you must depend on neighbors to be home who will call the police in the event the local alarm is triggered.

Varieties, brands, and price tags for home alarm systems vary widely. You will want to contact a local alarm company to inspect your home and provide you with system options that fit your needs and finances. Above all, you want to be sure that you are dealing with a company that is reputable—a few things to check are whether the company is licensed by the state, how long it has been in operation, whether its installations are supervised and the company warranties its work, what central station services it provides and if these services are provided on a twenty-four-hour basis, and whether you can obtain references of other satisfied customers. A call to your local Chamber of Commerce or the Consumer Protection Division of the State Attorney General's Office can supply you with much valuable information.

Renters

If you are a renter and your lease restricts the number of alterations you are allowed to make on your residence, you may think you are limited when it comes to personal safety measures. However, many local police departments have locking ordinances and security lighting ordinances that require landlords to provide safe, well-lit residences for their tenants. Check with your local police department for any such ordinances in your area, and have their crime prevention personnel visit your apartment to evaluate its current safety features.

A Word on Liability

It is your right to live in a safe home; however, the law forbids taking measures to secure your dwelling that are *intended* or *designed* to harm another—even a trespasser or intruder who is on your premises illegally. One anecdote recounts the experience of an elderly man who had been the victim of numerous burglaries, all committed while he was away from home, where in each case the intruder had broken and entered through the front door. Sick of replacing damaged frames and fed up with being repeatedly victimized, he rigged a shotgun aimed at his front door, designed to go off the moment the door was disturbed. True to form, the next would-be intruder was wounded by the shotgun blast—and the homeowner was held liable for injury. Any device that is designed to cause harm to others, even in the course of protecting one's home, poses serious legal problems, not to mention danger to innocent lives.

Neighborhood Watch

One security measure that we highly recommend is joining or forming a Neighborhood Watch organization in your community. These programs bring neighbors together, under the supervision of the local police department, to become educated about crime in their area and learn how to look out for each others' safety and the safety of their homes and property. Neighborhood Watch organizations can request instruction and information on special topics of concern as well, such as domestic violence or stalking, in order to help guard against such crimes in their area.

The potential effectiveness and support of neighbors cannot be emphasized enough, as one stalking victim learned somewhat after the fact. Her stalker tried to use her neighbors to gather information about her activities and routines, posing as a friend of hers and "chatting up" various individuals on her block to learn more about her. Not having been made aware of her stalking situation, her neighbors were only mildly suspicious if at all, and it was only after she explained her ordeal to them that she became aware of how frequently her stalker had been approaching them and how often he had been cruising her street when she was not at home.

Neighbors in the know can be an invaluable extra set of eyes and ears and can help both protect against and record suspicious behavior. Indeed, equipping a trusted neighbor with a video camera can help record evidence of loitering, trespassing, or forced entry by your stalker—a film of his activities can be powerful evidence at the local precinct or in court. Although victims may feel reluctant to advertise the fact that they are being stalked, given the false stigma of shame or blame discussed in Chapter 5, it is important to remember that stalking is a crime, even if you know the perpetrator, and that crime affects the entire community; it is everyone's problem. A neighbor who has been the victim of a burglary is not blamed or stigmatized for being singled out; in fact, the nearness of the crime makes clear to others the reality that their homes may be next. The crime of stalking is no different: everyone is hypothetically at risk of being a stalker's next target. A good Neighborhood Watch organization can provide support and protection, and reinforce the truth that crime is not a private ordeal, but a community issue.

Safety Kits

Despite your many home security options, there may be times when you feel the need to leave your home to find safety—sometimes quickly and without much forewarning. It is a good idea to keep a safety kit near your door for the possibility of wanting or needing to escape in a hurry. In moments of fear it can become a monumental task to try to think of important items one needs. Seconds drag like minutes, concentration blurs, decision-making can feel paralyzed. A safety kit at the ready saves time and reduces the process to two simple steps: grab the bag and go.

A safety kit should include both immediate overnight necessities, as well as important papers and items that you may need if you are prevented from returning home or if you will need to make a report to the police. Some items to include are the following:

- checkbook, cash, or credit cards
- identification you will need, such as driver's license, work ID, voter registration card, welfare ID, green card or passport, or social security card
- copies of restraining or protective orders
- copies of—or better, your original records of—the stalking behavior, including a copy of your police report if you have one. Stalkers have been known to break into a home specifically to destroy records of evidence against them.
- address book or a list of important phone numbers of friends, relatives, counselors, support groups, attorney, and police
- keys to car, home, and safe deposit box
- any medicines you need, prescriptions for prescription drugs, and, if appropriate, medical records and health insurance information
- spare set of eyeglasses or contact lenses if you need them
- overnight items such as a toothbrush, comb, sleepwear, extra shirt or sweatshirt, and "special" items such as a good book or bubble bath. As one victim put it, "The emergency may be over in minutes—but when I'm safe at a friend's place or in a hotel room, I've got the rest of the night to get through. I want things around me that help me feel less dislocated, that can help soothe and relax me.

It's my way of taking care of myself, pampering myself after I've come through the crisis."

Making a safety kit is not a symptom of running scared or being paranoid—it is being coolly sensible and prepared in the event of an emergency. If you never need to use it, so much the better. The sight of a safety kit gathering dust should be a constant positive reinforcement and reward.

Telephones

We are giving telephones their own special section, because the telephone is so often a stalker's weapon of choice. It is the easiest device by which to invade your home and your life, the simplest way by which a stalker can command your attention and recharge your fear at any hour of the day or night. Telephone harassment can turn a benign tool, normally associated with social communication, into a hellish intrusion, a constant violation. The experience of one victim, who was receiving up to sixty abusive and threatening phone calls per day, is not uncommon. Worse, stalkers often seem to possess uncanny powers to discover unlisted or new numbers. This same victim reports, "I had my already unlisted number changed, and *that same evening* the phone rang again with taunts of 'Ha, ha, guess you gotta change your number again.'" Another victim's stalker, who remains unknown to her, was even able to obtain and harass her via her private pager number, along with her home number, work number, and the phone numbers of her family and friends.

Michael D. Smith, Director of the LaMarsh Centre for Research on Violence and Conflict Resolution at York University in Ontario, Canada, conducted a study in 1992 of obscene and threatening telephone calls to women as part of a national survey on sexual violence at home and in the workplace. This study was conducted randomly, using a geographically representative sampling of Canadian women.

Smith's results were striking, though his findings will touch a common chord in the experiences of women everywhere. He found that almost 67 percent of the 1,990 *random respondents* to his survey had received one or more obscene or threatening calls, and over half of the women who reported having received at least one "silent" call in the previous twelve months had received between two and five such calls. Over a third had received six or more. In short, telephone harassment is not only a common occurrence for large numbers of women, many women also suffer them frequently and repeatedly.

The types of calls the respondents identified as most disturbing were most often obscene or threatening (78 percent), but the number of silent calls (22 percent) were equally unsettling to the recipients. Most came after dark, when the woman was alone and in her own home, although Smith points out that over 8 percent of the most disturbing phone calls were received at work at least some of the time. When asked to describe their feelings on receiving these calls, Smith's respondents came back with "an outpouring of emotion," emphasizing in particular the intense and powerfully negative impact of even harmless hang-up calls. Over 90 percent reported feelings of fear, anger, violation or lack of control, with descriptions such as the following:

"[I felt] uneasy, very uneasy, you know, creepy. . . ."

"It almost made me feel like someone outside was watching me."

"Upset. I was paranoid when I walked to my car, thinking that someone was watching me, going to do something to me."

"These silent calls bother me the most because they are coming at work. I'm alone for the most part at work and I get the impression that someone is coming in and casing the place."

"Very uneasy. Do they know that I'm here or is this at random?"

"Frightened. It went on for months. Nobody ever said anything, just silence."

"Really scared. He called many times and even talked to my kids about me, asking them questions about me."

"Scared, really scared. It happened right after my husband left for work, at six-twenty in the morning, and it came as he was leaving the driveway, which made me think someone was watching."

"Frightened. It was as if they were right outside my door. One of them said he could see me. I was in the office and the lights were on in other office buildings. I was worried what his next move might be. . . ."

"Disgusted, infuriated, very mad, sick. It was from my ex-husband, verbally harassing me, saying things he was doing with other women."

"It made me feel like someone was watching me and knew when I would be home. I was very frightened."

"The call came when I was at work in the evening. He said he knew I was in the office alone, and he said he was coming to kill me."

"Frightened, not knowing what the motive was, or whether it was someone I knew or whether it was random."

"Really nervous. I went and made sure that my doors were locked. I was nervous that if he got my number, he could get the address. . . ."

"First I was stunned, then I was scared after I hung up, scared that they knew my phone number and my house."

"I felt that my privacy was violated."

"Degraded. Terrified."

"I couldn't believe it was happening."

"I felt watched. . . . It was invasion of my privacy. He was attempting to control me or at least get some sort of response from me."

"Invaded. Here I am in my own home and someone is phoning me. . . . I'm supposed to feel safe in my own home, but I went around and made sure all the doors were locked."

Clearly, terrorizing phone calls are a problem for all women, whether they are established victims of a single stalker or targets for random harassment. Yet law enforcement agencies are still largely at a loss about how to deal with this pervasive issue. Even more discouraging than Smith's statistics are his reports on the responses women received when they reported these calls to the police or the telephone company. Smith states:

> Approximately four out of every ten police and three out of ten phone company responses were in the form of advice, much of which was impractical (for example, Don't answer, Get an unlisted number), cost money (for example, Change your number, Get a CMS [call management/display system]), or both. The second most common response was that they could not do anything to help.

What *can* you do if you are at the receiving end of telephone terrorism, particularly if it is part of a pattern of harassment and other stalking behavior? There are no foolproof ways to avoid the intrusion of obscene, threatening, or silent calls—but there are some ways in which you can manage their impact on your life, and even use them to work for you as valuable records of evidence.

Answering Machines

First, an answering machine—equipped with a packet of extra cassettes—can be a valuable tool for both screening calls and recording threatening or abusive messages. Keep all tapes on which such messages occur in your "stalking file," marked and dated—some machines include a programmable timer, which automatically records the time of the call. Slip a fresh cassette into your answering machine every time you receive a harassing call or series of calls, to avoid mixing them with personal messages or accidentally erasing them. Some recommend a carefully worded outgoing message—preferably in a male voice. One single woman who lived alone asked a male friend to record the following outgoing message for her machine: *"Hi, we're home. If we want to talk to you, we'll pick up the phone. You can start talking after the beep."* This left the caller unsure of who and how many people were home, or who might or might not be hearing the message.

For victims subject to ongoing phone harassment, the temptation to change their number is strong. As we saw before, however, this is not always successful. Moreover, a stalker obsessed with making contact with his victim, if frustrated or unable to connect via the phone, may try more direct (and potentially dangerous) measures to confront his victim. Much stalking behavior involves a pattern of escalation—from relatively indirect contact by phone or mail, to more immediate approaches such as leaving objects on doorsteps and surveilling the home, to face-to-face confrontations and the potential of ultimate violence. Keeping the phone lines open *is no guarantee that escalation will not continue,* but it can help monitor and record the stalker's attentions—and sometimes provide clues to his intentions.

Unlisted Numbers

Jane McAllister, founder of Citizens Against Stalking in Richmond, Virginia, recommends installing a second (unlisted) phone line for private use. Keep the old number—attached to an answering machine with spare cassettes—to receive and record harassing calls. This will be your "stalker line," and you can disconnect the ring and lower the answering machine volume to keep it from intruding on your life—the phone will be your silent partner, collecting and recording evidence of calls. Give your new line number *discreetly* to friends and family, and use the new line exclusively as your personal line. You might also consider installing this line in your bedroom or a "safe room" discussed in a later chapter. A second line in the home can provide a lifeline to help that cannot be disabled by an intruder lifting the receiver from another room.

Caller ID

Another self-defense phone device is the call management/display system, commonly known as "Caller ID." This is an extra service provided (by subscription and at a price) by telephone companies in many areas of the country, by which the telephone number from which a call is made appears on a display device attached to the receiver's telephone. In addition, some companies offer "Caller ID with Name," which also displays the caller's name, whether listed or unlisted. In Smith's study, women who used a CMS (call management system) did so to screen calls and to keep on file the number or numbers from which harassing calls were made. This was particularly helpful in the case of "silent" or "hang-up" calls in which no recorded message was left.

The drawbacks of Caller ID are that it is not yet established in all areas of the country, and will only identify callers phoning from exchanges covered by the service. Often the service is also limited to one area code. This means that if your caller phones from a location that is not covered by the system—even the next county over—or from another state, the display panel will simply read "Out of Area." Some callers can also block the device with a code, again rendering it inoperable. In theory, however, Caller ID is a good device for monitoring and managing calls, and we hope it will be expanded and perfected in the future.

Tracing Calls

In the meanwhile, some states already offer other services for monitoring or tracing incoming calls. The "Customer Originated Trace" is a feature that is becoming available to customers in more and more areas. Under this system an individual can trace the origin of the last call received by simply entering a touch-tone code after hanging up. An automatic trace occurs, and a voice computer will come on the line to announce whether or not the trace was successful. In certain states the individual can then phone the telephone company office on the next business day to receive information about the trace. Although most companies are prohibited from revealing specific numbers or names—some laws require that all evidence must be passed on to law enforcement first—they can inform an individual whether the call or calls were made locally, from the same number, and so on. Above all, they provide an important source of information for police investigators—and phone company representatives emphasize that victims *should always* file telephone harassment complaints with the police. The Customer Originated Trace can offer a fast, accurate method of identifying incoming calls, and although there is a charge, often users will only be billed for successful traces or, if the problem is frequent, they can subscribe to the service on a monthly basis for a flat rate.

Telephone traces conducted independently by the police or the telephone company present a further option. Usually, if a representative from the telephone company's security division receives a complaint of threatening telephone calls—especially if the caller appears to single out an individual or know specific details about the residents or home—they will direct the recipient to the police department to file a complaint. The police then have the option of installing a trace on the line and can usually do so promptly, from twenty-four to forty-eight hours. If not, the individual can call the phone company with the complaint number, and the telephone company will send paperwork for a trace request to the individual. This can take far more time to process and evaluate, but it does pose an option if the police, for whatever reason, decline to instigate their own trace. Be sure you inform yourself of what a telephone company trace will cover and how long it will be in effect. Provide them with as much information as possible if you suspect you know who might be making the calls or where they may be coming from. All such information is kept confidential but can help the phone company focus its efforts more effectively.

A trace, however, is only as good as the people implementing it, and tales of frustration aren't hard to find. One victim, terrorized for over a decade, recalls her dashed hopes when she finally arranged for a tracing system: "I was told there was a trap on my phone at work, to keep logs of any times [the stalker] called. I was excited when I had six or eight calls. I later found out the policeman I was working with, a specialist in phone harassment, had forgotten to phone the telephone company to put the trap in place." Remember that all companies—and law enforcement agencies—are a chain of command. If you are dissatisfied with the results on one level, ask to speak to someone higher up until you get the help you need.

Access

Theories abound regarding how stalkers manage to get victims' telephone numbers in the first place, or manage to discover unlisted and new numbers, even sometimes after the victim has moved to another state. In one case, police were baffled by how one victim, a media personality, kept receiving harassing phone calls in which the anonymous caller knew not only phone numbers but intimate details about the victim's family out of state. Extensive investigations revealed that the harasser actually worked for the telephone company and had used company phone records to keep tabs on her victim.

Yet even without it being an inside job, one representative of a telephone security department explains that the task may be a simple one for anyone who wants a phone number badly enough and is willing to practice a bit of deception to get it. Often simply approaching the victim's friends or parents, posing casually as a friend or employer, can result in unsuspecting individuals carelessly giving out a victim's number. If the victim has moved away, a visit to old neighbors—again, posing as an old friend, realtor or insurance agent—can yield much information about the victim's new address, employment, and phone number. A more elaborate ruse involves a stalker phoning his victim's workplace during a time he knows she will not be there, and faking an emergency—claiming that a family member or spouse has just been in a terrible accident, and that he represents the police or hospital emergency room and must reach her immediately. In the agitation of the moment, a careless fellow employee might easily be duped into giving out the number.

Even without such deceptive measures, people are seldom aware of how often and to how many individuals and agencies they give out their telephone numbers without thinking. Phone numbers on checks, for instance, are commonplace—and canceled checks go through a lot of hands before they are returned. Credit card receipts often ask that you include your telephone number; one plan is to use only your work number on open documents like checks and receipts. Even an ordinary event like filling out an application for a check cashing card at your local supermarket presents opportunities for your home phone number to circulate. After you leave, the cashier may hand your card to the stock boy to take to the office—and who knows how long it will stay in his pocket, or lie on the office counter where passersby might have the leisure to inspect it? This is not to say that every agency is careless—but human error is a fact of life. Be cautious and aware whenever giving out your private number.

One avenue by which personal information can be accessed with startling ease is currently under investigation at the federal level. In 1993 a bill was introduced to Congress to change the current policy which allows state motor vehicle departments to give out information about license holders to random callers. In the past, any individual could obtain someone's name, address, and telephone number—indeed, any information that appears on a driver's license—simply by submitting a license plate number and paying a small fee. In the tragic case of Rebecca Schaeffer, her stalker obtained her home address by simply hiring a private investigator, who contacted the Department of Motor Vehicles for the information. Measures are now being taken by Congress to restrict access to such information without the consent of the license holder.

Telephones and Personal Safety

Whereas the telephone can be a stalker's simplest weapon, it can also be *your* best weapon and a lifeline to safety. If your home phone includes an automatic-dial feature, encode important numbers you may need in the event of an emergency, in the order you will need them: 911 may be your first number, the police department or the number for the detective on your case may be the second, a neighbor or family member the third, and so on. In a crisis or moment of fear, scrambling to find important phone numbers can be a distressing project and waste valuable time. Automatic dial puts the numbers you need at your fingertips.

Jane McAllister also strongly recommends getting a car phone if you can afford it. If you are approached while in your car, or stranded, you can call for help without leaving the vehicle. A good thing to remember is that all cellular phones will direct you to the nearest state police if you call 911, and all pay phones will let you call for help free of charge. Simply dial 0 (Operator) or 911. Unlike police departments, which can and do select and prioritize calls, 911 must respond, regardless of the nature of the case. One victim tells of an astonishing breach of this policy, when her stalker appeared one morning and confronted her from her neighbor's yard. She called 911, then a friend for help.

The stalker eventually left, but still she waited for the police to come. Finally, calling 911 again, she learned that the dispatcher had not considered her case serious enough and had decided not to alert the police! The victim complained, as is her right, and we assume that dispatcher has since been fired. The policy is clear: *911 must respond to all emergency calls.*

Watchdogs

How often have we heard the old injunction, "Just get a dog!" as a cure-all for personal protection? Dogs are in fact remarkable animals, and there are plenty of heartwarming stories of their loyalty, intelligence, and often heroic efforts to protect owners in trouble. The mere appearance of certain breeds will intimidate: Dobermans, Akitas, Rottweilers, German shepherds, and Great Danes all look fierce and have a deep, threatening bark. Many of these dogs also have a natural protective temperament, although breeders are quick to add that all dogs can sense danger and, in a crisis, will often try to protect the human partners they love. At the same time, owning a dog is a lifelong commitment; they are living beings that take a great deal of time, love, and care. Getting a dog on impulse, without knowing that you can commit to its care and needs, can be both cruel to the animal and frustrating to you.

If you have been seriously considering a dog—or if a dog is already part of your household—the question might arise whether guard dog training is appropriate for your animal. Opinions are divided regarding private citizens owning attack dogs, or enrolling their dogs in a program of attack training. On the one hand, trusting that your friendly golden retriever—who normally responds to visitors with a lick and a wag—will defend your life if a stalker approaches may leave you realistically uneasy. On the other hand, attack training for dogs is serious business—it is a strenuous and demanding program that requires professional supervision, and is only fully successful with certain animals. Moreover, it is designed to alter the temperament of your animal; lone attack is *not* natural behavior for a dog. In attack training he is *conditioned* toward aggressive display and vicious attack; he is taught to distrust and, when his trigger has been pulled, he is trained to fight to the finish. In a very real sense, an attack dog is no longer a pet, but a professional working animal, and his safety around children and visitors can become an issue. As one kennel owner puts it, "An attack-trained dog is a loaded gun. That owner had better know how to clean that gun and know where the safety lock is."

Short of putting your pet through an actual attack training course, there are mild commands to teach ordinary dogs that can serve to intimidate a would-be intruder. Dogs can be trained, for instance, to respond to one of two commands when barking at a doorbell or stranger. The command "Quiet!" means "Stop barking," whereas "Watch him!" signals the dog "Continue to bark." Trained in this command, your dog will continue to make a ruckus—and even if he is only doing so happily in the hopes of getting a treat, both the sound of ongoing barking and of your repeated command, "Watch him, Rover! Watch him!" can be threatening to an intruder.

Regardless of the role your dog plays in your plan of self-defense, remember to have good identification on your pets, and keep a current photo of your dog available. Pets have been stolen and injured by stalkers—often stalkers will target something precious to the victim as a means of terrorizing, controlling, or inflicting pain. You must be aware of the potential dangers to your pet, and take reasonable measures to ensure their safety as well as your own.

CHAPTER 9

Self-Defense II

What You Need to Know About Weapons

> Let me tell you the ways he tried to find me. . . . He called employers, ex-employers, friends, ex-friends, boyfriends, ex-boyfriends, family members, places I shop, veterinarian, police, school, library, mail, post office, IRS, social security —everybody. . . . He would pretend he was a police officer and burst into friends of mine's houses and say he had a warrant for me and search their house looking for me . . . and he'd call and say he was my husband. He would burst into classes trying to find me. . . .
>
> Stephanie, stalking victim shot three times by her ex-boyfriend

> It was like living under siege. You know, you tell your children when they're little, you tuck them in bed and you say, "Don't worry, there's no monsters, it's okay." And as an adult I have to look at my daughter and say, "There is a monster and he's outside this house and he's going to come and get somebody. We don't know how, we don't know when, but he's going to do it and there's nothing that can stop him."
>
> Sherron, Stephanie's mother

In the past two decades, riding on the crest of the second wave of the women's movement in the 1970s, the book market has been swamped with advice books on personal protection for women. Everybody and her sister seems to have suggestions for how you can defend yourself against ski-masked rapists and subway leches using bobby pins and credit cards, judo kicks and umbrella handles. Many of these books are good—many are not. Here is where your consumer savvy must be at its sharpest, and your reality check abilities at the ready. Let's take a walk through the maze of personal protection items.

Everyday Weapons

Some of the most innocuous, bizarre objects have been recommended over the years as everyday weapons for women's self-defense: hat pins (who wears *hat pins* anymore?), rolled-up newspapers (assuming that, under attack, you'll have the time to roll up that copy of the *Wall Street Journal* you've been reading), credit cards, and the list goes on. We've even heard of slinging one's shoes at an attacker! Amusing as these items may be in themselves, it is worth remembering that in a struggle *anything* at hand *can* be used as a weapon—what is important is force, survival, and determination. As the saying goes, "It's not the size of the woman in the fight, it's the size of the fight in the woman."

Still, there are one or two common items worth discussing for their potential (or lack of potential) to protect and defend.

Keys, pens, and pencils. Jabbing at an attacker with car keys or writing implements will do negligible damage, but since these objects are often in one's hands anyway, why not? Hold a key ring in the palm of your hand with one key projecting from between the fingers of your fist. Jab forcefully at an attacker's face and eyes to distract him. Hold the pen in the fist and jab upward to soft parts under the chin and throat.

Whistles and handheld sirens. More in the order of an alarm device, unless you can find one powerful enough to damage an attacker's eardrums—in which case you too will be wearing a hearing aid after the fight is over. As alarm devices, you must be realistic about their effectiveness. The sound of a whistle or small siren *may* alert a passerby who, if you are lucky, will be knowledgeable and helpful enough to call the police or come to your aid. At the same time, the chances are as good that strangers—inured to odd noises or simply unwilling to investigate—would turn away. Ask yourself: If *you* heard a faint whistle blast from a block away, would *you* rush to dial 911? Personal alarms, however, can be effective in a prearranged scenario, such as when walking from one's car to one's door, if neighbors and family have been alerted to the fact that your whistle will be a signal for help. Have your alarm consistently at the ready—an attack from behind will leave you no time to fumble in your purse or pocket for the device.

Umbrellas. For some reason, we don't know why, umbrellas keep coming up in discussions of personal protection devices. Perhaps many self-defense advisers live in the Pacific Northwest where it rains a lot—or perhaps it's a masked nostalgia for the "olden days" when women carried parasols as a matter of course. Once again, in the clinches you should be prepared to use anything at hand, but an umbrella is not a good item on which to stake your safety. The point on an ordinary umbrella is never sharp enough to do real damage, and it is too lightweight an object to use effectively as a club. Ironically, the best use might be to *open* the umbrella in your attacker's face, distracting him for a split second. Not a very impressive martial arts move, we admit.

Long objects—broom handles and canes. Broom handles and canes might be tempting objects to jab into an attacker's midriff to keep him at bay; used this way, they are just as easy for an attacker to grab and knock you off balance or turn against you. One self-defense group recommends using the "golf-swing" technique with a cane or walking stick, striking hard and low at the attacker's ankles and calves. This makes the weapon harder to take away, and the "whipping" action of low, fast swings can generate more painful force—though a smack on the shin is hardly likely to disable a hardy assailant. Brooms and mop handles are obviously far more unwieldy used in this (or any) manner.

Belts. Oddly, belts can provide a quite effective tool by which to distract and hold back an attacker who is at arm's length, and can be especially useful if he is armed with a knife or club, where your life may depend on keeping him at a distance. Use the leather end of the belt (hold the buckle end in your hand), and snap the belt into his face, as if you were snapping a rolled wet towel. Do not *whip* the belt—this action does little damage and makes the belt far easier to take away, and do not use the *buckle* end toward the assailant—it is bulky and inaccurate and will jerk back and hit you instead. Snap sharply at his face and eyes rather than at other vulnerable areas such as the groin. An assailant can cover his privates with one hand and still come at you, but he cannot protect his face without impeding his vision.

Clothing. Clothing you are carrying, such as jackets or sweaters, can be unexpected means of protection in an emergency situation. Some recommend throwing loose clothing at an attacker's face to surprise and distract him—but frankly we feel this tactic is little more than a good way to lose your wardrobe. In the event that you are confronted with a knife, however, a loose jacket or sweater can help deflect serious wounds. Wrap the clothing quickly around your weak hand and forearm (for example, if you are right-handed, your left arm) and use your padded arm to block knife jabs. Some women have also used purses and bags successfully to block knife attacks, and while these won't win the fight for you, they may buy you valuable time and give you some protection against immediate, serious injury.

As you can see, everyday weapons can be used imaginatively, but they seldom provide more than an element of distraction or temporary protection. If you fight, by all means fight hard and with everything at your disposal—dirt flung in the eyes, hurled ashtrays, household cleaning sprays, whatever. But relying solely on these makeshift weapons to protect you is a thin plan of self-defense.

Commercial Sprays

Much has been made of commercial sprays ("chemical defense weapons") such as mace, tear gas, and capuscin (pepper) sprays. These small, handheld sprays work by squirting a stream or aerosol fumes of some irritating substance at the attacker, which upon contact with eyes, skin, or mucous membranes produces a burning, stinging sensation and profuse tearing, leaving the assailant temporarily blinded and disoriented. Advertisements for such items are dramatic and sound eminently convincing—"When Danger Lurks, the Paralyzer Works"—and ad copy frequently heralds the product's effective use by police and military, promising instant, fingertip-ready defense for civilians as well. Opinions on their effectiveness, however, are divided.

Self-defense expert Massad Ayoob, in his book *In the Gravest Extreme,* insists that commercially available sprays are diluted for public use, after a rash of complaints about eye damage to suspects followed their original manufacture in the 1960s. Moreover, he claims that in real-life situations, "Mace-type sprays have proven to be much less effective than once believed. Many people can take several streams of the stuff square in the face with no immediate ill effects." Others point out that individuals under the influence of alcohol or narcotic drugs can be virtually immune to the effects of disabling chemical sprays as well.

We feel, however, that this relatively inexpensive item is certainly a more powerful device than keys or credit cards, and, provided it is used correctly, can be a useful part of a self-defense plan. Some sprays come attached to key chains, which makes them handy—

but you must be careful if your keys lie about unattended as potential playthings for children. Others come with small carrying cases that attach to a belt, also hypothetically providing easy access; however, in our experience some of the clips securing the canister in its case require a bit of fumbling to unclip. Try out the cases of a number of brands at the store—most army surplus stores carry a variety of incapacitating aerosol products—until you find one you are comfortable with. Remember, no defense item does you much good if it is not ready at hand and easy to use.

When using a mace-type spray, remember to hold the canister in front of you and, if possible, to protect your own face by turning away or shielding your face with your free hand. Know that using such a product in an enclosed space (such as a car), at very close quarters, or with the wind against you can disable you as well as (or instead of) your attacker. And, as with any weapon, sprays can also be taken away from you in a struggle and used against you. Finally, you must know the laws in your area concerning chemical defense weapons; some states limit the type and strength of self-defense sprays citizens are allowed to carry.

Stun Guns

A dramatic and potentially disabling weapon is the stun gun, which works by applying a stream of electricity, generated between two electrodes, to the attacker's body. While such weapons have been used by law enforcement agencies, they are not generally recommended for personal protection. Paxton Quigley, author of *Armed and Female,* looks at some of their drawbacks.

> . . . a stun gun will only work if the victim manages approximately three seconds of constant application into a major muscle group or nerve center. . . . The public needs to understand that you must be physically close to the assailant—belly to belly—so that you can wrap your arm around him and dig the small electrodes into him and hold the position for three seconds. During that time, a man trained in violence is going to do a great many unpleasant things to you. . . . Also, anyone wearing a leather or heavy wool jacket, as well as very obese people, or people with a high pain tolerance, are not affected by a stun gun. These are all enough reasons not to rely on the stun gun to deter an assault.

In addition to complicated legalities concerning owning and using a stun gun, the impracticalities and risks of such a weapon make it a less than desirable choice for the average individual.

Guns

For a variety of reasons—ethical, political, and practical—we are not ourselves advocates of guns as weapons for personal self-defense. The depiction of guns on television and in the movies too often underplays their true destructive capability, while overplaying their magic as a quick fix to power, control, or personal safety. In these Hollywood-fabricated scenarios, the hero pulls out his .357 Magnum, the bad guys freeze in their tracks, the situation is suddenly his to command. Or, if an adrenaline-charged gunfight ensues, viewers see casualties drop like dominos in sanitized, virtually bloodless fashion. Both scenarios are dangerously far from the truth. Indeed, if television were to show the actual effects on a human body of a bullet from a .357 Magnum, which travels at a velocity of over a thousand feet per second and on impact at close range creates enough hydrostatic shock to turn a melon into juice, ratings would most likely plummet.

For women in particular, the image of a gun as a magic wand for self-protection is tempting. Just buy one, just keep it in your nightstand or purse, just be ready to show it when you need to, and you'll be safe in any situation—no one will mess with you. But guns are not magic amulets. They are highly technical, lethal weapons that require training and ongoing practice to use, care and maintenance to function correctly, and vigilant safety habits for responsible ownership.

Despite our hesitations, gun ownership for personal protection is at present every woman's option—and indeed, although the statistics are still speculative, it may be one that more and more women in America are choosing to exercise. According to Paxton Quigley, author of *Armed and Female*, the numbers of women who own guns in this country went up 53 percent between 1983 and 1986 alone. Elizabeth Swayze, Director of Women's Issues at the National Rifle Association in Washington, estimates that today between fifteen and twenty million women own guns for self-protection. These figures, however, are not supported by National Opinion Research Center surveys, which found that the percentage of female gun owners has remained roughly the same over the last thirteen years.

If you are considering getting a gun, there are a number of issues you should think through carefully in making your decision. These include personal issues, legal issues, and practical issues of ownership, skills training, and safety.

Personal Issues

Understanding your own personal issues surrounding guns must be your first step in deciding whether this choice is right for you. Many of the women interviewed in Quigley's book—and Quigley herself—went through a conversion in their attitudes about guns, from neutrality or even an antigun position to a conviction that handguns were appropriate and effective items for their personal protection. Their reasons and motivations range from a sense of survival, personal empowerment, a refusal to be victimized, or healing from the trauma of past assaults. But in each case, these women knew fully what their choice involved—owning a gun for self-protection means they must be prepared to use it, and if necessary be prepared to kill.

The myth that simply showing a gun in a crisis situation will stop an assault is just that—*a dangerous myth.* According to some experts, the element of surprise and fear that a gun evokes may as easily escalate an assault—if you show a gun, you must be prepared to fire it if the assailant continues to advance. If not, you run the very real risk of having that deadly weapon taken from you and, worse, used against you. Statistics confirm that even those with extensive gun skills are not immune to this risk. According to the FBI Uniform Crime Reports, in 1989 one in four of all law enforcement officers killed with handguns were killed with their own weapons. Similarly, in a life or death situation measured in seconds and blurred by fear and confusion, believing that you will have the cool judgment, shooting skill, accuracy, and opportunity to "just wound" or "scare" an assailant is another myth. Skills of self-defense gunmanship—also known as "combat shooting" or "practical shooting"—involve first and foremost shooting to stop an oncoming assailant by aiming at the major body mass, the chest. Although a bullet to this area may simply wound, it is just as likely to kill. The personal issues surrounding psychological readiness to use a weapon, and the ethics of killing, even in self-defense, are issues that you must decide for yourself—*but you must decide.*

You should know, moreover, that merely living in a household with one or more guns can be dangerous. According to a 1993 study by Arthur Kellermann of Emory University and others, *the presence of a gun in the home nearly tripled the risk of homicide in that home,* with three-quarters of the homicides committed by intimate partners or family members. Despite the fact that most gun owners in this country keep a gun for self-protection, the authors found that keeping a gun in the home offered no protective benefit to the gun owner. If keeping a gun doesn't protect a gun owner, but rather increases the risk of harm to him or her, states Kellermann, then "the advisability of keeping firearms in the home for protection must be questioned."

Legal Issues

If you have made the decision that you would be able and ready to use a gun in a crisis, and if despite such statistics you want to continue investigating gun ownership, the next realities you must be aware of are the legal issues surrounding the use of lethal force in self-defense. Paxton Quigley writes:

> In no state is it a crime to defend oneself, and though local laws may differ somewhat in interpretation of what kinds of threats justify what kinds of responses, nowhere is it considered unreasonable to use lethal force by any means available to stop a threat that may endanger your life or the lives of innocent people, or that may result in grave bodily harm.

At the same time, however, certain definitions and restrictions to self-defense apply. First, the danger of death or grave injury must be *immediate* and *inescapable.* If an estranged spouse telephones and threatens your life or the lives of your children, and you, taking him at his word, drive to his home and shoot him, you are not acting under the legal definition of self-defense. The danger of death in this case was not immediate (as it would be if he were standing in your living room, holding your child at knifepoint), nor was there "no hope of your escaping the attack"—in fact, a jury would most likely find that your driving to his home constituted your opening a confrontation, and your use of deadly force in this case to be manslaughter or even premeditated murder.

Quigley cites self-defense expert Massad Ayoob, who outlines three necessary qualifications for the use of deadly force to defend oneself. First, the attacker must have the *ability* to endanger his victim's life—in short, he must have the physical power to kill or injure, or be equipped with a weapon that could be lethally used. (This also constitutes what is called the "seriousness" of the impending attack.) Second, the attacker must have the *opportunity* to inflict harm immediately; he must be within range of his victim. (Elsewhere, this is termed the "imminence" of the attack.) Finally, the attacker must be exhibiting behavior that any reasonable person would interpret as an intent to attack—he must be posing *jeopardy* for the victim. All three conditions—ability, opportunity, and jeopardy—*must be present* for the victim's use of deadly force to be justified under the law as self-defense.

Understanding these conditions—and being mentally ready to assess the danger of an assault situation in the seconds it takes to unfold—are crucial responsibilities if you are planning to rely on a gun for self-defense. Ensuring your protection in a short-term, immediate crisis is sadly inadequate if, due to misjudgment or ignorance of the law, you end up serving prison time for murder.

Several other facets of the right to self-defense are especially applicable to victims of stalkers. Most important of these is the fact of law that states *"past incidents may not be the cause for a present use of lethal force."* Quigley explains:

> We have all heard tragic stories about people asking for and being denied police protection from individuals who made repeated threats upon their lives, later to have those threats fulfilled. . . . *However, the subject of someone's harassment, or the victim of previous assaults, cannot assume that previous threats or even beatings are grounds enough to use deadly force unless*

> *the aggressor displays all the conditions of immediate, unavoidable attack.* (Italics added)

This means that, despite a stalker's repeated threats—or even repeated attempts to kill or injure the victim—in order for deadly force to be legally defensible in a given situation, that situation must be judged independently and must meet the three self-defense conditions of ability, opportunity, and jeopardy.

Suppose Alice's stalker has left dozens of death threats on her answering machine, and has tried on several occasions to run her off the road. Alice is convinced he is serious about his threats, and she begins to keep a gun in the glove compartment of her car for protection. One evening, as she pulls into her driveway on her way home from work, she sees her stalker standing a mere five yards away, on the sidewalk in front of her house. She panics, pulls out the gun, and before he has a chance to move toward her, she shoots him dead. Has Alice acted in self-defense? Legally speaking, no. Although past incidents certainly made Alice believe in her stalker's intent and ability to harm her, he was neither at this time within physical range to do so (assuming he was unarmed), nor was he right then behaving in a manner that a neutral witness would interpret as immediate, unavoidable attack. Had he been holding a baseball bat, shouting, and running toward her to close the gap, the scenario would have been very different.

Despite the apparent strictness of this rule, however, the growing number of cases involving self-defense and domestic violence seem to be making courts more sensitive to ways in which past incidents and threats heighten the danger to the victim and may impact her "honest and reasonable belief" that her assailant poses a grave threat. In the criminal jury instructions for Michigan regarding self-defense trials (see end of chapter), the guidelines invite juries to take all factors into consideration when evaluating a plea of self-defense. Notice that the threat of forcible rape qualifies as "serious injury" here and is, therefore, included under the right to self-defense. California (see end of chapter) includes some unique differences regarding the right to "stand one's ground" in self-defense. Interpretations and conditions for self-defense vary from state to state, and copies of jury instructions for your state are available through law libraries or any county prosecutor's office. If you do request information about guidelines for using lethal force in self-defense, *do so discreetly and anonymously if possible*—in no way do you want to be suspected of premeditation simply because you are informing yourself of the law!

Moreover, despite the apparently expanding flexibility of the courts, no jury outcome is ever guaranteed—and discrimination still haunts our system. We highly recommend an excellent, and chilling, study by Cynthia K. Gillespie titled *Justifiable Homicide: Battered Women, Self-Defense, and the Law,* which traces case after case of astonishing inequity when self-defense law tries to accommodate the unique circumstances of women victims. The realities of a judicial system in a society still struggling to reach equal rights for women are grim and can carry painful consequences.

Lethal force is unlawful in two other important situations. First, it is never justified in protecting property alone. If a victim surprises her stalker in the act of defacing her home, vandalizing or even stealing her car, shooting to kill is not legally justifiable.

Unless he is threatening her life directly and immediately, she cannot claim self-defense. Second, the use of deadly force is almost always unjustified if you initiate an attack, or if you chase an attacker (see unique exceptions in California at end of chapter). If you pursue an assailant, even after he has just attacked you but is now leaving the scene, in general the law sees you now as the aggressor and him as the victim.

Imagine a case in which a stalking victim, we'll call her Doris, awakes one night to find her stalker standing beside her bed. Despite her efforts to resist, he beats her severely, rapes her, and as he leaves, promises her more of the same tomorrow night. Before he is to the front door, Doris reaches into her nightstand for the loaded revolver she has kept there for weeks, steps into the hallway and fires six slugs into his back. Self-defense? Not in the eyes of the law. Indeed, the moment her assailant turned from the initial confrontation, Doris's actions are legally considered "carrying the fight to him"—in short, opening a new confrontation in which, ironically, he now has the right to defend his life without penalty under the law.

The legal issues surrounding self-defense are intricate and can carry heavy consequences. Interpretations vary, courts differ, attorneys debate, the position of judges and juries is never guaranteed. Despite the fear, the violation and desperation that stalking can inflict on a victim, he or she must be absolutely aware of the dangers and legalities of using lethal force in personal protection.

In addition to understanding the laws governing actual self-defense, those who choose to own guns must be aware of the particular laws and regulations concerning gun ownership in their individual states. Laws vary widely on such issues as carrying a concealed weapon or transporting handguns across state or county lines. It is your responsibility to know and follow the gun laws for your area.

Practical Issues

Let's say you have thought about these issues carefully and still think that a gun is the right choice for you. You feel that your survival is at stake; you deserve the right to self-protection and to protect the safety of those around you. You understand the risks and legalities of lethal force, have studied the gun laws in your area, know that you would be a capable and responsible owner of a weapon and, most importantly, that you would be prepared to use it if faced with a life-or-death situation. What now?

Your next steps in the process involve selecting a gun, becoming trained to use it, preparing for self-defense situations, and learning the invaluable safety rituals of gun ownership.

Many women—or people in general unfamiliar with firearms—make the mistake of allowing someone else to select a weapon for them, whether it be a well-meaning male friend or family member, or by asking for a store owner's recommendation. But choosing a handgun, especially as a lifeline to one's personal protection, is an intensely individual decision. The weapon you may have to rely on to save your life must be, among other things, powerful enough to be effective, yet appropriate for your particular hand size and strength. That flashy 9mm Luger semiautomatic with the power to stop a locomotive does you no good if you lack the grip strength to depress the hammer or disengage a jammed cartridge. Nor will the handy little Saturday Night Special that fits your toiletries case so well be much good if you need the accuracy and force to stop an intoxicated assailant hurtling toward you down twenty feet of dark hallway. Shopping for a gun involves listening to many recommendations and trying out a number of firearms before making your choice. Just remember, as Paxton Quigley notes, "Everybody and his brother has an opinion about which gun and what ammunition is best, and most of those opinions are dead wrong."

We highly recommend Quigley's chapter "Buying a Gun" in her book *Armed and Female.* The author, a noted expert in handguns and a security consultant, provides a lucid and informative discussion of gun types, makes, and calibers, along with specific brand recommendations; an overview of choices in ammunition; and an excellent explanation of things to look for in making sure you have selected the most suitable handgun for you and your needs.

Above all, buying a gun means you are purchasing a tool that must be maintained with regularity—and committing yourself to skills that must be learned and practiced with regularity. There are numerous training classes available throughout the country, including specialized schools for what is called "practical shooting" or "combat shooting," in which instructors focus on the special skills needed for self-defense. An appendix at the end of this chapter lists a few of these programs nationwide; others may exist either as independent programs in your area or as training sessions offered by your local police department.

If you have trouble finding training programs in your area, don't be afraid to approach the police department or local media to create such a program. Quigley tells the story of how in 1987 the *Orlando Sentinel Star* newspaper in Florida and Orlando's

Chief of Police Carlisle Johnstone, following a hunch that there might be an interest in gun-training classes for women, advertised such a course to be held in a city park. To their surprise, *over 2,500 women* showed up on the given day! You too may be astonished at how many individuals are interested in developing knowledge and skill with handguns, and you may find valuable social and support networks stemming from the participants you meet.

Self-defense shooting, it must be noted, involves very different skills and concerns than simple target shooting, or pistolcraft for sport. The life-or-death conditions in which combat shooting takes place are often less than optimal. If you keep a gun for protection in the home, you may be shooting in an enclosed space—which presents the danger of ricocheting bullets—or firing at uncomfortably close range at a rapidly, erratically moving target. Confrontations often occur at night, in darkened rooms where aim has to be instinctive and "point shooting" your only option. You may be forced to defend yourself from behind cover or lying down, shooting sideways or upside down—there may be no time or room to assume a proper shooting stance, and in a pinch or struggle, you must be ready to use either hand to fire. Even more than in the calm conditions of a target range, you must be aware of what is around you and beyond your target, including bystanders or walls to other rooms. Stray bullets can pass through a wall and into a child's bedroom or a neighbor's apartment, endangering other lives. Most important, in self-defense shooting the time element for decision and judgment is compressed, and fear and confusion are added to the situation.

All these considerations are addressed and prepared for in practical shooting classes, but many can also be practiced on your own. Quigley recommends practicing at special combat ranges if you can find one in your area, or practicing a number of "dry run" scenarios in your home with an unloaded pistol. MAKE SURE IT IS UNLOADED! She advises going through your home in the dark for a few nights in order to learn its layout and obstacles instinctively, for when you may need to move quickly and unimpeded through unlit rooms. Then, with the lights on, check the arrangement of each room for positions of cover—sofas, dressers, the side of the refrigerator—from which you can command a view of every entry to the room and shoot from a protected position if you need to. If a room lacks good cover, make some—rearrange furniture or slide that dresser over an extra six inches to give you the protection and unimpeded range you may need.

Another suggestion is to create a "safe room" in your house—usually the bedroom—equipped with a dead bolt, a set of house keys, and a separate telephone line, where you can retreat with family members if you hear an intruder, lock yourself in and telephone the police (without fear that the intruder can disable the phone line from another room). Let the police know the situation, and *let them know that you are armed.* Describe the layout of the house and where you are located and, if possible, explain that you can pass a set of house keys to them through the window. If the intruder attempts to break through the door before the police arrive, shooting will be your last line of defense.

We need to add a final word about guns and safety, particularly if you have children in the house. There is always a trade-off between having your gun immediately available—loaded and easily accessible in a crisis situation—and having the gun be safe from curious, playful fingers. Storing your gun in a complicated combination safe in your living room, with the ammunition hidden away on the top shelf of your linen closet, may make it relatively safe from children, but may do you little good in a sudden confrontation. Hiding places for guns—under mattresses, in lingerie drawers, and the like—are remarkably easy to discover, either by inquisitive children or by intruders themselves. There are no easy solutions to this dilemma of balancing accessibility with safety.

Quigley recommends that, rather than attempting to childproof guns, we instead create gunproof children—by carefully teaching our children about the power and danger of firearms, instructing them in safety guidelines, and in the case of older children or teenagers, even providing hands-on training in safe and responsible handgun use. Taking your child to a shooting range to witness the real force of what a gun can do can go far in satisfying their natural curiosity and teaching a healthy respect for these lethal weapons.

Quigley's recommendations are sensible—but even they are no guarantee. According to the National Center for Health Statistics, fifteen children aged nineteen and under are killed each day by guns. If you don't believe your children are ready to follow the guidelines you set, or if you cannot take the time to instruct them in handgun safety, then *don't get a gun.* Rather than securing your home, you may instead be turning it into a deadly playground.

If you wish to carry a gun with you for protection outside the home, you must know and follow the laws in your area for carrying a concealed weapon, including laws covering transporting a gun from one district to another. A wide variety of federal and state laws regulate the licensing and registration of firearms, and may require special permits for—or ban altogether—the carrying of a concealed weapon. It is important to familiarize yourself with the restrictions in your area before you purchase your gun.

The overall rule of gun ownership is discretion and responsibility. Don't show off your gun, don't pass it around among friends, or brag—even if you think you want your stalker to know that you own one. Announcing that you are armed may scare him, but it may just as easily enrage or pose a challenge, ensuring that if he does approach you, he too will be armed and ready.

Your true weapons are surprise, accuracy, good judgment and determination. A gun won't protect you—you, however, may be able to protect yourself with a gun.

Michigan Criminal Jury Instructions (2nd Ed., v. 1, 1989)

Use of Deadly Force in Self-Defense*

(1) The defendant claims that she acted in lawful self-defense. A person has the right to use force or

*Pronouns have been changed to read "she" and instruction format of "killed/seriously injured/forcibly sexually penetrated" has been altered to read more narratively.

even take a life to defend herself under certain circumstances. If a person acts in lawful self-defense, her actions are excused and she is not guilty of any crime.

(2) You should consider all the evidence and use the following rules to decide whether the defendant acted in lawful self-defense. Remember to judge the defendant's conduct according to how the circumstances appeared to her at the time she acted.

(3) First, at the time she acted, the defendant must have honestly and reasonably believed that she was in danger of being killed, seriously injured, or forcibly sexually penetrated. If her belief was honest and reasonable, she could act immediately to defend herself even if it turned out later that she was wrong about how much danger she was in. In deciding if the defendant's belief was honest and reasonable, you should consider all the circumstances as they appeared to the defendant at the time.

(4) Second, a person may not kill or seriously injure another person just to protect herself against what seems like a threat of only minor injury. The defendant must have been afraid of death, serious physical injury, or forcible sexual penetration. When you decide if the defendant was afraid of one or more of these, you should consider all the circumstances: the condition of the people involved, including their relative strength; whether the other person was armed with a dangerous weapon or had some other means of injuring the defendant; the nature of the other person's attack or threat; whether the defendant knew about any previous violent acts or threats made by the other person.

(5) Third, at the time she acted, the defendant must have honestly and reasonably believed that what she

did was immediately necessary. Under the law, a person may only use as much force as she thinks is necessary at the time to protect herself. When you decide whether the amount of force used seemed to be necessary, you may consider whether the defendant knew about any other ways of protecting herself, but you may also consider how the excitement of the moment affected the choice the defendant made.

Duty to Retreat to Avoid Using Deadly Force

(1) By law, a person must avoid using deadly force if she can safely do so. If the defendant could have safely retreated but did not do so, you can consider that fact, along with all the other circumstances, when you decide whether she went farther in protecting herself than she should have.

(2) However, if the defendant honestly and reasonably believed that it was immediately necessary to use deadly force to protect herself from an imminent threat of death, serious injury, or forcible sexual penetration, the law does not require her to retreat. She may stand her ground and use the amount of force she believes necessary to protect herself.

No Duty to Retreat While in Own Dwelling

If a person assaulted the defendant in the defendant's own home or forcibly entered the defendant's home, the defendant did not have to try to retreat or get away. Under those circumstances, the defendant could stand her ground and resist the attack or intrusion with as much force as she honestly and reasonably believed necessary at the time to protect herself.

California Jury Instructions—Criminal (5th ed., v. 1)

Justifiable Homicide in Self-Defense

The killing of another person in self-defense is justifiable and not unlawful when the person who does the killing honestly and reasonably believes:

1. That there is imminent danger that the other person will kill her or cause her great bodily injury; and

2. That it was necessary under the circumstances to kill the other person to prevent death or great bodily injury to herself.

In order to justify killing another person in self-defense, actual danger or great bodily injury is not necessary. On the other hand, a mere fear of death or great bodily injury is not sufficient.

Justifiable Homicide—Lawful Defense of Self or Another

Homicide is justifiable and not unlawful when committed by any person in the defense of herself or her ______________ [insert relationship of other party defended] if she honestly and reasonably believed that the individual killed intended to commit a forcible and atrocious crime and that there was imminent danger of such crime being accomplished. A person may act upon appearances whether such danger is real or merely apparent.

Homicide in Defense of Member of Family

The reasonable ground of apprehension does not require actual danger, but it does require that the person about to kill another be confronted by the appearance of a peril such as has been mentioned; that such appearance arouse in her mind an honest conviction and fear of the existence of such peril; that a reasonable person in the same situation, seeing and knowing the same facts, would have, and be justified in having, the same fear; and that the killing be done under the influence of such fear alone.

Self-Defense—Assailed Person Need Not Retreat

A person threatened with an attack that justifies the exercise of the right to self-defense need not retreat. In the exercise of her right of self-defense such person may stand her ground and defend herself by the use of all force and means which would appear to be necessary to a reasonable person in a similar situation and with similar knowledge; and such person may pursue such assailant until she has secured herself from danger if that course likewise appears reasonably necessary. This law applies even though the assailed person might more easily have gained safety by flight or by withdrawing from the scene.

Self-Defense—Actual Danger Not Necessary

Actual danger is not necessary to justify self-defense. If one is confronted by the appearance of danger which arouses in her mind, as a reasonable person, an honest conviction and fear that she is about to suffer bodily injury, and if a reasonable person in a like situation, seeing and knowing the same facts, would be justified in believing herself in like danger, and if that individual so confronted acts in self-defense upon such appearances and from such fear and honest convictions, such person's right of self-defense is the same, whether such danger is real or merely apparent.

Self-Defense—When Danger Ceases

The right of self-defense exists only as long as the real or apparent threatened danger continues to exist. When such danger ceases to appear to exist, the right to use force in self-defense ends.

CHAPTER **10**

Self-Defense III

Services, Skills, and Tactics

Victim Protection Services' objective is to enable their clients to regain control of their lives by providing a viable response to violence that is proactive and preventive.

Wendy Collier, founder,
Victim Protection Services

By the time a woman graduates from this course, she's been 'mugged' about twenty times.

Janet Berry, course instructor for
Bay Area Model Mugging/Self-Defense (BAMM)

Personal Protection Services

On June 22, 1992, Wendy Collier knew she needed more help than the police, her friends, or her family could offer. That was the day her ex-husband was sentenced for assaulting and holding her hostage for eight hours with a double-barrel shotgun. It was the day she realized that fairness doesn't come easily, the day she learned the motto, "the weak seek revenge and the strong seek justice."

Wendy's married life with Frank Taylor had been a saga of violence—during three years she had received frequent severe beatings, had been sexually and psychologically abused, her pets tortured and her life threatened verbally and physically. Like so many battered women, Wendy had tried to escape from her batterer several times during the course of those years—but every time she left, Frank stalked her relentlessly, tracked her down, and terrified her with threats to her life and the lives of her family, until time and again she complied with his demands and returned.

Finally, on March 5, 1989, the violence grew so bad that she knew she either had to make a permanent break or die at the hands of her husband. Frank Taylor, in the course of an argument, grabbed and loaded his shotgun and held her at gunpoint in fear for her life for eight hours. Wendy recalls her ordeal vividly:

> . . . Loading the shotgun, he stood over me, silently seething. I felt keenly aware of all of my senses. I really thought I was going to die, and I wanted to be aware to the end. Frank began taunting me, daring me to give him an excuse to shoot me. Frank held me hostage with the loaded shotgun for the next eight hours. His rage escalated in waves and he screamed at me, his spittle flying. He continually pointed the shotgun at me, and pressed the barrels of the shotgun against my forehead, neck, breasts, and stomach. He tortured and beat me mercilessly. He threatened to kill me, my family, co-workers, and my dog.
>
> Escape from the house was impossible. I wasn't worried about being naked or running barefooted on the rocky driveway. I didn't think I could outrun the

> shotgun. I did everything I could think of to survive. I kept him talking. I pled for my life.

After Frank finally released her, gashed and wounded and with patches of hair pulled from her head from the beatings, Wendy knew her survival depended on escaping his control. With cunning and courage, over the next several weeks she finally managed to sneak out enough clothing and money to leave Frank for good. Her opportunity came when her employer asked her to travel to a convention in Las Vegas. Wendy took the chance; once there, she phoned Frank to tell him she was divorcing him.

But only half of her troubles were over. Frank began a nightmarish three years of stalking and harassment—following Wendy home from work, pounding on her door and shouting obscenities, leaving nails under her car's tires, phoning her with graphic threats, attempting to run her down with his car while she was walking her dog. Over and over he violated the restraining order she had been forced to take out against him, but the police seemed unable or unwilling to take any action.

> Every time I called the police I was informed that Frank was not violating the restraining order and therefore there was nothing that they could do. Once I was told that he was indeed violating the restraining order, but that the police had to catch him in the act. . . . Frank continued to blatantly disregard the restraining order with impunity. On July 10, 1990, Frank chased me in traffic and attempted to run me off the road while I was driving to work. Two separate police departments informed me that because the incident occurred while driving through two different

police jurisdictions, that neither jurisdiction would accept responsibility for filing a report.

Desperate and terrified, Wendy finally called on the courts for help. After a great deal of persistence, she was at last able to get the District Attorney's Office to investigate and charge Frank with felony menacing regarding the shotgun ordeal. A warrant for his arrest was issued in December 1990.

By now Wendy knew better than to feel relieved. Frank was violent. He was dangerous. And within eight hours of his arrest he was at large again, released on bond by a system that had seemed to fail her time and again. This man had repeatedly come close to ending her life; Wendy strongly believed that, given the chance, Frank Taylor could and would make good on his numerous death threats against her.

That was when Wendy Collier stepped into a series of events and choices that would change her life—and the lives of numerous other victims of domestic violence and stalking. Just before Frank's sentencing, still in terrified hiding, Wendy met a bodyguard through one of her neighbors. Out of kindness, and for no pay, he and two other protective agents offered to protect her during the tension-filled days before and during the sentencing. They escorted her to the hearing—at which she watched the system fail to protect her again. Although Frank Taylor was charged with a Class-5 felony—a crime carrying a maximum penalty of eight years in prison and a $100,000 fine—he ended up serving only forty-five days in prison, including time off for work and good behavior.

On the day of Frank's sentencing—June 22, 1992—Wendy Collier founded Victim Protection Services, a nonprofit, Colorado-based agency that provides a variety of personal protection services to victims of stalking, domestic violence, and harassment. For a low, sliding-scale fee, and using hand-screened, professionally trained bodyguards who work on a volunteer basis, Wendy's organization now offers escorts to and from court appearances, family visits, and other necessary travel, or around-the-clock protection if the threat of lethal danger is clear. Victim Protection Services also offers self-defense classes, educational brochures, a newsletter, community awareness programs, and security consultations. Above all, VPS provides viable, professional protection for victims who generally would not be able to afford the high cost of a bodyguard.

Wendy feels such services are vital for all victims experiencing the very real danger posed by violent, abusive partners. She writes:

> Victim Protection Services is not a replacement for or an alternative to law enforcement or battered women's shelters. Victim Protection Services fills a unique and vital niche in the services available to victims by ensuring their safety. Their objective is to enable their clients to restore empowerment and regain control of their lives while providing a viable response to violence that is proactive and preventive.

For herself, Wendy still fears Frank Taylor, but her ordeal has resulted in empowering outcomes: "I seek justice through the catharsis of helping other victims like myself. I've earned a lot of self-respect from knowing that I continue to transcend a horrible victimization, transforming it into something very positive."

Electronic Monitoring Devices

Another interesting development in personal safety includes the testing of electronic surveillance devices to monitor the movements of stalkers, particularly in situations of domestic violence where known abusers have repeatedly violated restraining or "no contact" orders. JurisMonitor, Inc., another Colorado-based organization, has teamed up with BI Incorporated, a firm specializing in electronic home-arrest monitoring technology with systems in over 550 jurisdictions worldwide. Together they have made dramatic strides in victim safety and law enforcement, by way of a system that combines technology with counseling and advocacy programs called JurisMonitor.

The offender is required by court order to wear an electronic ankle bracelet which will monitor whether or not he complies with the no-contact order prohibiting any proximity to the victim. The device provides electronic evidence of any violations, allowing the police to document and arrest the perpetrator without having to be on the scene to witness the violation. The victim receives monitoring equipment in her home, which includes a remote personal help button that will send an alarm signal to a central monitoring station, much like a home security alarm will register and transmit a signal to law enforcement. The police are called to the scene, and both the victim's advocate and supervisors of the perpetrator—such as his corrections officer or treatment provider—are also notified of the violation.

These electronic monitoring devices are successful on a number of levels. For law enforcement, they provide a reliable source of evidence, allowing them to arrest and prosecute following restraining order violations that had previously been difficult to record without secondary witnesses. For community safety, the electronic bracelet allows courts to determine more accurately whether a potentially dangerous perpetrator can stop violent or invasive behaviors on their own, or whether they require full incarceration. In this way, it provides a much-needed middle step between prison time and unsupervised release of the offender into the community.

But it is victims themselves who applaud the success of these devices, despite the fact that the technology still does not extend beyond the home. Realizing its limitations, however, victims still report a far greater feeling of safety and effective legal recourse against violent partners who repeatedly violate restraining orders. One victim reports, "I was in and out of court until my head was spinning. Every time, I couldn't prove he was guilty beyond a reasonable doubt, until he wore the ankle bracelet and set off the alarm. Then they took me seriously and the judge understood I was in real danger." Another writes, ". . . having that little button to press to call for help when I am outside or in the house does make me feel better even though I know its limitations."

JurisMonitor is more than a simple technological device, however. It involves a complete and well-integrated community effort, which includes advocacy and support for the victim, the involvement and education of the courts and law enforcement, treatment programs and supervision of the perpetrator, and community training and intervention programs —all working together to protect the victim and foreground the dangerous nature of invasive crimes like stalking. According to George Wattendorf, Prosecuting Attorney for Dover, New Hampshire, "The

JurisMonitor program is much more than an electronic alarm system for stalkers. It is also a community policing program that facilitates law enforcement by helping develop community bonding to prevent stalking crimes from escalating. . . . The JurisMonitor program is one model of community policing at its best. Technology and laws alone cannot solve the problem of stalking. The community and law enforcement coordinating a response together is the key."

JurisMonitor selects additional project locations to implement and test their program across the country. Your community may be an ideal spot to introduce this outstanding system of intervention, technology, and protective assistance.

Skills Courses

We now move into an area that holds promise as a self-defense strategy for everyone. Courses in physical skills of self-defense—fighting skills—are highly recommended as a way to develop strength, confidence, personal growth, and "street-smarts"—not to mention life-saving abilities. Of course, as with all protection measures, these programs too must be evaluated realistically and selected with care.

Martial arts have long been known in this country, intriguing men and women alike by their blend of grace, power, and the rich traditions of a centuries-old discipline. Schools and varieties of martial arts abound, each with its own distinctive style and philosophy; the list is far too extensive to mention here. Martial arts can be a beautiful sport, and an excellent avenue to fitness and mental discipline; however, along with its many benefits, it holds several practical drawbacks to those seeking a primary, practical, and immediate mode of self-defense.

Most importantly, martial arts take many years of instruction and practice for an individual to perfect and be able to use with confidence and sure success in a real-life fighting situation. Many times the moves taught in martial arts classes—particularly the more advanced kicks and blocks—are impressive, complicated sequences designed for exhibition rather than for actual fighting. For reasons of safety, moreover, students train without making full-force contact or at less than fighting speed—and the inclination to "draw" punches may not be so easily overcome in a real, life-or-death situation. Most importantly, martial arts as a rule teaches a style of "standing" fighting in which equal opponents face each other from a prescribed distance, a scenario seldom replicated in actual attack situations, particularly the ways in which women are attacked.

The limitations of martial arts were demonstrated graphically in the experience of black-belt martial arts expert Matthew Thomas who, in 1971, launched a new avenue in women's self-defense. A woman in Thomas's karate class, who was herself an exhibition-level martial arts competitor, was assaulted and raped. Sadly, in this real combat situation, her considerable martial arts talents could not protect her. Upon returning to her class, as the story is told, she *apologized* to her teacher for not having been able to use her skills successfully; she felt she had let down her teacher, her fellow students, and her system of study! Thomas saw something wrong with this picture: Rather than *her* having betrayed the system, he felt that it was the *system* that had betrayed *her*.

Thomas set about studying the ways women are actually attacked in the real world of home, street, and workplace. His examination of nearly three thousand assaults against women resulted in his designing the first Model Mugging Women's Self-Defense course, which is now available through approximately thirty chapters throughout the United States, Canada, and Switzerland. In contrast to martial arts, the course takes relatively little time to complete—usually requiring approximately two weeks of intensive study rather than years of instruction and practice. The fighting techniques taught in Model Mugging focus on *women's* unique strength, via leg kicks from a prone position—since most often women are taken to the ground when attacked or raped—a thorough knowledge of disabling techniques to an attacker's vulnerable points, and the use of leverage to compensate for the usually unequal strength between a woman victim and her assailant.

The most unique feature of the course is that participants engage in "real" fighting, using full force against a padded male "mugger," throughout the course of the program. The fights are designed to simulate real-life scenarios of rape, surprise, escalation of violence, and attack from behind—often including loud verbal abuse and unexpected moves—in order to strengthen and prepare the woman for the highly adrenalized confusion and fear of a real attack situation. The type of "muscle-memory" learning and true confidence this builds are incomparable aspects of the Model Mugging technique.

Indeed, in the decades of its existence, the success rate of this style of self-defense has been astonishing. The organization's headquarters, Bay Area Model Mugging in San Francisco, reports that Model Mugging chapters across the country have graduated over eight thousand individuals. Of fifty documented participants who had subsequently been attacked, all but two have successfully resisted their assailants by either physically deterring the attack or disabling their attackers. Five hundred other graduates report having successfully deflected violent attacks through verbal de-escalation, another technique taught in Model Mugging training.

The numbers are only part of the story, however. From our own experience, this is not simply a course in fighting techniques—it is a program of emotional growth, attitude building, and a release of the power and confidence all women have within. It is truly an exceptional course of study, and can provide the foundation for any woman's plan for self-defense and empowerment.

How to Disappear

There are times when all available protection seems to have been exhausted, when a victim fears so strongly for her life or has become so worn down by constant vigilance and terror, that she decides her only choice is to "disappear." Many victims consider this option of moving to a new town, county, or even state, in order to try to escape their stalkers and start a new life elsewhere. It is the rare stalking target who hasn't visualized erasing her identity, leaving the stalker's reign of terror for good by simply packing up and going.

But in the experience of numerous victims who have tried to elude their stalkers, this option seems sometimes to have more loopholes than advantages. If a victim can get beyond the obvious obstacles of leaving a home and friends, changing jobs, enduring the cost and burden of relocating themselves (and sometimes their families as well)—even if these are all overcome, victims frequently report that their stalkers were able to find them again, sometimes with alarming ease, no matter how far they had moved.

Why are stalkers so often able to track down their victims again—whether they've moved twenty minutes down the road or two thousand miles away? Victims have been known to flee from city to city, state to state, only to have their stalkers find them again and again—each time leaving them with fewer resources and fewer support circles to fall back on. Knowing some of the ways that persistent stalkers can find out personal information about an individual may help guide your choices if you are a victim, and if moving or attempting to disappear seems like your most viable—or only—option. There are no airtight formulas for erasing one's identity; even the FBI's prestigious and experienced Witness Protection Program cannot claim a hundred percent success. There are, however, certain basic precautions you can take to reduce the chance of your being traced and found.

Few citizens realize how simple it is to obtain information about virtually anyone today, given our proliferation of public documents and records. Moreover, we tend too quickly to assume that "private" or "classified" personal information is actually safe from investigating eyes. Take "unlisted" telephone numbers: most of us assume an unlisted number means a number that is not available to the public, right? What we don't realize is that any unlisted number *becomes* public information when it appears on a public record, such as a driving record, registration, deeds and titles, agreements and affidavits, divorce papers, licenses, and numerous other documents. These also often reveal an individual's address and social security number—important pieces of information that, though assumed to be private, are in fact relatively easy to obtain. Erasing your identity, if your safety or life depends on it, must begin by identifying and plugging up the leaks in the system that make private information available to public scrutiny.

The post office, for instance, is an obvious way to trace the whereabouts of an individual who has moved—and here would be a first step to wiping out the paper trail by which your stalker might track you down. The U.S. Postal Service will provide anyone with an individual's new address for a small fee, provided that individual filed a change-of-address form within the last eighteen months. If you need to truly "disappear," *do not file a change-of-address form* with your local post office. You may lose those last few months of that magazine subscription, or miss the postcard forwarded from an old college friend—but in return you may be gaining your safety.

Another notoriously leaky crack in the information system is the Department of Motor Vehicles. In fact, the DMV seems to have become such a sieve for private information that the recent National Institute of Justice report on model antistalking legislation (1993) called for a dramatic analysis and tightening of DMV information disclosure policies, in the interests of public safety. As it stands, in most states the name and address of any licensed driver are part of the public record, available on request. Driving records, accident reports, and motor vehicle registrations are considered public documents as well; these files can obviously contain much information about an individual's location, history, or current livelihood.

If you are moving and need to change DMV documents, one private investigator suggests you find or hire an attorney who will allow you to use his business address in place of your "new" mailing address when renewing public documents like drivers' licenses or vehicle registrations (as well as on other documents, discussed later in this chapter). Although often drivers' licenses need not be renewed for up to eight years, motor vehicle registrations need to be renewed annually. Simply list your attorney's address as your new address. Any important information from the DMV (such as next year's registration forms or this year's stickers) will be sent to your attorney, who can hold or forward such mail on to you. If your stalker attempts to find out your new address through the DMV records, however, the farthest he will get is face-to-face with your lawyer.

The post office and DMV are only two of a host of agencies that hold—and often inappropriately release—important private information about you. In order to truly "erase your identity," you have much more homework to do. You must familiarize yourself with all these agencies, carefully screen your own paper trail of documents and public records, and be extraordinarily vigilant about how and where you register your new address. The appendix for this chapter lists a number of excellent and eye-opening books that can help you locate the leaks in your own information system. Some address specifically the topic of changing your identity; others approach the field from the opposite direction—how anyone can find another individual. In either case, these publications should provide you with a number of crucial tips on how to disappear.

Private investigator Joe Culligan, author of *You, Too, Can Find Anybody* and *When In Doubt, Check Him Out,* offered us a few ideas for women who feel they need to flee an abusive or life-threatening situation, yet want to prevent their harassers from tracking them down. First, Culligan strongly recommends that the victim list her new telephone number under an assumed name—preferably an extremely common name like "Mary Smith"—so that even the assumed identity will be further buried among the hundreds of other Mary Smiths in the phone book. Second, and extremely important, Culligan advises that victims tell the telephone company in their new location that they have never had a telephone before. The phone company will request a deposit of about $200 for one year, in order to cover the credit risk of a first-time client, but Culligan says this is a relatively small price to pay for the gain in privacy it affords. Apparently anyone who had your old telephone number (stalkers included) can obtain your new number from the phone company that installed your new line.

Even if you "unlist" your new number, sometimes a simple bit of trickery on the part of someone bent on obtaining this information may be enough to cause a slip. A stalker who has learned of your new city but does not know your telephone number could call the phone company, posing as your relative or spouse, who "just happened to forget" the home phone number newly installed. Although many phone companies will never permit the release of such information, it isn't inconceivable that human error could make available the information you've worked so hard to keep private.

Culligan insists that victims should place *all* new bills and services—such as electric, gas, cable, etc.—in their "new" name (Mary Smith), and should *never* give their telephone numbers to companies like cable TV or electric, even if requested to do so. These records are fairly easy to gain access to—constituting another dangerous leak. Instead, Culligan suggests giving either a fictitious number or the number of some other individual like a relative or attorney, in order to deflect your stalker should he manage to track you as far as your cable company or other home service provider. Finally, Culligan recommends listing your attorney's address instead of your own *wherever* you must by law use your real name on a record, deed, or public document such as on a voter registration or library card.

In addition to these fairly basic precautions, Culligan makes a special point of advising victims to look closely at their habits, hobbies, and lifestyle patterns. He warns that these could easily be the "weak link" that allows a determined stalker to find his victim. According to Culligan, "You can change your identity, but you're not going to change your habits" unless you are extremely vigilant and alert. In Culligan's own distinguished career locating missing persons, it is their hobbies and interests that have given away their whereabouts, time and again.

Do you own a dog? Dog licenses are easily accessible to the public, providing an owner's name and address. Do you fish or hunt? Licenses here can also be major sources of personal information. Do you bowl in a league? Belong to a quilting club, book club, fan club, shopping club? Do you carry membership in an association? There are 17,000 different clubs and associations listed in the *Gale Research Index*, each of which is easy to contact for information about its members. Culligan's advice may seem severe, but it is ultimately sound: Don't belong to any clubs or organizations if you are attempting to guard your identity and whereabouts.

You may, in addition, need to be especially vigilant for a while about pursuing hobbies and interests that may help your stalker find you, even without his resorting to agency or association files. If your stalker has had you under surveillance in the past, he may know unique details about your lifestyle and habits—perhaps that you prefer attending evening aerobics classes, that you made a habit of jogging in the park at a particular time of day, or that on Saturdays you enjoyed going to the mall to shop and see a movie. Banking on the chance that old habits are hard to break, he might be able to find you in a new city simply by hanging around local parks or gyms or shopping mall theaters for a few weeks, knowing your habitual times for exercise or recreation. Being alert to—and changing—your old routines could help deflect a determined stalker. And, of course, the *most* common way that stalkers seem to find their victims who move is through the careless giving out of information by past neighbors, employers, friends, and family. Be *extremely* careful about who knows your new whereabouts, and make absolutely sure they understand the need for complete secrecy.

Disappearing is a complex and major undertaking in today's too-public world, but it is not impossible. It does require a good deal of savvy and considerable sacrifice, along with ceaseless vigilance and determination. But if you feel it is a matter of your personal safety, even of your life, then disappearing may be the most powerful self-defense strategy you can undertake. It's not a bad joke to suggest that, in some very extreme stalking cases, it's far better to go underground than to wind up there.

CHAPTER 11

License to Pursue

Stalking and Society

> There are many theories about why men hurt women, but no matter how much sense they make, they cannot heal our fear or blunt our outrage. Every time I read of a woman stalked and killed by her ex-husband, every time an acquaintance confides that she was raped, every time my attacker invades my dreams, my heart burns with the old, bitter question: Why?
>
> Victoria Loe,
> *Dallas Morning News*

> Violence and its threat sabotages the fundamental human need for a sense of security and place in the world. While the temptation to take strong actions against violence after the fact is attractive to many, a wiser and ultimately more effective course is that which looks at prevention.
>
> Michael Resnick, Ph.D.,
> Sociologist, University of Minnesota

Media representation of stalking, while valuable in focusing public attention on this crime, we believe has also fostered a number of misperceptions and myths about stalking—myths that we hope this book has helped uncover and dispel. Media reports often focus only on the more sensational cases or those with extreme and tragic outcomes—homicide, multiple murders, or workplace killing sprees. In addition, the stalking of celebrities and public figures tends to receive a disproportionate amount of media attention, since audiences are always eager for stories about stars and public leaders. As a result, the thousands of ongoing cases involving ordinary individuals, victims of a whole spectrum of stalking behavior, remain largely invisible to the public eye. Most potentially misleading, however, is the trend in many media reports to portray stalking *only* as the product of individual psychosis—the "sick mind," the abnormal individual—rather than as a continuum of behavior that may stem from a range of social and cultural causes.

Challenging these views is not to say that violent, extreme levels of stalking do not exist. On the contrary, one reason antistalking laws were passed with such speed across the country is the fact that lawmakers acknowledge the extreme threat such criminal behavior can pose. The awareness of lawmakers is keen, because the potential lethality of stalking *has* been overwhelmingly documented. Moreover, as we have seen in previous chapters, public figures *are* the targets of stalkers, and indeed some stalkers do suffer from mental illness, delusional or obsessive disorders. However, the vast majority of stalking occurs between ordinary people, often people who have known each other or had some form of prior relationship. And much of this criminal behavior, it appears, is *not* the product of psychosis, but may stem in part from cultural messages about men and women in a society that seems to offer some of its members a license to pursue.

It can be argued that we live in a culture that romanticizes pursuit. The messages are all around us—in the movies, in television shows, song lyrics, even in advertisements for products as remote as perfume, like Calvin Klein's Obsession for Men campaign—the subtle or blatant word is that pursuit is appropriate, heroic, and ultimately rewarded. Over and over the images that construct our world depict women as vulnerable and available, men as being most manly when they are invincible and aggressive. Moreover, the more difficult the chase, the tougher the conquest—the greater, we are told, the rewards will be.

Stalking expert Gavin de Becker comments that one of the powerful messages that continues to come from Hollywood films is that "no means yes"—that pursuit, even pursuit that ordinarily ought to be considered invasive and abnormal, is glamorized as noble and adventurous. From classic movies like *The Graduate* to contemporary blockbusters, the pattern is clear: obsessive behavior wins the prize of romantic love. According to de Becker, the Hollywood formula today seems to be:

Boy Meets Girl,
Boy Loses Girl,
Boy Stalks Girl,
Boy Gets Girl.

It is interesting to note too that this message is usually a gendered one. This dangerous license to pursue, in short, is not given to all members of society. While male characters who pursue are often romanticized, or at least depicted as engaging in "normal" persistent courtship, when the tables are turned and a *female* character attempts to make the same type of repeated unwanted contact, she is depicted as no less than a monster. Films like *Fatal Attraction, Play Misty for Me,* or *The Hand That Rocks the Cradle,* present scenarios in which female characters seem suddenly unable to understand the meaning of no, and pursue the attentions of men who are either unwitting or unwilling. In each case, the behavior is seen to be crazy, terrifying, potentially lethal, and certainly abnormal.

But there are even exceptions to this rule, which ironically end up being exceptions that *prove* the rule of pursuit as desirable and rewarded. De Becker points to the comedy *Housesitter* as one instance in which a female character's obsessive behavior also results in her "winning out" in the end. In this film, the main character, played by Steve Martin, undergoes an ordeal that in real life would be considered nightmarish—a woman (Goldie Hawn) with whom he had an impersonal, one-night affair pursues him to his newly built home, moves into the house while he is away, illegally charges furnishings to his credit cards, dupes his family and neighbors into believing that she is his wife, spins a series of extraordinary tales about him, disrupts his existing relationships, and effectively takes over his life—all utterly without his consent. Martin, throughout, plays the exasperated victim—nothing he can do or say can remove her from his world. And the outcome of this abnormal, overwhelming invasion? When Hawn finally does retreat, Martin realizes that he "cannot live without her," and the two fall into a blissful embrace. The message, however comic and slapstick, seems to be that persistence, however excessive, will succeed; pursuit, however insane, will ultimately result in romance and reward.

A Mild Drug for Most

In addition to how interpersonal pursuit is portrayed in the entertainment industry, the industry itself may have changed the very way we as a public understand such concepts as accessibility to others, forms of admiration, and notions of fame and idolatry. De Becker argues that over the last several decades, audience behavior in a range of public events seems to have altered dramatically. He points to a turning point that may have taken place sometime around the 1940s, with the emergence of such idols as Frank Sinatra, in the singer's days as a crooner who could inspire mass frenzy in his female fans. Admiration for public performers, which used to be expressed from afar, seems to have become more direct and extreme with the evolution and marketing of such superstars. Whereas before, behaviors such as fans screaming, pulling off clothing, attempting to clamber onstage, or young fans dropping out of school and abandoning their lives in order to follow a performer around the country—all these would have been considered insane and utterly exceptional behaviors, to say the least. Yet in the emerging age of superstardom, such extreme expressions of idolatry began to crest into a cult; according to one psychologist of the time, the American public seemed to be suffering symptoms of "mass frustrated love" in regard to its celebrities. In Gavin de Becker's words, "Elements in society were pioneering the skills of manipulating emotion and behavior in ways that had never been possible before, electronic ways. The media was *institutionalizing* idolatry—and new ways to express it."

The dangers of such unbounded idolatry were clear even in the 1940s. During that decade America witnessed perhaps its first publicized case of celebrity stalking, in which a young woman, Ruth Steinhagen, developed an obsessive attachment to her baseball idol, Eddie Waitkus, then of the Chicago Cubs. Steinhagen began to follow Waitkus to all his games, believing that he belonged to her exclusively. De Becker traces the details of the case:

> Even though they'd never met, Ruth devoted her life to Eddie. He was of Lithuanian descent so she tried to learn that language. He was number 36 on the Chicago Cubs, so Ruth became obsessed with that number, buying every record she could find that was produced in 1936. She collected all press clippings about Eddie, slept with his picture under her pillow, attended every game she could, and sent him letter after letter, even though he never responded. Often Ruth arranged the chairs at dinner so that there was an empty one facing hers; she told her sister that Eddie was in that chair. When Eddie was traded to the Philadelphia Phillies, Ruth stated she could not live if he moved away from Chicago.

But it was not merely a thwarted desire for Waitkus's attentions that fueled Steinhagen's persistence. De Becker points to her deluded need for fame, prominence, the attention of the public itself. In June of 1949, Steinhagen checked into the hotel where Waitkus was staying while on tour, then sent a note to his room asking the athlete to meet with her. Generously, Waitkus agreed to see her, thinking her just another avid fan. When he arrived at her room, however, Steinhagen announced, "I have a surprise for you," then shot him in the chest with a rifle she had hidden in the closet.

Astonishingly, however, Steinhagen did not flee the scene, but stayed there, calling out to bystanders that she had shot Waitkus, frustrated when they did not immediately give her the spotlight of fame she felt she deserved. In her own account of the moments following the shooting, Steinhagen recalled:

> Nobody came out of their rooms. You would think they would all come rushing out. I got mad. I kept telling them I shot Eddie Waitkus but they didn't know who Eddie Waitkus was. . . . After that the police came, but I was burning because nobody was coming out of those other rooms. *Nobody seemed to want me much.* I could've walked right out of that place and nobody would have come after me.

Steinhagen later admitted, "I wanted attention and publicity for once. Now all my dreams have come true."

De Becker points out the deeper impulses underlying such delusions: Not only have celebrities become more desirable and accessible to fans, but the very concept of public prominence has become a prize to be won, a type of affirmation of identity for the anonymous, even if achieved at the cost of violent or deranged acts. "Since Ruth Steinhagen," says de Becker, "we've seen many people seek to prove their 'love' through public acts of violence. When all else failed to give them the identity they hoped a relationship would bring, the handgun would be sure to do it—John Hinckley, forever linked with Jodie Foster; Robert Bardo, forever linked with actress Rebecca Schaeffer; Arthur Jackson, forever linked with Theresa Saldana, and so on."

While not all fans suffer such delusions or take out their frustrations in violent ways, clearly our culture does hold out to all of us the extreme glamor of celebrity, and welcomes almost an atmosphere of worship surrounding the stars. It is hard to imagine a rock concert, sports event, or celebrity function today without its screaming masses of fans. For most of us, de Becker acknowledges, such excitement is a mild drug—but it is a drug that can prove to be a poison for a seemingly growing number of individuals who cannot distinguish between appropriate reality and frustrated fantasy. Andy Warhol's often-quoted phrase about each person's fifteen minutes of fame seems grimly real in an era where felons reap royalties for writing their life stories, where serial killers become the stars of comic strips, where the more grisly the crime, the more likely it is to be the subject of the next television movie of the week. Perhaps our admiration for our public figures has indeed become a type of uncritical idolatry whose consequences are just beginning to be felt.

A Legacy of Violence

Most victims of stalking, however, are ordinary people, not superstars surrounded by the glitter of the spotlight. As we have seen in previous chapters, the highest percentage of stalking cases occurs within a context of domestic violence, and as part of a larger pattern of violence between individuals. Domestic violence, like stalking, also represents a once-invisible crime that has since become the focus of much attention, legislative action, and efforts at education —however, simply bringing it to light has by no means eradicated its existence. Indeed, studies show that both the practice and the tolerance of domestic abuse is a legacy of violence now being passed on to the next generation.

In a number of studies of adolescent violence, researchers revealed that physical abuse among dating teens seems to be a rising trend. Psychologist Barrie Levy—author of *Dating Violence: Young Women in Danger* and *In Love and Danger: A Teen Guide to Breaking Free of Abusive Relationships*—reports that an alarming 25 percent of teenagers surveyed say they have experienced physical violence in a dating relationship. Other researchers estimate that this figure is actually conservative, and that the percentages of young people who are victims of dating violence, particularly in urban areas, are even higher. The *Boston Globe* reports that, in one ten-month period, courts in Massachusetts issued 757 restraining orders against teens engaged in threatening, stalking, abuse, or outright assault of their young partners. The trend in dating violence was so notable in Washington, D.C., that it impelled the superior court to implement a separate domestic violence treatment program for teenagers, as they were seeing more and more batterers among boys between the ages of thirteen and eighteen. Some states have recognized the problem enough to make the topic of dating violence prevention a mandatory part of the public school curriculum.

According to Fern Shen of the *Washington Post,* "Researchers are at a loss to provide a definitive explanation for teenage dating violence, though many see it reflected in the sexual stereotypes that permeate American youth culture in its music, movies and videos. . . . Many researchers consider teenage dating violence an extension of the sexual stereotyping and violence that infects U.S. society on all levels . . . as part of a continuum that ranges from sexually harassing jokes and comments to stalking, serious assault and rape." What is clear, however, is that in cases of dating violence, the patterns of power and control have been set early—often these include extreme jealousy and surveillance, physical beatings and threats, campaigns of stalking and harassment if the young woman attempts to leave the relationship. Much as in adult domestic violence, the cycle of domination and intimidation creates a dangerous and tightening trap.

Most poignant is when messages from culture or peers have resulted in a type of resignation among young women themselves to the fact of interpersonal violence, a deep misunderstanding of their own boundaries and rights. Consider the lessons about men and women we must be teaching our children that could shape the following comment from one young victim: "If a guy really loves you, he hits you to let you know how much he loves you." A culture in which violence continues to be portrayed as an effective solution to problems, and in which abuse is misperceived as an expected part of intimacy, is sadly a culture that will continue to be confronted with these crimes.

Education is clearly needed for young men and women, not just toward the prevention of physically violent relationships, but to instill a general understanding of the spectrum of inappropriate attachments. In the following piece, Gavin de Becker outlines an ideal high school course that would teach young men and women the parameters of appropriate relationships—how to *hear* the word NO, as well as how to say it. Learning these lessons early can make the difference between acquiring healthy social skills or beginning a potentially dangerous pattern of manipulation and control.

Rejection 101

by Gavin de Becker

Stalking and unwanted pursuit demonstrate dramatically that interpersonal boundaries in Western society have moved far in recent decades. What once was clearly inappropriate is now routine. What once was extraordinary behavior is now familiar to many of us.

The news media attention on stalking began because of a few cases involving famous people. We shuddered to see that someone would be so obsessed with a media figure that it might escalate to stalking, and even violence. Perhaps the erosion of personal boundaries which affects so many regular people was initially modeled for us by the famous.

Though I've testified for stalking laws in many states, I'd trade them all for a high school class that would teach young men how to hear "No," and teach young women that it's all right to decide who is in their lives—and all right to express that decision explicitly. If the culture allowed women to explicitly reject, or if more women took that power early in every relationship, stalking cases would decline dramatically.

The curriculum for that class would include one clear rule that can be applied to all cases of unwanted pursuit: *Do Not Negotiate.* Negotiations are about possibilities, and once a woman has made the decision that she doesn't want to pursue a relationship with a particular man, it needs to be said one time, explicitly. Otherwise, almost any contact that follows can be seen as a negotiation.

If a woman tells a man ten times that she doesn't want to talk to him, that is talking to him. She has entered into nine negotiations that betray her resolve in the matter. When a pursuer leaves thirty messages for a woman who doesn't return his calls, and then she finally gives in and calls him back, no matter what she says, he learns that the cost of reaching her is leaving thirty messages. For this type of man, almost any contact will be seen as progress.

The way to stop contact is to *stop contact.* But some victims are worried that by not responding they'll provoke him, so they try to "let him down easy." The result often is that he believes she is emotionally invested, that she really likes him but just doesn't know it yet.

When a teenaged girl rejects a boy with a crush, and he says, "But don't you think I'm cute?" and she says, "Yes, but I don't want a boyfriend right now," the young man hears only the words "yes" and "right now." To him, this means she *will* want to be in a relationship later. If she says, "You're a great guy and you have a lot to offer, but I'm not the girl for you; my head's just not in the right place these days," he hears: "She really likes me; it's just that she's confused. I've got to prove to her that she's the girl for me."

The rejection *should* be: "I don't want to be in a relationship *with you.*" Unless it's just that clear—and sometimes even when it is that clear—he doesn't get it, or doesn't believe it. When a woman explains *why* she is rejecting, this type of man will challenge each reason she offers. Conditional rejection doesn't work, because he'll just change to fit the conditions.

The excellent opening scene of the film *Tootsie*, illustrates this so well. Dustin Hoffman plays an actor reading lines at an audition. A voice from offstage tells him he isn't getting the part.

VOICE: The reading was fine, you're just the wrong height.

HOFFMAN: Oh, I can be taller.

VOICE: No, you don't understand. We're looking for somebody shorter.

HOFFMAN: Oh, well look, I don't have to be this tall. See. I'm wearing lifts. I can be shorter.

VOICE: I know, but really . . . we're looking for somebody different.

HOFFMAN: I can be different.

VOICE: We're looking for somebody *else*, okay?

This last line offers no reasons and begs no negotiations. But women in this culture are virtually prohibited from speaking it. They are taught that speaking it clearly and early will lead to unpopularity, banishment, anger, and maybe even violence.

Women are taught to be nice when they are rejecting, and men are taught to be nice when they are pursuing. The result often is that men and women aren't speaking the same language. This is most alarmingly expressed by the millions of fathers (and mothers), older brothers (and sisters), movies and television shows that taught many men that "when she says no, that isn't what she means."

Someday, Western culture may evolve to the point that NO means NO. Then, perhaps, we won't get our definitions from fantasy entertainment, but from the dictionary, the one book where all definitions of the word are clear. I have yet to read a dictionary that defines NO in any of these ways:

MAYBE	I'M CHANGING MY MIND
GIVE ME TIME	KEEP THE PRESSURE ON
NOT SURE	TRY AGAIN
YES	PROVE YOU LOVE ME

Conversely, I have seen many movies that used one or more of these interpretations of NO—and some that used them all. Men in the movies—and very often in real life—apply their own twist to the word, projecting onto the speaker any number of conflicting emotions and intentions.

In *The Graduate,* Dustin Hoffman applies a courting strategy that is at the core of every stalking case: *persistence.* His pursuit of marrying Katherine Ross became the model for a generation of young men. In the film, Hoffman shows up outside her classes, he refuses to accept NO when she declines to marry him. He does not give up. When he learns she is going to marry someone else, Hoffman uses stalking techniques to find her. He pretends to be a family friend and a priest to learn the name of the church. Ultimately, he breaks into the church just seconds after Katherine Ross is pronounced the wife of another man.

And what happens? She runs off with Dustin Hoffman, leaving her family and new husband behind her. Also left behind was the notion that a woman should be heard, the notion that NO means NO, the notion that a woman has a right to decide who will be in her life.

The belief that persistence will succeed has permeated our society. The belief that if you stay with it, even if you offend her, even if you treat her like trash (and sometimes *because* you've treated her like trash), even if she's in another relationship, you'll eventually get the girl. Just stay with it, persistence will win the war *Against All Odds*—another movie which proves the rule, by the way, just like *The Heartbreak Kid, Flashdance, 10, The Piano,* and many other movies about hard-won romance.

But there's another movie that bears mention: *Casablanca* with Humphrey Bogart and Ingrid Bergman. It is such a shining example of *reason* in the movies. A politically motivated woman, dedicated to her idealistic husband, amazingly *doesn't* choose the owner of the sleazy gambling joint, and does choose to stay with her husband. Even though Bogart helps her decide, the key word here is CHOOSE. That's what women are rarely allowed to do. Typically, they are swept along by the desires and intent of the man.

Back to our definition of NO. Though it will doubtless appear harsh to some, here's an unconditional rejection: "No matter what you may have assumed up to now, and no matter for what reason you assumed it, I have no romantic interest in you whatsoever. I am certain I never will. I expect that, knowing this, you will put your attention elsewhere, which I understand, because that's what I intend to do."

There is only one appropriate reaction to a rejection like this: acceptance. However he communicates it, the basic concept would ideally be: "I hear you. I understand, and although I am disappointed, I certainly will respect your decision." This is the only appropriate reaction. Unfortunately, there are hundreds of inappropriate reactions, and while they take many forms, their basic message is, "I do not accept your decision."

If a man who scares a woman debates, doubts, negotiates, or attempts to change her mind, it should be recognized for what it is. It should be clear that:

a) She made the right decision about this man. Instead of her resolve being challenged by his response, it should be strengthened.

b) She obviously would not want a relationship with someone who does not hear what she says and who does not recognize her feelings.

c) If he failed to understand a message this clear and explicit, imagine how he would have reacted to anything ambiguous, or to being "let down easy."

Students in that ideal high school class I envision would learn all this and could choose a different cultural casting. It's true that ours has long been a patriarchal society; it's true that the criminal justice system is way behind the criminal; it's true that the media is motivated by money, not morals. We can't change any of that easily, but each of us can change ourselves, so that we model a new type of male/female interaction for our children.

And maybe it will get better for the next generation, for victims of stalking, and for those who need never become victims at all.

Sign Language

Learning to convey and accept messages about interpersonal rights and boundaries is not only a lesson for the young. In a changing society such as ours, adults also often find themselves struggling to interpret the parameters of male/female relationships. Is communication between men and women, as linguist Deborah Tannen has suggested, truly a case of "cross-cultural" communication, speaking across what almost amounts to two separate languages? Do expectations and interpretations really differ so widely between the sexes?

Social psychologists have turned these questions to their study of one particular area of contemporary concern—sexual harassment in the workplace—in an attempt to understand the causes of the growing levels of inappropriate behavior in this area. Some of their findings might point to possible clues about the rising instances of stalking and other instances of sexual invasion or abuse outside the workplace as well.

Most interesting is the current application of what is termed "misperception theory" to male/female interactions, both at the workplace and in other social settings. In studies where male and female respondents were asked to view videotapes of actors engaging in neutral, professional scenarios—an office manager speaking with an employee, say, or a professor discussing a grade with a student—researchers found that male respondents tended far more to misinterpret neutral or merely friendly professional interactions as *sexual interactions.* In particular, women's friendliness was more frequently misperceived as a sexual "come-on," and completely neutral gestures were misinterpreted as being sexually motivated cues of the woman's interest.

Such differences in interpretation between men and women, moreover, are not limited to the workplace. One study examining social interactions among college-aged students found that 72 percent of women and 60 percent of men had experienced some incident of misperception or misinterpretation about sexuality in social interactions. In most of these cases, verbally clearing up the misunderstanding solved the situation. In others, however, the misperception escalated into sexual coercion, intimidation, or rape.

What makes initial misperceptions about interest and sexual availability move beyond mere misunderstanding into possible harassment, coercion, or sexual violence? Do some individuals have a higher propensity for misreading neutral interactions as sexual? Social psychologist Margaret Stockdale has studied such cases extensively, and her findings show that certain subjects not only have a greater tendency to misinterpret situations, but also to carry out their misperceptions in inappropriate ways.

Stockdale finds this tendency is based in part on the subject's preset attitudes about men and women. These include a belief in sexual aggressiveness—that is, that sexual relationships between men and women are innately adversarial and unequal, that men are *supposed* to conquer women, and that women *should* submit. Other attitudes that come into play include the belief that women should continue to hold traditional roles, and that it is a man's place to assume positions of authority in the workplace and continue to be "king of his castle" at home. Finally, this individual sees and enjoys women more as sexual objects rather than as human beings, friends, and companions.

This "sexual aggression belief system," according to Stockdale, results in far higher instances of sexual misperception. Even in completely neutral interactions, these individuals view women as seductresses, coming on to men, and wanting it, however subtly. Much like the selective hearing process of the person with inappropriate attachments, it is as if the situation *must* be made to fit into a prearranged set of expectations, despite any evidence to the contrary. As a result, even ambiguous or innocent actions and gestures are interpreted in a sexual manner—and often, subsequently, as a license to pursue. These individuals also report a high level of tolerance for sexual harassment, and even, in some studies, a high level of tolerance for rape. Indeed, the continuum between such "scripting" of expectations and the justification for sexual coercion is not difficult to trace.

It is important to note that these individuals are not sick, abnormal, or psychotic; belief systems about sexual aggression are socialized beliefs—learned behaviors and attitudes that, despite some changes in our thinking, are often more widely held than we would like to admit. Moreover, these are not only "old-guard" attitudes held by adults. In an astonishing study of sixth, seventh, and eighth graders, when asked whether they felt a man had the right to force sex with a woman for whom he had bought a ten-dollar dinner, 33 percent of these young respondents answered yes! Sexual aggressiveness, it seems, is a set of attitudes and lessons that continues to be passed on to our children. It may be a kind of cultural "script" that subtly condones and continues to lay the groundwork for inappropriate and invasive relationships between men and women.

Workplace Violence

The workplace is not only the site of sexual harassment, but is becoming an arena for violence of all forms. As our earlier chapters indicated, often the workplace becomes the target of choice for the stalker, as a place where he knows his victim must appear. But stalking also occurs between employees and employers, among co-workers, and across gender boundaries. And it is joined by an alarming rise in other forms of threat and assault in the workplace. In a recent study by the Northwestern National Life Insurance Company—reportedly the first comprehensive examination of violence and fear in the workplace—it was discovered that 25 percent of full-time workers in America had experienced some form of harassment, intimidation, or assault on the job in one year. According to NWNL findings:

> More than 2 million Americans were victims of physical attack at the workplace during the past year. Another 6 million American workers were threatened, and 16 million were harassed. Between July 1992 and

July 1993, one out of four full-time workers was harassed, threatened, or attacked on the job.

To what can we attribute this surge in workplace violence? What are some of the motivating factors that are putting workers at such risk for their health and safety? How can we effectively address and prevent instances of threat on the job, including the danger of stalking? The workplace looms large in most of our lives, as a place in which we seek to establish our identities, be valued as members of a community, receive rewards and recognition for our efforts, and create social bonds that validate who we are. We spend an enormous amount of our lifetime at the workplace; consequently, its atmosphere can be a powerful influence on how we perceive ourselves and how we feel about our lives in general. Workplace environments that present conflict or alienation, that offer only criticism without support, that rob us of control or identity can quickly instill a deep dissatisfaction and stress.

Researchers have discovered that rates of workplace violence decrease dramatically when employers follow a number of guidelines to create more supportive work environments. These include promoting harmony and teamwork among employees, allowing employees greater control over their work, providing training in how to address and solve interpersonal conflicts, affording adequate protection and security for workers, and having an effective grievance process in place. Although no formula can completely prevent the occurrence of workplace violence, corporations are beginning to take these statistics very seriously, and many are acting not only to improve their existing security systems, but also to address ways in which the work environment might help stop dissatisfaction and stress even before it escalates to violence.

Drive-by Shootings on the Information Superhighway

While the alienation of the workplace may be one issue to address, our society is currently moving into a far wider network of interpersonal communication that may present many of the same problems as other arenas for social interaction. There are currently over five million subscribers to on-line information and communication services such as Prodigy, CompuServe, and America Online, and an estimated 30,000 to 40,000 computer bulletin boards throughout the United States alone. This huge and growing electronic network truly represents a new frontier in interpersonal communication as we near the twenty-first century. But as with any frontier, this "Information Superhighway" is beginning to have its own share of renegades and outlaws.

"You name a crime in the penal code, it happens on-line," says Detective Frank Clark of the Fresno, California, Police Department, who holds a national reputation for investigating computer crime. More than 1,300 incidents were reported on the Internet system in 1993 alone, and the FBI reports that approximately 90 percent of all computer crime occurs on the Internet airwaves. Those crimes include soliciting children for sex, peddling child pornography, fraud, theft, harassment—and even stalking.

The most notorious "electronic stalker," and the first apprehended, used the code name "Vito" to terrorize and threaten a series of victims across the country in 1993 and 1994. Laurie Powell was one such victim. A North Carolina mother, Laurie initially joined the network to communicate with other parents on the topic of raising children. Instead, she began receiving harassing messages from a mysterious user who simply called himself Vito. Soon these annoying communications escalated to graphic pornographic threats against her and her young son, which the stalker distributed widely to other users across the Internet system—then attempts to ruin her credit electronically and accost her friends and acquaintances through the system as well. Finally, what began to emerge were more serious hints that he intended to do her harm. It became clear to Laurie that Vito knew intimate, real life details about her and her activities—her travel plans, her whereabouts, the name of her employer, her address. Laurie was convinced he was beginning to follow her with terrifying closeness, and that his threats against her life were very real. "I am frightened," she told the media in March 1994. "This guy knows my name, where I live, and what I do for a living. . . . He has made it his business to find out everything about me."

New Yorker Larry Greenberg was another of Vito's victims. Not only was Greenberg subjected to a series of on-line insults and graphic ethnic hate mail, the stalker also sent a defamatory fax to Greenberg's employer, falsely accusing Greenberg of being a child molester and convicted rapist. Vito also disseminated messages throughout the Prodigy service, claiming that Greenberg was infected with the HIV virus—all bizarre untruths designed simply to terrorize and disrupt his target's life. Calling the stalker a "psychopath," Greenberg commented, "I am afraid that he's going to come out from behind the computer and hurt somebody."

It was only recently that Detective Frank Clark, after months of investigation, was able to crack the case of Vito—who, he believes, may have been stalking many more victims under a number of computer aliases and from a variety of locations in different cities. The suspect, a part-time teacher, was finally apprehended in Fresno, California. When police searched the man's affluent suburban home, they discovered over 180 separate subscriptions to the on-line service, evidently Vito's way of escaping detection and eluding authorities.

Other victims of electronic terrorism abound. Thirty-seven-year-old Carolyn Fleming of Texas found herself the target of threats and insults after she innocently posted a message asking for information about used cars. He stalker even sent a lurid message to Fleming's nine-year-old daughter, describing his desire to sexually assault the child. Another victim, a fourteen-year-old girl, was driven off the network by repeated and invasive sexual messages from an anonymous user. Other children find themselves the targets of sexual solicitation or graphic pornographic images and descriptions that seem to be able to travel the Information Superhighway unchecked, uncensored, and largely unpunished.

For the many who initially welcomed this new technology as a way to create a truly global community, opening the lines for friendship and information exchange across the world, this darker side of cyberspace comes as quite a shock. But perhaps culture cannot so easily leave behind its deviants and criminals, even as it optimistically advances toward a new age. The anonymity of electronic communications, combined with its potential ability to invade even the most private areas of the user's life, may be providing precisely the blend of secrecy, immunity, and access in which a crime like stalking can continue to flourish. It is sad to admit that even here we must learn to guard ourselves and our children from the potential harm that just one unmonitored contact can impose.

Breaking the Silence

To what, then, can we attribute the range of invasions and threats posed by the crime of stalking? Are its sources environmental, in the increased access others have to our lives, the paradoxical new closeness of the information age? Is it the alienation of the workplace and the stress of modern society that drives individuals to crimes of harassment, revenge, or violence? Or must we look deeper, to cultural messages about male/female relationships and the violation of personal boundaries, that seem to afford certain members of society the license to pursue? Could the solution lie in enhanced education for the young, clearer messages about self-esteem and the parameters of healthy and unhealthy attachments? How pervasive is the influence of the media on our mentality, as it promotes both a cult of idolatry and celebrity, and appears to glamorize violence as a solution to interpersonal conflict? Has our world simply become so anonymous, and our need for identity so great, that it drives some to the twisted validation of crime?

Human nature is complex, and there may never be a formula for uncovering the sources of deviant behavior—particularly in regards to a crime like stalking, which can take so many forms and cover such a wide spectrum of profiles and behaviors. To the extent that we can, however, we need to recognize the ways in which our society may contribute to and collude with inappropriate and damaging invasions into the lives of others. Laws alone will not change the future directions our culture takes. Real change involves an adjustment in attitudes and beliefs, a new look at how individual rights and personal boundaries are defined in today's world. The crime of stalking shows, at the very least, how much we have left to learn about each other and ourselves.

ENDNOTES

INTRODUCTION

1 *Rebecca Schaeffer died within minutes, of a massive bullet wound to the heart.* "Investigative Reports/ Stalking: The Assassins Among Us," *Arts and Entertainment Network,* October 29, 1993.

2 *These behaviors have existed in our society for a long time, but we're just now starting to put a label on them.* Lane, John. Ibid.

3 *. . . items like . . . the head of a coyote.* Dietz, Park Elliott, M.D., M.P.H., Ph.D., et al. "Threatening and Otherwise Inappropriate Letters to Hollywood Celebrities," *Journal of Forensic Sciences,* Vol. 36, No. 1, January 1991, pp. 197–8.

3 *. . . the high number of cases in which stalking victims are ordinary citizens.* Interview with Gavin de Becker, December 23, 1993.

3 *. . . all accidents combined, including motor vehicle accidents.* Biden, Senator Joseph R. Opening remarks, Hearing Before the Committee on the Judiciary, United States Senate, One Hundred Sec-

ond Congress, Second Session on S. 2922, September 29, 1992, p. 1.

The number of people who died in 1990 due to accidents, including automobile accidents, was 91,983. *Statistical Abstract of the United States* (Lanham, MD: Bernan Press, 1994), p. 98.

3 . . . *one in twenty American women will become victims of stalking at some time in their lives.* Puente, Maria. "Legislators Tackling the Terror of Stalking," *USA Today,* July 21, 1992, p. 9A.

3 *Some experts estimate that 75 to 80 percent of stalking cases emerge from domestic situations.* National Organization for Victim Assistance statistics; cited in Lewin, Tamar. "New Laws Address Old Problem: The Terror of a Stalker's Threats," *New York Times,* February 8, 1993, A1, B10.

3 . . . *30 percent of female homicide victims in 1990 were killed by intimate partners. Crime in the United States, Uniform Crime Reports for the United States,* 1990 (Washington, D.C.: Federal Bureau of Investigation, U.S. Department of Justice, 1991), p. 13.

3 . . . *some authorities put the number as high as 90 percent.* Micklem, Ruth. Virginians Against Domestic Violence, cited in Beck, Melinda. "Murderous Obsession," *Newsweek,* July, 13, 1992, pp. 60 & ff.

5 . . . *known to more than* one billion *people.* Interview with Gavin de Becker, December 23, 1993.

CHAPTER 1

9 Header quotes from "Investigative Reports/ Stalking: The Assassins Among Us," *Arts and Entertainment Network,* October 29, 1993.

10 . . . *Brian Framstead, who had also assaulted their twenty-one-month-old child, sending both of them*

to the hospital. Anderson, Janine, "Police Link OC Deaths to Persecution," *The Orange County Register,* March 11, 1990, p. J4.

10 *"What does he have to do," she cried, "shoot me?"* Corwin, Miles. "When the Law Can't Protect," *Los Angeles Times,* May 8, 1993, p. A1 & ff.

10 . . . *recalls Lieutenant John Lane of the Los Angeles Police Department.* Interview with Lieutenant John Lane, Threat Management Unit, Los Angeles Police Department, December 23, 1993.

10 . . . *as many attacks on public figures by people with mental disorders had occurred in the previous twenty years as had occurred in the preceding 175 years.* Dietz, Park Elliott. "Public Figures as Victims of Harassment, Threats, and Attacks," presented by Gavin de Becker to the National Conference of Personal Managers, October 18, 1989. Cited in John C. Lane, "Threat Management Fills Void in Police Services," *The Police Chief,* August 1992, p. 27.

12 *"I'm not just coming after your possessions, you'll be the next thing damaged."* Connelly, Michael. "Ex-Boyfriend Jailed Under Stalking Law," *Los Angeles Times,* June 10, 1991, p. B1 & ff.

12 *Bleakley was sentenced to one year in jail and six months in a rehabilitation facility.* Quinn, James. "Man is Sentenced for 'Stalking' Ex-Girlfriend," *Los Angeles Times,* October 25, 1991, p. B3.

12 . . . *a terrifying standoff with police SWAT teams.* Streshinsky, Shirley. "The Stalker and His Prey," *Glamour,* August 1992, pp. 238–67.

13 *That expression of what she'd been through, you could see it on the faces of the members of the committee.* "Investigative Reports/Stalking: The Assassins Among Us," *Arts and Entertainment Network,* October 29, 1993.

14 . . . *burning a hole in the ceiling of my mobile home. The list goes on and on.* Written testimony of "Judi M.," State of Montana Senate Judiciary Committee Hearings, March 8, 1993.

14 . . . *not knowing if my abuser or any [of the abuser's] friends might be outside.* Written testimony of anonymous victim, State of Hawaii Hearings on HB 2610—Relating to Harassment, February 3, 1992.

15 *What do you say to your child when they ask you a question like that?* Written testimony of Sherry Schunk, State of Hawaii Hearings on HB 2610—Relating to Harassment, February 3, 1992.

15 *My whole life has changed.* Testimony of Erin Tavegia, State of Connecticut House of Representatives Judiciary Committee Hearings, March 23, 1992.

16 . . . *very often he was up there at the corner, never saying anything, just staring at us.* Testimony of RoseAlyce Thayer, State of Connecticut House of Representatives Judiciary Committee Hearings, March 23, 1992.

17 . . . *he shot her to death. . . . The list goes on and on.* Testimony of Representative Tom Homer, Third Reading of HR Bill 2677, a Bill for an Act to Amend the Criminal Code of 1961, May 20, 1992.

17 . . . *the repetitive, often escalating nature of crimes like stalking.* National Institute of Justice, "Project to Develop a Model Antistalking Code for States," National Criminal Justice Association, October 1993, pp. 12–13.

19 *Would you be willing to sit back and wait for that to happen to your son or your daughter?* Testimony of Sandra Poland, Hearing Before the Committee on the Judiciary, United States Senate, One Hundred Second Congress, Second Session, on S. 2922, "A Bill to

Assist the States in the Enactment of Legislation to Address the Criminal Act of Stalking Other Persons," September 28, 1992, pp. 34–38.

21 . . . *continue for at least thirty days, but rejected these approaches.* Cahill, David. "Legislature Gives Stalking Victims New Protections," *MTLA Quarterly,* Vol. 27, No. 1, Winter 1993, p. 1.

21 . . . *which could even be "separated by an hour or less."* Ibid., p. 28.

21 *". . . two or more acts [must be] separated by at least 36 hours, but [occur] within one year."* Ark. Stat. Ann. 5–71–229(a), (b)&(c), 5–13–301, 5–71–208 & 209.

22 . . . *behavior that is "willful," "knowing," or "purposeful,"* National Institute of Justice, "Project to Develop . . ." p. 21.

22 . . . *California penalizes a course of conduct that is* "willful, malicious *and repeated,"* California Penal Code, 646.9.

22 . . . *Washington prohibits "intentionally and repeatedly" following another.* State of Washington, Engrossed Substitute House Bill 2702 (52nd Legislature, 1992 Regular Session), p. 1.

24 . . . *of those seven cases, five stalking victims were men stalked by women.* Zona, Michael A., M.D., Kaushal K. Sharma, M.D., John Lane, Lt., "A Comparative Study of Erotomanic and Obsessional Subjects in a Forensic Sample," *Journal of Forensic Sciences,* (date)

25 *Marchant, who had previously threatened his wife, later killed himself at his father's home.* "Husband kills wife, her boyfriend, self," AP, July 5, 1994.

25 *Wilhite later killed himself.* Mann, Charles C. "The Walking Wounded," *Self,* August 1994, pp. 142–45.

25 *Ultimately the couple's marriage dissolved under the weight of their ordeal.* Ibid., p. 158.

26 *He, like Kenneth Marchant and David Wilhite, later committed suicide.* Miller, Bryan, "Thou Shalt Not Stalk," *Chicago Tribune,* April 18, 1993, p. 14 & ff.

26 *". . . we walk right through them, unaware that the season has turned to winter."* Mann, Charles C. "The Walking Wounded," p. 146.

CHAPTER 2

28 Header quote. Bardo, Robert. "Investigative Reports/Stalking: The Assassins Among Us," *A&E Network,* October 29, 1993, and Dietz, Park Elliott, "Threatening and Otherwise Inappropriate Letters to Hollywood Celebrities," *Journal of Forensic Sciences,* Vol. 36, No. 1, January 1991, p. 205.

29 *To me, my victim wasn't a stranger.* "Investigative Reports/Stalking: The Assassins Among Us," *A&E Network,* October 29, 1993.

29 *. . . she broke into his car and drove it around for several days.* "Letterman Nemesis Arrested for 8th Time," *Orlando Sentinel,* July 8, 1998, p. A2; and Axthelm, Pete. "An Innocent Life, A Heartbreaking Death," *People,* July 31, 1989, p. 66.

29 *. . . a woman he believes to be confused and in need of help. USA Today,* December 14, 1993.

30 *. . . Evans has gone into hiding and will not disclose where she lives.* Ellis, David, et. al. "Nowhere to Hide," *People,* May 17, 1993, pp. 66–68.

31 *This evil world, wrote Jackson, was too ugly for such a "beautiful angel."* Saldana, Theresa. *Beyond Survival.* (Toronto: Bantam Books, 1986), p. 12.

31 . . . *even from prison he has repeatedly threatened to kill Saldana when he is released.* Bacon, Doris. "When Fans Turn Into Fanatics, Nervous Celebs Call For Help From Security Expert Gavin de Becker," *People,* February 12, 1990, p. 106.

32 *Altogether his staff has assessed some 16,000 people who may pose a threat to clients.* Correspondence with Gavin de Becker, April 6, 1994.

32 *"Nowhere in history," says de Becker, "could you completely 'know' someone like you can now 'know' Johnny Carson."* Axthelm, Pete, et. al. "An Innocent Life: A Heartbreaking Death," *People,* July 31, 1989, p. 66.

32 . . . *de Becker and his staff have collected over 300,000 bizarre letters and "gifts" sent to stars by clearly obsessed fans.* De Becker, April 6, 1994.

32 . . . *containers of urine or semen, dead animals, even human body parts.* Dietz, "Threatening and Otherwise Inappropriate Letters to Celebrities," pp. 197–98; De Becker, April 6, 1994.

33 *In the course of about a year, Fox received* 6,200 *such letters from Ledbetter.* De Becker, April 6, 1994.

33 . . . *otherwise, she claimed, Fox would die.* Toufexis, Anastasia. "Fatal Obsession with the Stars," *Time,* July 31, 1989, p. 43.

34 . . . *attempting to telephone as well as write.* Dietz, "Threatening and Otherwise Inappropriate Letters to Celebrities," p. 208.

34 *Then he wrote, "We'll see Jesus together."* Miller, Bryan. "Thou Shalt Not Stalk," *Chicago Tribune,* April 18, 1993, pp. 14 & ff.

35 *". . . I'm not sure I want to go back into public life and risk going through that again."* Ibid.

37 . . . *Valerie has since learned that Dave has returned to the area and has been asking about her.* Interview with Valerie Martin, May 10, 1994.

37 *When confronted, however, she admitted to making the calls and agreed to undergo counseling.* Interview with John Lane, March 1993.

38 *". . . members of Congress receive a steady stream of hostile and inappropriate mail, telephone calls and visitors."* Dietz, Park Elliott, M.D., et. al. "Threatening and Otherwise Inappropriate Letters to Members of the United States Congress," *Journal of Forensic Sciences,* Vol. 36, No. 5, September 1991, p. 1446.

38 . . . *photographs of the subject masturbating, and containers of blood or semen.* Ibid., p. 1464.

38 *"I am sure," he continued, "[that] millions of people witnessed this occurence."* Ibid., p. 1451.

39 *". . . slam—and if I have to slam—I'll destroy them all."* Ibid., p. 1450.

39 . . . *stabbed herself in the eye with a pen while composing her letter.* Ibid., p. 1451.

39 . . . *letter writers who threatened a member of Congress were statistically less likely to approach that public figure.* Ibid., p. 1460.

40 *At that moment, Kathleen recalls, Tom snapped.* Testimony of Kathleen Krueger, "Hearing Before the Committee on the Judiciary," March 17, 1993, p. 24.

40 *One day Humphrey himself appeared and gripped the startled Kathleen in a long, eerie hug.* Ellis, David, et. al. "Nowhere to Hide," *People,* May 17, 1993, pp. 63–64.

40 . . . *I've hired a killer to put a .22-caliber to your head while you lay sleeping next to your wife.* Kathleen Krueger testimony, p. 25.

41 *"Then you'll know there is life beyond the flesh."* "On Thin Ice," *People,* March 30, 1992, p. 77.

41 . . . *his aim was not as deadly as his intent, and Seles survived the attack.* Ellis, David, et al. "Nowhere to Hide," *People,* May 17, 1993, p. 71.

42 *The children's room was heated by an open grate, through which they had full view of the parents' activities.* Rubenstein, Bruce. "Stalker Could Go Free: Ralph Nau's Case Reveals Flaws in System," *Illinois Legal Times,* April 1992.

42 *"It was my first and last time in bed with a girl."* Ibid.

43 *. . . often amounting to several letters a day. Chicago Tribune,* August 20, 1989.

43 *. . . another woman, "Maria," was watching over these letter-writing interchanges and would punish any unruly correspondent.* Rubenstein, Bruce. "How Ralph Nau Terrorized Hollywood Celebrities: At War with a Witch Named Maria," *Illinois Legal Times,* May 1992.

43 *Nau set out for Los Angeles to do just that.* Ibid., and Horton, Sue. "Secret Admirer," *L.A. Weekly.*

43 *. . . they were able to surveille Nau's room, which appeared to be "a shrine to Olivia Newton-John."* Rubenstein, May 1992.

44 *"They should all be six feet under."* Ibid.

44 *. . . whom Nau believed it was his responsibility to kill next. Chicago Tribune,* August 20, 1989.

44 *In 1983, Nau went so far as to travel to Australia, believing that Newton-John was there.* Correspondence with Gavin de Becker.

44 *Nau was comitting acts of bestiality with his dog.* Rubenstein, *Illinois Legal Times,* June 1992.

44 *. . . I swung at it with the ax and hit it in the head."* Ibid.

44 *. . . Nau was diagnosed as suffering from paranoid schizophrenia. Chicago Tribune,* August 20, 1989.

44 . . . *an illness whose symptoms can include severely disordered thinking and behavior. Diagnostic and Statistical Manual of Mental Disorders (DSM-III-R)* (Washington, D.C.: American Psychiatric Association, 1987), pp. 188–89.

45 . . . *and he was writing to Nadia Comaneci.* Rubenstein, June 1992.

45 *Nau has written to Marie Osmond, Madonna . . . People,* July 31, 1989, p. 64.

45 . . . *Heather Locklear, and Whitney Houston. USA Today,* August 24, 1989.

45 . . . *sent him messages through* Wheel of Fortune puzzles. UPI, December 12, 1989.

45 . . . *communicated with him via the television.* UPI, June 2, 1990.

45 . . . *others spoke to him through their album covers.* UPI, March 1, 1991.

45 . . . *claimed to be the father of Farrah Fawcett's child, and to be engaged to Marie Osmond. People,* September 25, 1989, p. 113.

46 *On each screen, Perry had drawn a staring eye. People,* February 12, 1990, pp. 105–106; correspondence with Gavin de Becker.

46 . . . *persecutory, somatic, jealous, grandiose, erotomanic. DSM-III-R,* p. 199.

46 . . . *relates to feelings of love given to and received from another. Comprehensive Textbook of Psychiatry,* Vol. 1, Fifth Edition (Baltimore: Williams & Wilkins, 1989), p. 825.

47 . . . *go to extraordinary lengths to find and make contact with the loved one.* Zona, Michael A., M.D. "A Comparative Study of Erotomanic and Obsessional Subjects in a Forensic Sample," *Journal of Forensic Sciences,* Vol. 38, No. 4, July 1993, p. 894.

47 . . . *she believed the King to be signaling her.*

Enoch, M. David and W.H. Trethowan, *Uncommon Psychiatric Syndromes* (Bristol: John Wright & Sons, 1979), pp. 22–23.

47 *"Prognosis," writes Zona, "is considered poor for these individuals."* Zona, Michael A., M.D. Op. cit., p. 895.

47 . . . *a few erotomanics have responded positively to the psychiatric medication Pimozide.* Ibid.

47 . . . *other medications ultimately helped dispel her erotomanic feelings.* Munro, Alistair, M.D., James V. O'Brien, M.B., and Dawn Ross, M.D. "Two Cases of 'Pure' or 'Primary' Erotomania Successfully Treated with Pimozide," *Canadian Journal of Psychiatry,* Vol. 30, No. 8, December 1985, p. 620.

48 . . . *they increase the likelihood that their harassing behavior will bring them into contact with the police.* Interview with John Lane, December 23, 1993.

48 . . . *were the most likely to seek out a celebrity at home and to stalk that celebrity.* Zona, p. 899.

48 . . . *the delusional phone caller continued to attempt to make contact even after undergoing psychiatric counseling.* Interview with John Lane, March 1994.

50 . . . *"a pattern of maladaptive behavior"—a personality disorder.* Interview with Robert Fein, April 12, 1994.

50 . . . *but individuals in each of the forms are likely to share some common characteristics. The Columbia University College of Physicians and Surgeons Complete Home Guide to Mental Health,* Kass, Frederic I., M.D., John M. Oldham, M.D., and Herbert Pardes, M.D., eds. (New York: Henry Holt & Co., 1992), pp. 185–87.

50 . . . *they are also apt to have difficult personal relationships. Comprehensive Textbook of Psychiatry,*

Vol. 2, Fifth Edition, Harold I. Kaplan, M.D., and Benjamin J. Sadock, M.D., eds. (Baltimore: Williams & Wilkins, 1989), p. 1352.

50 . . . *"not so much troubled themselves [as] troublesome to others."* Bruno, Frank J. *The Family Mental Health Encyclopedia* (New York: John Wiley & Sons, 1989), pp. 292–93.

51 . . . *he said that his name and phone number were in Schaeffer's date book on the day he murdered her.* Tharp, Mike. "In the mind of a stalker," *U.S. News & World Report,* February 17, 1992, p. 30.

52 . . . *those words represented more favorable contact with a woman than he'd ever known in his life.* Interview with Gavin de Becker, December 23, 1993.

CHAPTER 3

53 Header quotes. Interview with Julie Owens, December 3, 1993, and Stephanie Sund, "Sally Jessie Raphael Show," January 5, 1994.

54 *In 1984 the Surgeon General declared domestic violence as this nation's "number one health problem."* Cited in "Domestic Violence and Stalking Statistics," publication of Victim Protection Services, Denver, CO.

55 . . . *beaten with hammers, broom sticks, gun butts, and metal pipes, and thrown from moving cars. Violence Against Women: A Week in the Life of America,* A Majority Staff Report, October 1992, pp. 3–25.

55 . . . *they insist that their partner "generally account for every moment of her time."* Walker, Lenore E. *The Battered Woman* (New York: Harper & Row, 1979), p. 38.

55 *Finally, Teresa left the relationship.* Ellis, David, et.al. "Nowhere to Hide," *People,* May 17, 1993, p. 72.

56 . . . *killed Teresa and two co-workers, then killed himself.* Ibid.

56 . . . *have a 75 percent higher chance of being killed by their partners . . . Factsheet on Domestic Violence,* The Domestic Violence Project, Inc., SAFE House, Ann Arbor, MI, 1990.

56 . . . *experts report that 90 percent of women who were killed by their husbands in 1991 were stalked prior to being murdered.* Micklem, Ruth. Virginians Against Domestic Violence. Cited in Melinda Beck, "Murderous Obsession," *Newsweek,* July 13, 1992, pp. 60 & ff.

57 *". . . to tell her what to do and where to go."* Interview with Julie Owens, December 3, 1993.

57 *"I have the right to enforce this any way I see fit."* Ibid.

57 *"I'm a hunter."* Interview with Kathryn Chaney, December 10, 1993.

58 *"No! This is war."* Johnson, Allen. "Diary of a Stalker: How I Killed My Wife," *Chicago Tribune,* June 26, 1992, p. 1.

58 *". . . oh of course see her sweat it out and die."* Ibid., p. 14.

58 *". . . 'So lucky Connie . . . I'll be back.'"* Ibid.

58 *". . . she fell like a rock."* Ibid.

59 . . . *a "male emotional funnel."* Stordeur, Richard A., and Richard Stille. *Ending Men's Violence Against Their Partners: One Road to Peace* (Newbury Park, CA: Sage Publications, 1989), p. 39.

59 *Others who witness—or feel the effects of—his rage may experience it as impulsive and erratic.* Ibid.

59 . . . *they believe far more often that others are hostile or rejecting them.* Ibid.

59 . . . *in and out of their immediate families—as being unassertive.* Ibid., p. 40.

60 . . . *instead projecting blame onto other people and external factors, such as alcohol or stress.* Ibid., pp. 41–42.

60 . . . *even suicidal in an attempt to prevent what he sees as an abandonment.* Ibid., p. 45.

60 . . . *had her restraining order in her purse when she was shot.* Corwin, Miles. "When the Law Can't Protect," *Los Angeles Times,* May 8, 1993, p. A1 & ff.

61 . . . *Dorescenzi had shot Beverly Mertz over twenty times, once even stopping to reload.* Jones, J. Harry. "Slaying Suspect's Former Wives, Girlfriends Tell of Stalking, Terror," *San Diego Union-Tribune,* March 9, 1993, p. A1.

61 . . . *then turned the gun against himself.* Lardner, George. "The Stalking of Kristin," *Washington Post,* November 22, 1992, pp. C1–10.

63 . . . *"end up going back because he won't leave her alone."* Interview with Linda van den Bossche, February 3, 1994.

63 . . . *has encountered literally hundreds of stalking cases among its clients.* Interview with Kathryn Chaney, December 10, 1993.

63 . . . *so many domestic-violence-related stalking cases they were "too numerous to count."* Interview with Julie Owens, December 3, 1993.

63 . . . *"when the woman first leaves the battering."* Interview with Bonnie Gainer, December 10, 1993.

64 . . . *leaving themselves particularly vulnerable when the stalker resurfaces and the terror begins again.* Collier, Wendy. "The Cycle of Stalking," publication of Victim Protection Services, Denver, CO.

64 . . . *claiming remorse and promising change.* Walker, pp. 56–70.

65 . . . *someone who is not yet alert to their dangerous patterns and treachery."* Collier, "The Cycle of Stalking."

65 *He kept a log on her.* Interview with "Pamela," August 12, 1993, and August 13, 1993.

66 *"People who get restraining orders get destroyed."* Ibid.

67 *But it was also a cry of relief, because I was getting away.* Ibid.

67 *"Some day, in some way, we'll be together."* Ibid.

67 *". . . 'Hi, I'm a homicidal maniac, baby.'"* Germer, Fawn. "Stalked: Victims Pull Together," *Rocky Mountain News,* March 8, 1993, p. 12.

68 *(which only serve to remove inhibitions that modify behavior).* Collier, Wendy. "Stalking: An Overview," publication of Victim Protection Services, 1993, p. 15.

75 *That's a pretty heavy statement about the current system's lack of power when it comes to protecting its citizens.* Testimony of "Erica."

CHAPTER 4

78 Header quotes. "Investigative Reports/Stalking: The Assassins Among Us," *Arts and Entertainment Network,* October 29, 1993, and Trebilcock, Bob. "I Love You to Death," *Redbook,* March 1992, p. 103.

79 . . . *or perhaps may just know about her.* Interview with Robert Fein, April 11, 1994.

79 *He was trying to "win me back."* Interview with Beverly Hannon, April 8, 1994.

80 *". . . he knew me, and figured, well, I knew him, too."* Ibid.

80 "*. . . I didn't know what he looked like at all.*" Ibid.

80 "'*. . . I'd never want to meet him in an alley at night.*'" Ibid.

81 *That was the one and only time I ever saw him.* Ibid.

81 "*. . . 'It's this guy. He's out there.'* Ibid.

82 "*. . . until I saw his obituary.*" Ibid.

82 "*. . . 'I want to marry you.'*" Interview with Jane McAllister, July 15–16, 1993.

82 *. . . unfortunately,* he *remembered* her. Ibid.

83 *And with that [the stalking] escalated and became very hostile.* Ibid.

83 *. . . passing back and forth, "constantly, day and night."* Ibid.

83 *. . . "there was nothing I could do to stop him."* Ibid.

84 "*. . . and the police won't be here when I decide to give it to you.*" Ibid.

84 *. . . I realized it was not a random survey.* Interview with "Lori," November 15, 1993.

85 *"Did you think I couldn't get your dog, babe?"* Ibid.

85 "*. . . I stay locked in the house, afraid to go out on my own.*" Correspondence from "Lori."

86 *. . . "just as a reminder that he's there."* Interview with "Lori," November 15, 1993.

86 "*. . . I ended up going out with one of his best friends, and this is when it all started.*" Interview with "Carolyn," October 14, 1993.

87 "*. . . 'You love him. You know you love him.'*" Ibid.

87 *"The car chases were the big thing," she recalls.* Ibid.

87 "*. . . They basically kidnapped me.*" Ibid.

88 . . . *who have refused—for a variety of reasons—to make an arrest. Ibid.*

88 *"It ruined our lives," she said.* Ibid.

89 *"You don't really mean it."* Interview with "Erin," August 19, 1993.

89 *". . . he rarely entered into a lot of conversation about anything other than work."* Ibid.

90 . . . *this . . . continued for over a year.* Ibid.

90 *". . . You don't know what's going to put somebody over the edge."* Ibid.

91 . . . intentional killings *in the workplace have gained prominence.* Windau, Janice and Guy Toscano, "Workplace Homicides in 1992," U.S. Department of Labor, Bureau of Labor Statistics, p. 1.

91 . . . *the leading cause of death for American* women *in the workplace.* Ibid.

92 *". . . When she did not refuse in a cordial way, I felt I had the right to bother her."* Trebilcock, Bob, p. 103.

92 *". . . to hell with the consequences."* Ibid., p. 112.

92 *He is now on death row in California.* Ibid., p. 114.

92 . . . *three thousand calls from other victims who had also suffered or were themselves suffering the threatening obsessions of stalkers.* Chew, Sally. "Hide and Stalk," *Lear's,* June 1993, p. 27.

93 *". . . And I had trouble breathing."* Safran, Claire. "A Stranger Was Stalking Our Little Girl," *Good Housekeeping,* November 1992, p. 263.

93 . . . *calling her names like "slut."* Ibid.

94 . . . *"wanted to get [his] foot in the door early."* Ibid., p. 266.

94 . . . *a variety of "stalker-type videos" depicting young children.* Hevesi, Dennis. "Tennis Coach Begged Girl to Forgive His Obsession," *New York Times,* April 29, 1993, p. B3.

95 "*. . . she was on the town swim team.*" Interview with RoseAlyce Thayer, August 31, 1993.

95 . . . "*a great treasure to us, a much-appreciated person.*" Ibid.

96 *She was frightened. She was a child.* Ibid.

96 . . . *the perpetrator himself claimed he was merely "yucking around.*" Ibid.

96 . . . *I want her to have just women teachers next year.* Ibid.

97 "*. . . I imagine he was thinking either my husband or I would not [walk up] with her.*" Testimony of RoseAlyce Thayer, State of Connecticut House of Representatives Judiciary Committee Hearings, March 23, 1992

97 "*. . . and it was hunting season.*" Interview with RoseAlyce Thayer, August 31, 1993.

97 "*Well, I guess I can stand you waiting with me.*" Ibid.

98 "*. . . I'm deciding which of my friends gets my dolls and books when the man who's been following me gets me.*" Ibid.

98 "*. . . Rachel said Caty gasped and began to cry.*" Interview with RoseAlyce Thayer, May 24, 1994.

98 *And that is why it is so ghastly.* Interview with RoseAlyce Thayer, August 31, 1993.

98 *She had been repeatedly sexually assaulted, mutilated, and beaten to death.* Ibid.

99 *It took me at least five minutes to get the knife out of her hand.* Interview with Beverly Crawford, September 1, 1993.

100 . . . *I just never let her out of my sight.* Ibid.

100 . . . *they knew where I was going so they could contact me instantly in case anything happened.* Ibid.

101 . . . *the one who had visited Beverly three days earlier.* Ibid.

102 *". . . Is it safe to go outside most days? Of course it is."* Chira, Susan. "High-Tech Safety: Will Parents Buy It?" *New York Times,* February 17, 1994, p. C6.

102 *"Most people are safe, but some are like lightning storms."* Ibid.

CHAPTER 5

121 *. . . the end point when energy reserves are depleted and breakdown occurs.* Waites, Elizabeth. *Trauma and Survival: Post-Traumatic and Dissociative Disorders in Women* (New York: Norton, 1993), p. 24.

121 *. . . a sense of hope and fairness in life; strong commitment to our goals.* Cramer, Kathryn D. *Staying on Top When Your World Turns Upside Down* (New York: Penguin, 1990), p. 35.

122 *. . . they are not crazy or alone if they experience some of the following symptoms of I.S. trauma.* Waites, E. *Trauma and Survival,* pp. 23–34.

125 *. . . when dangers are shared through support and through the victim's knowledge that she is not alone.* Ibid., p. 32.

126 *Working with others to achieve your goals constitutes the final phase of reaching out and claiming control.* Cramer, K. *Staying on Top,* p. 35.

127 *. . . recurring thoughts of death or suicide.* Copeland, Mary Ellen. *The Depression Workbook.* (Oakland, CA: New Harbinger, 1992).

128 *. . . but it doesn't mean you will never catch that bus again!* Ibid.

130 *. . . breaking out in a sweat, for instance, or beginning to shake.* Waites, E. *Trauma and Survival,* p. 37.

132 *What will I do in another catastrophe?* Figley, Charles R. *Trauma and Its Wake,* v. 2 (New York: Brunner/Mazel, 1986), p. 45.

CHAPTER 6

139 Header quote. Kuehl, Sheila. "Sonya Live," CNN Transcripts, May 26, 1993.

149 *. . . particularly given the dangers of perpetrators remaining at large.* Robeson, George. "Carrying a 'love' obsession too far can now be illegal,' *Long Beach, CA, Press-Telegram,* June 11, 1991.

159 *. . . and you'll find police interventions or TRO's, or both.* De Becker, Gavin. "Intervention Decisions—The Value of Flexibility: A White Paper Report Prepared for the Attendees of the 1994 CIA Threat Management Conference," 1994, p. 11.

161 *Kristen's stalker subsequently followed her and shot Kristen to death in the middle of the day on a busy Boston street.* Beck, Melinda. "Murderous Obsession," *Newsweek,* July 13, 1992, p. 61.

161 *He was apprehended waiting for his victim outside her gym and, fortunately, taken into custody before he could do her more harm.* Ibid.

162 *. . . 223 technical violations of the electronic monitoring system he had been placed on to insure that he stay away from her.* Ingrassia, Michele. "Stalked to Death?" *Newsweek,* November 1, 1993, p. 28.

163 *". . . the system can be successful. I've seen it."* Schultz, Suzanne. "Sonya Live," CNN Transcripts, May 26, 1993.

CHAPTER 7

168 *"The law is here to serve us."* Quote by Judge John Watson, currently of the Orange County Superior Court. Interview with John Watson, May 6, 1994.

168 Header quote. . . . *the loss of the quality of life.* Interview with Judge John Watson, May 6, 1994.

169 . . . *she must be harassed and followed.* Kansas Statute Ann. 95 & 96 (1992); West Virginia Code 61–2–9a (1993 Revisions) 61–2–9a to 61–2–9k.

169 *Washington State, for example, prohibits repeated following.* State of Washington, "Engrossed Substitute House Bill 2702," Chapter 9A.46 RCW, p. 1.

169 *Maryland prohibits approaching or following . . .* State of Maryland, Senate bill 7, Chapter 205, House bill 433.

170 *North Carolina prohibits following or being in the presence of another person without legal purpose . . .* General Statutes of North Carolina, Ch. 14–277.3.

170 . . . *Connecticut prohibits following or lying in wait.* General Statutes of Connecticut, Sec. 53a–181c and 53a–181d.

170 . . . *requiring that a prior intimate relationship between perpetrator and victim exist in order for a claim of stalking to be made.* 1992 Acts of the West Virginia Legislature. Ch. 61, Art. 2, 61–2–9a.

170 . . . *that the stalker cease his behavior before she can press antistalking charges.* N.C. General Stat. 14–277.3 (1992).

170 . . . *after she has reported any one act to the police.* Tex. Penal Code Ann. 42.07, Tex. Code Crim. Proc. Ann 17.46, 42.12, 42.8, Tex Gov't. Code 501.006.

170 . . . *can be charged with the crime.* Cal. Penal Code 646.9 (1992).

170 . . . *if a victim fears that her (or another's) property will be damaged.* RCW 9A.46.110 "Stalking."

171 . . . *delivering an object to, property owned, leased, or occupied by that individual.* Cahill, p. 28.

171 "*. . . makes legally enforceable the traditional idea of privacy as 'the right to be let alone.'*" Ibid.

172 . . . "*the threat is the last thing that happens before the person is harmed.*" Truppa, Mike. "Suburban Prosecutors Call Stalking Law Too Strict," *Chicago Daily Law Bulletin,* February 12, 1993, p. 1.

172 . . . *in 1993 lawmakers struck both the "credible threat" and the "threat to cause great bodily injury" sections of that law.* State of Rhode Island, Public Laws Chapter 93–358.

174 . . . *even though he may never have spoken a threatening word.* Testimony of Gavin de Becker, Hearing Before the Committee on the Judiciary, United States Senate, 102nd Congress, Second Session, on S. 2922, "A Bill to Assist the States in the Enactment of Legislation to Address the Criminal Act of Stalking Other Persons," September 28, 1992, p. 90.

175 . . . *and that actually causes the victim to feel terrorized, frightened, intimidated, threatened, harassed, or molested.* Cahill, p. 1.

182 *By 1993 . . . that number had climbed to 434.* National Abortion Federation factsheet, "Incidents of Violence & Disruption Against Abortion Providers," 1994.

183 . . . *their license plate numbers traced for identifying information, and their families and employers harassed.* Ramsey, Ross, et al. "Anti-Stalking Bill Becomes Texas Law," *Houston Chronicle,* March 20, 1993, p. A25; Amy Hagstrom Miller, cited in "Morning Edition," *National Public Radio,* June 14, 1993; David Van Biema. "In Your Town, In Your Face," *Time,* July 19, 1993, p. 29; Maureen M. Smith. "Operation Rescue Trainee in Court: May Be Charged

Under State's New Antistalking Law," *Star Tribune,* June 29, 1993, p. 2B; Bob Ortega, "Stalking Laws Used to Fight Abortion Foes," *Wall Street Journal,* April 7, 1993, pp. B1 & B10; Sara Rimer, "Abortion Foes in Boot Camp Mull Doctor's Killing," *New York Times,* March 19, 1993, p. A12; Maureen M. Smith, "Court Further Limits Abortion Protesters," *Star Tribune,* June 30, 1993, p. 1B; Andrea D. Greene, "Legal Barricade Staked Before Abortion Foes," *Houston Chronicle,* June 25, 1993, p. A29; Andrea D. Greene, "Protesters Distanced from Physicians," *Houston Chronicle,* June 30, 1993, p. A22; Rick Pluta, " 'Informed Consent' Abortion Bill Before the Michigan House," UPI, July 7, 1993, Domestic News section.

183 . . . *the NAF logged 188 reported acts of stalking.* National Abortion Federation factsheet, "Incidents of Violence & Disruption Against Abortion Providers."

183 *Some legislators . . . moved to exempt such activists from the law.* Pendered, David. "Georgia Legislature 1993 House OKs Revised Anti-Stalking Bill," *Atlanta Journal and Constitution,* March 18, 1993, p. F3.

184 . . . *and unrequested deliveries from local restaurants.* Interview with Lorraine Maguire, May 17, 1994.

184 . . . *trying to gain further background information on the director.* Ibid.

184 " '. . . *If you don't, you'd better watch out when you go out.'* " Ibid.

184 "*. . . 'You sure do have a pretty little blond-headed girl,'* " *Maguire recalls.* Ibid.

185 "*. . . and let her know how it feels to have your child killed?*" Ibid.

185 "*I think you're gonna be next.*" Ibid.

185 . . . *within five hundred feet of Maguire or her family or any clinic staff person and his or her family.* Ibid.

185 . . . *at a store next to that clinic.* Mac Dougal, David W. "Abortion protester arrested outside clinic," *News & Courier,* September 24, 1994.

186 . . . *but this doesn't have* anything *to do with abortion.* Interview with Lorraine Maguire, May 17, 1994.

187 ". . . *and it's really difficult for the police to protect them."* Mason, Julie. "Stalking Ordinance Proposed," *Houston Chronicle,* p. A34.

187 ". . . *then they should avail themselves of [the law]."* Interview with Lt. John Lane, TMU, LAPD, May 24, 1994.

188 . . . *having begun "their careers with chronic abuse and sexual assault crimes."* Norris, Joel and William J. Birnes. *Serial Killers: The Growing Menace.* (New York: Doubleday, 1988), p. 245.

188 ". . . *eventually become tomorrow's lurid newspaper headlines."* Ibid., pp. 246–47.

190 . . . *to intervene progressively as crimes of increasing severity were committed.* National Institute of Justice, "Project to Develop . . ." p. 1.

190 . . . *or that person's family in fear of great bodily injury or death.* Ibid., p. 43.

190 . . . *the NIJ observed, could continue to be prosecuted under existing harassment statutes.* Ibid., p. 48.

190 . . . *conduct which results in a victim's feeling fear should be sufficient for an arrest and prosecution.* Ibid., p. 45.

190 . . . *work together in a multidisciplinary approach to begin to address that problem.* Ibid., p. 69.

190 . . . *it would help foster greater public awareness of the problem's complicated roots.* Ibid., pp. 70–71.

CHAPTER 8

193 Header quotes. Lane, John. "Investigative Reports/Stalking: The Assassins Among Us," *A&E Network,* October 29, 1993, and Baty, Kathleen. Ibid.

196 *Stagner was finally taken into custody and eventually convicted of attempted kidnapping.* Ibid and Streshinsky, Shirley. "The Stalker and His Prey," *Glamour,* August 1992, pp. 238–267.

199 . . . *anyone handy with a screwdriver or pair of pliers.* Maxwell, Helen. *Home Safe Home: How to Safeguard Your Home and Family Against Break-Ins* (Far Hills, NJ: New Horizon Press, 1992).

206 *Over a third had received six or more.* Smith, Michael. "Obscene and Threatening Telephone Calls to Women: Data From a Canadian National Survey." Unpublished working paper, p. 9.

206 . . . *over 8 percent of the most disturbing phone calls were received at work at least some of the time.* Ibid., p. 12.

208 *". . . but I went around and made sure all the doors were locked."* Ibid., pp. 14–18.

209 *The second most common response was that they could not do anything to help.* Ibid., p. 13.

CHAPTER 9

220 Header quotes from the "Sally Jessie Raphael Show," January 5, 1994.

225 *Many people can take several streams of the stuff square in the face with no immediate ill effects.* Ayoob, Massad. *In The Gravest Extreme: The Role of the Firearm in Personal Protection.* (Concord, NH: Police Bookshelf, 1980), p. 37.

227 *These are all enough reasons not to rely on the stun gun to deter an assault.* Quigley, Paxton. *Armed*

and Female. (New York: St. Martin's Press, 1990), pp. 34–35.

228 . . . *went up 53 percent between 1983 and 1986 alone.* Quigley, Ibid. p. 8.

228 . . . *between fifteen and twenty million women own guns for self-protection.* Interview with Elizabeth Swayze, National Rifle Association, Washington D.C., November 1, 1993.

229 . . . *the percentage of female gun owners has remained roughly the same over the last thirteen years.* Henneberger, Melinda. "The Small Arms Industry Comes on to Women," *New York Times,* October 24, 1993, section 4, p. 4.

230 . . . *killed with handguns were killed with their own weapons. FBI Crime Reports, 1989,* from factsheet, "Women and Guns," Handgun Control, Inc.

230 . . . *with three-quarters of the homicides committed by intimate partners or family members.* Kellerman, Arthur L., et. al. "Gun Ownership as a Risk Factor for Homicide in the Home," *The New England Journal of Medicine,* October 7, 1993, Vol. 329, No. 15, pp. 1084–85.

230 . . . *keeping a gun in the home offered no protective benefit to the gun owner.* Kellerman, Arthur L., et. al., p. 1087.

230 . . . *"the advisability of keeping firearms in the home for protection must be questioned."* Kellermann, Arthur L., and Donald T. Reay. "Protection or Peril? An Analysis of Firearm-Related Deaths in the Home," *The New England Journal of Medicine,* June 12, 1986, Vol. 314, No. 24, p. 1557.

231 . . . *or that may result in grave bodily harm.* Quigley, *Armed and Female,* pp. 108–109.

233 . . . *unless the aggressor displays all the con-*

ditions of immediate, unavoidable attack. Ibid., p. 114.

234 . . . *when self-defense law tries to accommodate the unique circumstances of women victims.* Gillespie, Cynthia K. *Justifiable Homicide: Battered Women, Self-Defense, and the Law.* (Columbus: Ohio State University Press, 1989).

237 *". . . and most of those opinions are dead wrong."* Quigley, *Armed and Female,* p. 194.

240 . . . *fifteen children aged nineteen and under are killed each day by guns.* National Center for Health Statistics. Factsheet "Firearm Facts," Handgun Control, Inc.

CHAPTER 10

247 Header quote. Berry, Janet. In Mahoney, Lisa Coffey. "Attack! School teaches local women self-protection," *The Monclarion,* December 29, 1992, p. 9.

249 *I pled for my life.* Collier, Wendy. "My Story." Unpublished paper, p. 3.

250 . . . *neither jurisdiction would accept responsibility for filing a report.* Ibid., p. 5.

251 . . . *a viable response to violence that is proactive and preventive.* Collier, Wendy. "An Introduction to Victim Protection Services." *The Advocate,* No. 1, May 1993, p. 1.

251 *". . . I continue to transcend a horrible victimization, transforming it into something very positive."* Collier, "My Story," p. 8.

253 *". . . does make me feel better even though I know its limitations." JurisMonitor: Issues and Practices* (Summer 1993), in-house newsletter of JurisMonitor, Inc., p. 1.

254 *"The community and law enforcement co-*

ordinating a response together is the key." Ibid., p. 6.

263 . . . *if you are attempting to guard your identity and whereabouts.* Interview with Joseph J. Culligan, December 19, 1993.

CHAPTER 11

265 Header quotes. Loe, Victoria. "An Abused Woman Asks, 'Why?'" *The Arizona Republic,* July 11, 1993, and Michael Resnick, "Fear and Violence in the Workplace." Northwest National Life Insurance Company report, October 1993, p. 12.

270 . . . *Ruth stated she could not live if he moved away from Chicago.* De Becker, Gavin. Lecture, Indiana University at South Bend. March 18, 1994.

271 *I could've walked right out of that place and nobody would have come after me.* Ibid.

272 *". . . Arthur Jackson, forever linked with Theresa Saldana, and so on."* Ibid.

273 . . . *who are victims of dating violence, particularly in urban areas, are even higher.* Cited in Shen, Fern. "Battered: Therapists seeing an alarming rise in abusive teen dating practices," *Star Tribune,* September 2, 1993.

273 . . . *against teens engaged in threatening, stalking, abuse or outright assault of their young partners.* Locy, Toni. "Dates, families driven to court for protection from violent youths," *Boston Globe,* April 14, 1994.

273 . . . *make the topic of dating violence prevention a mandatory part of the public school curriculum.* Shen, Fern. "Welts Betray a Dark Side of Teen Dating," *Washington Post,* July 18, 1993.

274 . . . *a continuum that ranges from sexually*

harassing jokes and comments to stalking, serious assault and rape." Ibid.

274 *"If a guy really loves you, he hits you to let you know how much he loves you."* Ibid.

282 . . . *completely neutral gestures were misinterpreted as being sexually motivated cues of the woman's interest.* Stockdale, Margaret S. "The Role of Sexual Misperceptions of Women's Friendliness in an Emerging Theory of Sexual Harassment," *Journal of Vocational Behavior,* 42 (1993), pp. 84–101.

282 . . . *misinterpretation about sexuality in social interactions.* Abbey, A. "Misperceptions of friendly behavior as sexual interest: A survey of naturally occurring incidents," *Psychology of Women Quarterly,* 11 (1987), pp. 173–94.

283 . . . *this individual sees and enjoys women more as sexual objects rather than as human beings, friends, and companions.* Stockdale, "The Role of Sexual Misperceptions" p. 85.

283 . . . *a high level of tolerance for rape.* Ibid.

284 . . . *33 percent of these young respondents answered yes!* Cited by Senator Joseph R. Biden, "Hearing Before the Committee on the Judiciary, United States Senate, 103rd Congress, First Session on Combating Stalking and Family Violence." March 17, 1993.

285 . . . *one out of four full-time workers was harassed, threatened, or attacked on the job.* "Fear and Violence in the Workplace." NWNL report, October 1993, p. 2.

285 . . . *having an effective grievance process in place.* Ibid., p. 12.

286 . . . *30,000 to 40,000 computer bulletin boards throughout the United States alone.* Price, Wayne T. "Harassment Goes On-Line," *USA Today,* August 6, 1993.

286 . . . *who holds a national reputation for investigating computer crime.* Kennedy, Shirley Duglin. "The Stalking of Victims Goes On-Line," *St. Petersburg Times,* April 6, 1994.

286 . . . *90 percent of all computer crime occurs on the Internet airwaves.* Rendleman, John. "It's a Crime —And it Happens On-Line—Law officials seek to rid services of stalkers and thieves," *Communications-Week,* March 28, 1994.

287 *". . . He has made it his business to find out everything about me."* Rosenlind, Steven. "Stalkers on the Cyberwaves: on-line chatting turns sinister," *San Francisco Examiner,* March 13, 1994.

287 *"I am afraid that he's going to come out from behind the computer and hurt somebody."* Rendleman, "It's a Crime."

288 . . . *Vito's way of escaping detection and eluding authorities.* Kennedy, "The Stalking of Victims."

288 . . . *describing his desire to sexually assault the child.* Ibid.

288 . . . *by repeated and invasive sexual messages from an anonymous user.* Rosenlind, "Stalkers on the Cyberwaves."